ORDER
IN THE CHURCH

A MANUAL
FOR CHURCH
MINISTRIES

PAUL CHAPPELL

First published in 2004 by *Striving Together Publications*, a ministry of Lancaster Baptist Church, Lancaster, CA 93535. *Striving Together Publications* is committed to providing tried, trusted, and proven books that will further equip local churches to carry out the Great Commission. Your comments and suggestions are valued.

Striving Together Publications
4020 E. Lancaster Blvd.
Lancaster, CA 93535
(800) 201-7748

Cover design: Cary Schmidt and Jeremy Lofgren
Cover photo: Craig Parker
Layout: Craig Parker

ISBN 0-9652859-3-6

Printed in the United States of America

Contents

PART THREE

Going Beyond: *Outreach Ministries*

PART FOUR

Great Expectations: *Church Calendar & Events*

Special Thanks

This manual has been a team effort. Special thanks to Elizabeth Kinsfather, Craig Parker, Melinda Cazis, Danielle Chappell and others who helped in the editorial process. Thanks also to Cary Schmidt for his vision to reproduce the biblical methods and materials blessed by our Lord at Lancaster Baptist Church.

Dedication

To the staff of Lancaster Baptist Church who have labored with me to "equip the saints for the work of the ministry" and maintain "order in the church."

Introduction

When the Apostle Paul wrote to Titus, one of his own sons in the faith, the Holy Spirit of God inspired him to say, *"For this cause left I thee in Crete, that thou shouldest set in order the things that are wanting..."* (Titus 1:5).

It is the responsibility of a pastor to bring order to the local church. In Acts 20:28 the Bible says, *"Take heed therefore unto yourselves, and to all the flock, over the which the Holy Ghost hath made you overseers, to feed the church of God, which he hath purchased with his own blood."* As an overseer, the pastor is to see the needs in the church and follow the Holy Spirit's leading in bringing order to the church. This daunting task cannot be accomplished by the pastor himself. Growing churches are churches where a strong spirit of teamwork is exhibited. These are churches that are striving together for the faith of the Gospel.

In Ephesians 4:11-12, the Bible says, *"And he gave some, apostles; and some, prophets; and some, evangelists; and some, pastors and teachers; For the perfecting of the saints, for the work of the ministry, for the edifying of the body of Christ."* I believe the work of the ministry is primarily the preaching and teaching of the Word of God;

therefore, the pastors are to equip the church family in the vital areas of soulwinning and discipleship. However, beyond the actual ministry in the Word, there are many other service ministries in the local church, which must be set in order to support the on-going work of reaching people and edifying them in the faith of the Lord Jesus Christ.

Order in the Church has been compiled with the desire to help pastors and church leaders fulfill the great commission in an orderly fashion. It is our prayer that this book will be used to bring order and direction in churches desiring to equip the saints for the work of the ministry.

I recognize that there are many Bible-based methods that will not change and should not change in a church that truly desires to please the Lord. For example, God has chosen the foolishness of preaching to confound the wise. This is His method for proclaiming the Truth.

There are other methods; however, which must be updated from time to time in the church. For example, nursery registration procedures have changed radically as the American family continues to show signs of deterioration. A myriad of these changes face the pastor and the church in today's modern society as we organize youth activities, bus ministries, and even the flow of traffic in and out of the church on Sunday.

This book is simply a view of ministry through the window of a local church that is attempting to reach and disciple people for Christ while maintaining a strong commitment to the fundamentals of our faith. I will be the first to admit that some of the methods mentioned in this book may become outdated years from now. Methods are not always timeless. As one preacher said years ago, "Methods are many; principles are few. Methods may change, but principles never do."

Furthermore, I recognize that methods and organizational principles are not the key to ministry. Without the power of the Holy Spirit of God, lives will never truly be changed; therefore, it is not our desire to share some prescribed organizational principles that will "help you to grow the church." Any pastor or church leader who makes numerical growth his goal instead of spiritual growth will oftentimes compromise in his quest for success.

In today's success-oriented culture, we see an abundance of "seeker-sensitive" churches. It is my prayer that we will see a host of pastors in America who will once again have a great desire for a "Saviour-sensitive" church.

The fact is, however, that we can be a solid, fundamental, "Saviour-sensitive" church and still be a church that is helping men and women to understand the truth of the Gospel and to be assimilated into a church family that will lovingly disciple them in the ways of Christ.

The Bible specifically says in I Corinthians 14:33, *"For God is not the author of confusion..."* It is God's desire that *"all things be done decently and in order"* (I Corinthians 14:40).

As you survey this book and consider the concepts which we have employed in developing the various ministries of Lancaster Baptist Church, our ultimate prayer is that something gleaned from your reading might help you to bring honor and glory to the Lord Jesus Christ in your church.

Finally, I would like to give glory and honor to the Lord for any good thing that has happened at Lancaster Baptist Church or West Coast Baptist College. He alone is worthy of the praise, for it is from Him that all blessings flow.

May God richly bless you as you serve Him and prayerfully develop "order in the church."

Paul Chappell

Preface

Order in the Church is a "why do" and then "how to" manual. Every chapter includes three separate areas that, when combined, will give the reader a clear understanding of the purpose and production of each ministry.

Ministry Philosophies

Each chapter begins with the scriptural foundation and philosophy for that particular ministry. It lays the groundwork for the "why" and gives foundational ideas for how a ministry should be organized.

Ministry Handbooks

The handbook section follows the philosophy section and contains the actual ministry handbook that is given to a new volunteer at Lancaster Baptist Church. It will stand out to the reader because it has a bold header on top of each page. This section will provide information and ideas for the "how to" as well as information that can be used to train those who will serve in each particular ministry.

Ministry Helps

A companion CD is enclosed in the front cover. In each chapter of the book, the reader will be referred to the CD to view a particular form, flyer, or booklet that is used in that ministry. Example: (See CD 1.2 for a sample of a decision card). The CD number indicates the chapter and form. The companion CD has a corresponding number that will allow the reader to easily access whichever form he desires to view.

PART ONE

Growing in Grace:
Foundations for the New Believer

CHAPTER ONE

The Soulwinning Ministry

*"The fruit of the righteous is a tree of life;
and he that winneth souls is wise."*
Proverbs 11:30

In 1986, when my wife, Terrie, and I came to Lancaster, California, there was no need for a manual for ministries. The simple reason was there were no ministries in our church! With just a handful of people, we had one basic thought in mind—to reach others with the Gospel of Jesus Christ.

The compelling mission of reaching souls for Christ is common in the infant church. As a church begins to develop and grow, the need to organize various ministries becomes apparent. However, one of the dangers of growth and ministry development is the potential to lose sight of the first passion of the church, which was to reach people with the Gospel of Jesus Christ.

The Scriptures say that Jesus came *"...to seek and to save that which was lost"* (Luke 19:10). With His heartbeat in mind, we begin this book of ministry manuals where our ministry began eighteen years ago on the theme of soulwinning.

By God's grace, we have built and maintained a strong soulwinning fervor in our church over the years. This chapter will outline some of the philosophies and programs utilized in leading our church family to become effective witnesses for Christ.

Frankly, if a church is not reaching people, there will be no need for the other chapters in this book. While the various ministries of the church are beneficial, it is vitally important to remember that the heart of all ministry is reaching the souls of men.

The Mandate of the Soulwinner

Before Christ ascended to heaven, He gave a great challenge to His disciples, *"Go ye therefore, and teach all nations, baptizing them in the name of the Father, and of the Son, and of the Holy Ghost: Teaching them to observe all things whatsoever I have commanded you: and, lo, I am with you alway, even unto the end of the world. Amen."* (Matthew 28:19–20).

This mandate was given to His disciples and has been passed to every church since then through the Word of God. Soulwinning is not an option for the New Testament Christian.

As we study the order of the Great Commission, we must obviously go before we can teach! Mark 16:15 says, *"And he said unto them, Go ye into all the world, and preach the gospel to every creature."* Acts 5:20 says, *"Go, stand and speak in the temple to the people all the words of this life."* It is the responsibility of pastors and church leaders to mobilize and encourage the local church in this matter of going out and telling others about Jesus Christ.

The Ministry of the Soulwinner

The ministry of the soulwinner is first, and foremost, to follow the Lord Jesus Christ. In Matthew 4:19 Jesus said, *"And he saith unto them, Follow me, and I will make you fishers of men."* If we, as Christians, will follow the example of our Saviour, we will truly be conscious of the eternal destiny of this lost world. I also am convinced that a vital daily relationship with the Saviour must be the foundation for all truly spiritual activity.

In addition to following the example of Christ, we must seek the fullness of the Holy Spirit's power. In Acts 1:8 the Bible says, *"But ye shall receive power, after that the Holy Ghost is come upon you: and ye shall be witnesses unto me both in Jerusalem, and in all Judaea, and in Samaria, and unto the uttermost part of the earth."* To be an effective witness, we must have the power of the Holy Spirit in our lives. Jesus promised that the Holy Spirit would *"...guide you into all truth"* (John 16:13).

The soulwinning training and organized program at Lancaster Baptist have never been intended to take the place of walking in the power of the Holy Spirit. We do believe, however, that busy people in today's churches often benefit by having a time set apart for the specific purpose of witnessing in their communities. Thus, the soulwinning ministry of the local church helps Christians with a desire to obey the Great Commission of their Saviour.

The soulwinning handbook, which is displayed on the next several pages, will share some of the various approaches blessed by God in reaching thousands of souls here in southern California.

I know that some of the methodologies discussed here regarding soulwinning are scoffed at by modern-day church growth experts. This book, as we stated in the introduction, is not written from the standpoint of endeavoring to be "seeker-sensitive" as much as it is our desire to be "Saviour-sensitive" in our methods of ministry. Jesus confronted people with this need for saving faith, and we must walk in His steps as we establish a biblical pattern and philosophy of ministry.

The Soulwinning Ministry

Dear Friend,

Thank you for your interest in the soulwinning ministry here at Lancaster Baptist Church. In the upcoming days, I will share with you many scriptural principles that will help you become a more effective witness for Christ.

As you will learn at the soulwinning kick-off, there are two tracks of soulwinning training here at Lancaster Baptist. First, there is Track I Soulwinning, which begins the first week of September and covers the basic approach for leading a soul to Christ.

Also, there is Track II Soulwinning, which includes a variety of lessons that help us learn how to better witness to people steeped in religious traditions and false teachings.

It is my prayer that you and your soulwinning partner hear the lessons, involve yourselves in faithfully witnessing for Christ, and bear fruit in the power of the Holy Spirit.

Remember, if you have questions along the way, let me or one of our soulwinning trainers know. We will be glad to help you. Thank you, again, for yielding to the Lord in the all-important area of soulwinning.

Your friend,

Pastor

(Note to reader: All ministry letters are to church members and are typed on church letterhead.)

An Overview

T.E.A.M. Soulwinning stands for **Train Every Available Member**. II Timothy 2:2 says, *"And the things that thou hast heard of me among many witnesses, the same commit thou to faithful men, who shall be able to teach others also."* The T.E.A.M. Soulwinning program has been used of God to successfully train and encourage thousands of soulwinners since its inception. As you begin your journey in the T.E.A.M. Soulwinning program, we trust this course of instruction, combined with the practical application of witnessing, will be used of God in your life to help you reach others for Christ.

Philosophy

Soulwinning is better caught than taught. Thus, as a person becomes involved in sharing his faith, he will catch not only the excitement, but also the understanding of how to become a more effective witness.

Schedule

The T.E.A.M. Soulwinning training program is conducted each Tuesday morning and evening throughout the calendar year. The kick-off for the initial 15-week training course begins the first Tuesday of September each year. You will receive the text, *To Seek and To Save*, written by Pastor Chappell, as well as other printed materials related to the subject of soulwinning.

The Soulwinning Partner

As you become involved in the soulwinning program of Lancaster Baptist Church, our soulwinning director or your adult Bible class leader will partner you with another member of our church who will go with you to make various visits in the community. Normally, the partners are chosen from your adult Bible class and oftentimes the visits you will make are prospects whom we hope will visit your class as a result of your time with them. The purpose of having a soulwinning partner is that you might pray for one another, encourage each other, and grow to become better witnesses for the Lord. It is vital to have spiritual accountability whenever we desire to be used of God.

The Soulwinning Meeting

Once you have made the commitment to enroll in T.E.A.M. Soulwinning and have your partner, you should decide which weekly meeting you will attend. The meetings will be well-prepared and planned to utilize our time most effectively. Sometimes there will be a brief song and a few announcements prior to the training you will receive. Childcare will always be provided for those who have that need.

Upon arrival to T.E.A.M. Soulwinning, please be sure to register at the table. Additionally, you will notice a few supply tables next to the registration table. These tables will be supplied with Gospel tracts, maps of our area, and other literature that will be useful in your soulwinning endeavors. You can expect to see the following items at the supply table:

1. Sign-in sheet—Team members will be registered at the soulwinning kick-off meeting or at the first soulwinning meetings in January. A soulwinning secretary will take attendance as we arrive. This allows our soulwinning director and adult Bible class leaders to encourage us to be faithful throughout the year. Also, next to our names on the sign-in sheet, there is a place where we can make comments about the visits we have made so that accurate records can be kept (see CD 1.1 for sample).

2. Maps—City maps will be available for your use at the soulwinning tables. Please take one per team.

3. Decision Cards—Should the Lord allow you the opportunity to lead a person to Christ or help them in another spiritual decision, please fill out a decision card so our soulwinning secretary will have an appropriate record of the decision and help encourage you in the follow-up of this decision (see CD 1.2 for sample).

4. Gospel tracts—You will find Gospel tracts at each meeting that may be used during your soulwinning time.

Organizing Through the Adult Classes

At Lancaster Baptist Church, we believe the Sunday school is the church organized to fulfill the purpose of the church. Therefore, your soulwinning partner and visits will be structured through your adult Bible class.

We will all meet together for the soulwinning training time. After the training time is concluded, we encourage you to go to the place in the room where you will find a sign posted for your adult Bible class. Each adult class will have a small sign posted along with a basket below that sign that will contain calls prepared for you and your partner. Normally, your class leader or a representative will be standing there to assist you in the distribution of these visits.

In the basket you will find several types of visits.

- First—follow-up visits of those who visited your class the previous week. (See CD 1.3 for a sample follow-up visit. Each half-sheet follow-up visit should be attached to a map of where the visit is located.)

- Second—follow-up visits of people in your lifestage (age group—see LifeStages Handbook on page 50 for details) who visited the church the previous week (see CD 1.3).

- Third—highlighted maps from an area in our city designated specifically for your class to reach in an evangelistic effort (see CD 1.4 for a sample highlighted map). We do not believe in going "wherever." Our soulwinning director will prepare maps with specific streets highlighted for each of us to visit. As you and your partner knock on the doors of the homes on a particular street, we ask that you circle the portion of the street that is completed and turn the map in to the basket for your class at the end of your soulwinning time.

Periodically, someone will request the church not to visit his home. On your map you may find instructions that say, "Do not visit 1212 Elm Street." Please adhere to this instruction, as we desire to be good neighbors for those who request no visit.

- Fourth—community "new move-in" visits. These are people who have moved into the area assigned to your adult Bible class in recent weeks. (These new move-ins may be obtained from Homeowner's Marketing service at 800-232-2134.) If you receive one of these visits, there will also be a gift at the supply tables that you may pick up to deliver to the new move-in. The gift is usually a coffee mug, a city map, or a ballpoint pen.

A Few Final Reminders

Please remember to bring your Bible and soulwinning training materials to each T.E.A.M. Soulwinning meeting. In the event your soulwinning partner is not present, the soulwinning director will help pair you up with someone who is an experienced soulwinner. Thank you again for your participation in the Lancaster Baptist Church T.E.A.M. Soulwinning program.

Building and Promoting the Soulwinning Program

This section highlights some thoughts for those desiring to begin a soulwinning program in the local church.

At least once a year, it is vital to have a soulwinning kick-off night. It may be planned for a Tuesday or Wednesday evening, depending on the desire of the pastor.

The purpose of the kick-off is three-fold:

- First, to involve and train every available member

- Second, to raise awareness of the need of people everywhere to receive Christ

- Third, to motivate those who have slacked in their witness during recent months

Promoting the Soulwinning Kick-Off

The following steps are helpful in promoting the annual kick-off for the T.E.A.M. Soulwinning program.

1. Advertise—Use church announcements, bulletin inserts, and church-wide mailings to get the word out. Sometimes we have found it very helpful to have three or four families give testimonies telling how they were reached through the soulwinning ministry of our church, then encourage others to sign up and become a part of the soulwinning ministry.

2. Set up registration tables—We have found it helpful to have two or three registration tables in the church lobby so people may sign up on their way out of church after each service. They may sign up for Track I, which is the basic training, or Track II, which is the more advanced training. Sometimes members who have been in the church a while

sign up for Track I a second time so they can be refreshed in the basic principles for presenting the Gospel.

Sign-ups should begin six to eight weeks before the actual kick-off night. This will allow the soulwinning director to monitor the number of people signing up and individually encourage those who have not yet signed up for soulwinning.

3. Encourage—It is vital to encourage soulwinning throughout the year. As you approach the soulwinning kick-off, take every opportunity to encourage members of your church to participate.

Organizing the Soulwinning Kick-Off

The soulwinning kick-off night should include the following elements:

1. A good dinner—This should be a delicious, complimentary dinner. This is one way to encourage and invest into God's people.

2. Partner registration—Consider pre-assigning partners prior to the kick-off night and formally introducing the partners the night of the kick-off.

3. Material distribution—On the night of the soulwinning kick-off, every person in attendance will receive books and materials. Track I participants receive the book *To Seek and To Save*. Track II participants receive loose-leaf binders, which will hold a variety of lessons on soulwinning and witnessing to various religious groups. In addition, maps and other booklets may be handed out.

4. Order of service—After the meal is finished, the soulwinners register at the sign-in tables. Then the kick-off service begins, overviewing the soulwinning program. The order is as follows:

a. An exciting soulwinning song, normally sung by an adult ensemble
b. Welcome from the pastor
c. Congregational song (something evangelistic)
d. Prayer
e. Overview of the history and purpose of the soulwinning program given by the pastor
f. Explanation of the differences between Track I and II, the purpose of having a partner, and the role of the adult Bible class leader in distributing calls
g. A brief Bible challenge on the subject of soulwinning and faithfulness
h. Closing prayer

At the conclusion of the soulwinning kick-off, partners get together and share their testimonies with one another, then have a word of prayer committing to be faithful in soulwinning during this new season.

Prior to the soulwinning kick-off, hundreds of hours of preparation are necessary. If we are to see souls saved through the ministries of our local churches, the leaders must spend time and effort preparing to equip the saints for the work of the ministry. May God bless your planning and preparation for the soulwinning ministry!

Tracking Soulwinning Contacts

The pastor and/or soulwinning director must be intensely aware of every contact made by the local church and should steward those contacts until each individual has been approached with the Gospel and given the opportunity to be saved. Our desire is that no person be left behind or fall through the cracks as we endeavor to reach the world with the Gospel.

There are various church management software programs to help with this process; however, we have found the Microsoft

Access software to be a great tool in tracking each contact (see CD 1.5 for sample visitor report and tracking database). The following chart illustrates the care with which we oversee the process.

LifeStages Soulwinning Follow-Up Procedure

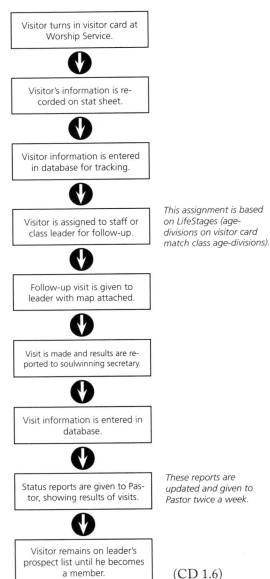

Visitor turns in visitor card at Worship Service.

Visitor's information is recorded on stat sheet.

Visitor information is entered in database for tracking.

Visitor is assigned to staff or class leader for follow-up.

This assignment is based on LifeStages (age-divisions on visitor card match class age-divisions).

Follow-up visit is given to leader with map attached.

Visit is made and results are reported to soulwinning secretary.

Visit information is entered in database.

Status reports are given to Pastor, showing results of visits.

These reports are updated and given to Pastor twice a week.

Visitor remains on leader's prospect list until he becomes a member.

(CD 1.6)

You will see from this chart that we follow the initial contact or visitor's card through a series of checkpoints until the prospect has had the opportunity to hear the Gospel. This level of tracking is a corporate responsibility that the local body must take very seriously.

In addition to the corporate responsibility, which is managed by the pastor and soulwinning secretary, each soulwinner should be trained to maintain a prospect list.

The Prospect List

The prospect list is a great tool that helps us focus on soulwinning. Sometimes it has been called a "Sweetheart List." Whatever it is called, it is simply a way of keeping track of individuals to whom you are witnessing.

For example, if I receive a visitation card from the soulwinning director, make the visit on a Tuesday night and find him not at home, I will place him on my prospect list and continue following up on that individual until there has been a decision made for the Lord or the prospect becomes a "dead end."

As a pastor, along with our staff and key lay leaders, I have endeavored to build and maintain prospect lists for many years. The goal of a prospect list is to develop a relationship with those with whom we have come in contact or met throughout the week. Yes, we will often attempt to lead them to Christ at a first meeting. But there are cases where we simply have a brief introduction to someone. In that case, we will either write, visit, or give them a phone call each week. The goal is to consistently share the Gospel and follow up with this person until he is saved and added to the church.

The form on the following page is commonly used amongst our church family as a prayer and tracking list for those people to whom we are witnessing.

Soulwinning Sweetheart List   for the month of: _____

Name: _____ Phone #: _____

Address: _____ Zip: _____

Date											
Contact											

PH=phone call   C/N=card or note   V=personal visit

Comments: _____

_____

- -

Soulwinning Sweetheart List   for the month of: _____

Name: _____ Phone #: _____

Address: _____ Zip: _____

Date											
Contact											

PH=phone call   C/N=card or note   V=personal visit

Comments: _____

_____

- -

Soulwinning Sweetheart List   for the month of: _____

Name: _____ Phone #: _____

Address: _____ Zip: _____

Date											
Contact											

PH=phone call   C/N=card or note   V=personal visit

Comments: _____

_____

(CD 1.7)

Conclusion

As we conclude this chapter on the soulwinning ministry, it is vital that the pastor, staff, and deacons of any church find themselves publicly engaged in the soulwinning ministries of the church. One of the great aspects of the public soulwinning meeting is that our church family can see the leadership of the church involved in this great endeavor. **We believe that people do what people see.** If our members see us actively involved, they will support the program with much more enthusiasm. Soulwinning is the "main thing" of the local church. May God continue to bless you as you keep the "main thing" the main thing by pointing others to the Lord Jesus Christ!

CHAPTER TWO

Baptism

"Then they that gladly received his
word were baptized: and the same day there
were added unto them about three thousand souls."
Acts 2:41

In recent years there has been much written about church growth, and various philosophies have been taught at seminars regarding "how to grow a church." Ironically, many of the fast-growing churches in America today are recording relatively few baptisms during these amazing growth years. This, of course, is indicative of the fact that often these churches are growing by receiving members from other churches or by not emphasizing the necessity of following the Lord in believer's baptism after salvation.

We believe that the stirring of the baptism waters is a good indication of the fact that a church is maintaining a heart and passion for souls. New believers should be encouraged to identify with their Saviour through baptism by immersion.

Each new believer should know what baptism symbolizes. Baptism, put simply, is "an outward sign of an inward decision."

It does not bring salvation or grant him "special rights" with God. It is a symbol of what has already taken place when he accepted Christ as his Saviour. When a believer chooses to enter the waters of baptism, he is identifying with the death, burial, and resurrection of Christ. He is also identifying with the body of believers where he is baptized. This identification can be compared to wearing a wedding ring. It identifies one spouse with the other, but it is not necessary to wear the ring to be married. In the same way, baptism identifies us as followers of Christ, but it is not necessary for salvation. It is, however, a command to the believer. Any Christian who refuses to be baptized is in direct disobedience to a command from the Lord Jesus Christ. Notice what Christ tells His disciples in Matthew 28:19–20:

> *Go ye therefore, and teach all nations, baptizing them in the name of the Father, and of the Son, and of the Holy Ghost: Teaching them to observe all things whatsoever I have commanded you: and, lo, I am with you alway, even unto the end of the world. Amen.*

Christ Himself commands us to be baptized! But notice the specific order He gives in the above verses. He tells us to win the people before we baptize them. They are to be saved, baptized, and then discipled.

Many churches today sprinkle infants and small children to assure their later salvation. Thus, it is very possible that your new convert has already been "baptized" and may wonder why he should do it again. The story of Philip and the Ethiopian eunuch in Acts is a good example of why conversion must precede baptism:

> *Then Philip opened his mouth, and began at the same scripture, and preached unto him Jesus. And as they went on their way, they came unto a certain water: and the eunuch said, See, here is water; what doth hinder me to be baptized? And Philip said, If thou believest with all thine heart, thou mayest. And he answered and said, I believe that Jesus Christ is the Son of God.*

*And he commanded the chariot to stand still: and they
went down both into the water…and he baptized him.*
Acts 8:35–38

In the above passage we see that when the eunuch asked to be
baptized, Philip told him that he had to believe on the Lord first.
The biblical order for Christian growth is conversion, baptism,
and discipleship. If one has just come to know the Lord, being
sprinkled as a child cannot identify him with his new-found
Saviour any more than wearing another's wedding band makes you
married to his spouse. Only after he believes can he take the first
step of believer's baptism.

Some new believers may question why your church baptizes by
immersion instead of sprinkling. In the Greek language, the word for
baptism, *baptizo*, literally means "to immerse." Acts 8 also gives us a
biblical precedent for this practice. If Philip and the eunuch had to
go down into the water, then later came up out of the water, it is only
logical to conclude that he was immersed in the water. If Philip were
only going to sprinkle the eunuch, stopping the chariot and going into
the water would have been unnecessary. Romans 6:3–4 also clarifies
this issue:

*Know ye not, that so many of us as were baptized into
Jesus Christ were baptized into his death? Therefore
we are buried with him by baptism into death: that
like as Christ was raised up from the dead by the glory
of the Father, even so we also should walk in newness
of life.*

When one is immersed in the water, he is identifying with
the death of Jesus Christ and His burial in the tomb. In being
raised out of the water, he identifies with the new life Christ gave
him when He rose from the dead. Sprinkling is never practiced
or alluded to in the Scriptures. To encourage new Christians to be
baptized as soon as possible after their salvation, Lancaster Baptist
Church is prepared to baptize after every service.

Now that the new believer understands why he is to be baptized, let us take a look at the mechanics behind what happens. First, have the new Christian come forward during the invitation at the end of your service and tell an altar worker that he wishes to be baptized. (If possible, you may take him personally.) He will be led to a changing room where he can leave his clothes and change into the baptismal gown. After he changes, he will be led to the baptistry. The pastor will be waiting for him and will ask him if he has accepted the Lord Jesus as his personal Saviour. When he affirms that he has, the pastor will say, "Based upon this public profession of faith, I now baptize you in the name of the Father, the Son, and the Holy Ghost—buried in the likeness of His death— raised in the likeness of His resurrection," and will immerse him in the water. Then he can be directed to the proper changing room.

Now, let us take a look at the Baptistry Ministry handbook. The first page is a letter sent to thank and encourage all who volunteer to be changing room attendants. The rest details the recommended procedures and gives other helpful material.

The Baptistry Ministry

Dear Friend,

I want to welcome you to the Baptistry Ministry! I am thrilled that you have decided to become a part of this ministry. I pray that the Lord will use you to encourage and even to calm the nerves of these new Christians who may be nervous about taking their first step in the Christian walk.

It is a privilege to be able to serve the Lord in any way or fashion here. As you serve in this ministry, I would like you to keep in mind what the Bible says in Colossians 3:23–24: "And whatsoever ye do, do it heartily, as to the Lord, and not unto men; Knowing that of the Lord ye shall receive the reward of the inheritance: for ye serve the Lord Christ." Always be mindful that your service is unto the Lord and whatever we do for Him should be our best.

The thought of a "commitment to excellence" comes to my mind when I read those verses. As servants of God, our attitude toward the Lord's work should be on a different level of excellence because of Whom we are serving—the Lord.

Finally, let me express how excited I am that the Lord has led you to serve in this ministry, and may the Lord bless you because of your faithfulness in this area of service.

Your friend,

Pastor

The Purpose

The First Step of Faith...

It is exciting to do something for the first time; even more so, it is thrilling to help a new believer take that first step of obedience to the Lord. Baptism is the first step of faith for the new Christian. By serving in this ministry, you are helping this new believer to grow spiritually.

Sometimes, when working in the Baptistry Ministry, it may be necessary to reinforce the reasons for baptism...

First, baptism shows obedience to God's Word. The following Scriptures clearly show God's heart on the matter.

> *Go ye therefore, and teach all nations, baptizing them in the name of the Father, and of the Son, and of the Holy Ghost: Teaching them to observe all things whatsoever I have commanded you: and, lo, I am with you always, even unto the end of the world. Amen.*
> Matthew 28:19–20

> *If ye love me, keep my commandments.* John 14:15

> *If ye keep my commandments, ye shall abide in my love; even as I have kept my Father's commandments, and abide in his love.* John 15:10

Second, baptism identifies the new believer with his personal Saviour, Jesus Christ.

> *Know ye not, that so many of us as were baptized into Jesus Christ were baptized into his death? Therefore we are buried with him by baptism into death: that like as Christ was raised up from the dead by the glory of the Father, even so we also should walk in newness of life.*
> Romans 6:3–4

Moreover, brethren, I declare unto you the gospel which I preached unto you, which also ye have received, and wherein ye stand; By which also ye are saved, if ye keep in memory what I preached unto you, unless ye have believed in vain. For I delivered unto you first of all that which I also received, how that Christ died for our sins according to the scriptures; And that he was buried, and that he rose again the third day according to the scriptures: I Corinthians 15:1–4

Third, baptism is an opportunity to follow Christ's example.

And Jesus answering said unto him, Suffer it to be so now: for thus it becometh us to fulfil all righteousness. Then he suffered him. And Jesus, when he was baptized, went up straightway out of the water: and, lo, the heavens were opened unto him, and he saw the Spirit of God descending like a dove, and lighting upon him: And lo a voice from heaven, saying, This is my beloved Son, in whom I am well pleased. Matthew 3:15–17

Fourth, baptism is one way to include the new believer in the church family. (Note: Children must have written permission from their parents to be baptized. See CD 2.1 to view the children's baptismal permission slip.)

Then they that gladly received his word were baptized: and the same day there were added unto them about three thousand souls. Acts 2:41

The following are some guidelines that include reminders and suggestions to help the new convert feel at ease.

The Baptistry Changing Room

The changing room should be as close to the baptistry as possible. This will make it quick, easy, and modest for those being baptized. It is best to have separate changing areas within the changing room.

These areas should have privacy walls. Our individual changing areas are divided like large showers with durable curtains separating the stalls. Stock each changing room with the following:

- Clean towels

- Baptismal robes in as many varying sizes as possible

- Hangers to hang the robes on once they are used so they do not mildew (The person laundering them can collect them from the hangers.)

- Hair dryers

- Brushes and combs (These should be cleaned after each use.)

- Hairspray

- Address labels (These are used as name tags on the gowns.)

- Decision cards (see CD 1.2) and pens

- Stapler for attaching children's permission slip to decision card

- Waders for the pastor in the men's changing room

The Baptism—The Soulwinner and the New Christian

Let us walk through the steps of getting a convert baptized from the soulwinner's perspective:

1. Discuss before the actual service, if possible, why the new Christian needs to be baptized. This helps to save time during the invitation.

2. At the invitation, walk with the new Christian down the aisle and tell the altar worker that he wishes to be baptized.

3. A worker may accompany you and the new Christian to the changing room where he will change from his clothes to a baptismal gown. While he is changing, fill out the decision card (see CD 1.2) completely. Give this card to the changing room attendant.

4. The changing room attendant may need you to write the new Christian's name on the provided address label and place it on his left shoulder after he has changed into the baptismal gown. Be ready to assist in this manner.

5. When it is his turn, he should carefully step down into the baptistry.

6. The pastor will call his name and ask if he has accepted Christ as his Saviour. He will then be baptized and return to the changing room.

7. Once in the changing room, he should change back into his clothes while you wait for him.

8. When he is ready to go, we recommend taking him aside and praying with him that God will help him to grow as a new Christian and will help him to stay strong and faithful.

Practical Reminders

These reminders will help ensure that you have a smooth experience every service.

1. The supplies need to be checked each week. This would include finding out if there are enough towels, decision cards, name tags, and baptismal gowns. The waders for the pastor also need to be in the men's baptistry area.

2. In the event that these supplies are running low, please submit in writing a request for more supplies to the outreach pastor.

3. After each baptismal service, dirty towels and baptismal gowns need to be placed in the laundry bag so they can be washed. A member of the Baptistry Ministry should be assigned to handle the baptistry laundry each week.

Baptismal Procedures

1. Discreetly leave for the baptistry area during the early part of the invitation and unlock baptistry doors.

2. Greet the new convert with a warm smile. (He may be a little nervous.)

3. Help the altar worker find the correct gown size so the new convert can get changed and then direct him toward an available changing area.

4. Remind the altar worker to fill out the decision card completely: name, age, address, phone number, birth date, marital status, etc. (see CD 1.2).

5. Fill out the name tag for the new convert legibly and place it on his left shoulder. (Use his first and last name.)

6. Instruct him about the actual procedure once he is dressed:
   a. Walk slowly.
   b. Hold on to the rails—it is very slippery.
   c. Relax.
   d. Speak clearly when answering.
   e. With one hand, grip the nose, and with the other hand hold onto the wrist (demonstrate for them).
   f. To help the pastor in baptizing, bend a little at the knees (demonstrate for them).

7. Workers on the men's side should assist the pastor in putting on the waders.

8. Communicate with the other baptistry area as to how many there are to be baptized. (It is helpful if phones can be placed in all changing rooms so that attendants can communicate with each other.)

9. Have towels ready to give to each person as soon as he comes out of the baptistry.

10. On the men's side, assist the pastor as he comes out of the baptistry.

11. Clean and straighten up the baptistry area. Hang up all wet clothing.

12. On the ladies' side, make combs and hair dryers available for their use. Make sure the brushes and combs are cleaned after each use.

13. Congratulate those who have just been baptized. After they have dressed, have a word of prayer with them.

The Baptism of Children

1. A parental permission slip is required before any child (under age 18) is baptized (see CD 2.1).

2. A visit to the home by the Sunday school workers is to be made with a three-fold purpose:

   a. Explain to the parents the biblical reasons for baptism and secure written permission with date and signature of either parent or legal guardian.

   b. Explain to the child the biblical reasons for baptism and make sure he understands the difference between their salvation decision and baptism.

   c. Share the Gospel with the rest of the family if they are unsaved.

3. Explain the procedures for actual physical baptism, including the following:

   a. How to get to the changing rooms
   b. The private stalls for changing into baptismal robes
   c. The procedure for being immersed into the water

4. Baptistry workers should receive the permission slip and staple it to the child's information/decision card, which is filled out when he is baptized.

5. These decision cards must be turned in to the changing room attendant who will place them in the church's decision card box. From there, the church staff will make a permanent record of the decision.

6. A child is never to be baptized without parental consent in written form.

Note: A detailed baptism brochure is available from *Striving Together Publications* for use in follow-up work. Contact *Striving Together* at 800-201-7748 or visit the website at www.strivingtogether.com for more information.

CHAPTER THREE

The Discipleship Ministry

"And the things that thou hast heard of me
among many witnesses, the same commit thou
to faithful men, who shall be able to teach others also."
II Timothy 2:2

The Lord left His marching orders to the church in Matthew 28:18–20. Throughout the course of church history, these verses have come to be recognized as "The Great Commission." Sadly, for many churches in our land, these verses represent the "Great Omission."

In many churches across America, these verses are sounded out to challenge our people in the area of soulwinning; however, care should be taken to recognize that "soulwinning" is merely the first step in this commission. There are four key thoughts contained in this passage. First, we are to GO. Second, we are to WIN, which is represented by *"teach all nations."* Third, we are to BAPTIZE those whom we have led to Christ. Still, even at this point the commission is not complete. Finally, we are commanded to DISCIPLE these converts as we teach them "to observe all things." It is vital that Bible-believing churches remember that ALL of the Great Commission is applicable to our ministries.

Paul gave Timothy a command as he was left to pastor the church in Ephesus. In Paul's second epistle to the young pastor, the aged Apostle admonished Timothy to take the things that he had learned from him and to commit those sacred truths to the next generation. More importantly, those truths were to be committed in such a way that this generation could teach the same principles to those following in their footsteps. We call this process biblical discipleship, and it is the means that God has given us to reach the world. Biblical discipleship is a necessary outgrowth of (and not a replacement for) biblical evangelism.

At Lancaster Baptist Church we have often said, "It is only as we develop others around us that we permanently succeed." We believe that a formal discipleship is one of the best tools to help nurture and ground people in the Lord Jesus Christ. We believe the preaching of God's Word is the primary tool for developing strong Christians; however, we have determined not to underestimate the powerful importance of one-on-one relationships for the purpose of teaching, encouraging, and mentoring people in their walks with Christ.

It is no coincidence that Peter refers to *"newborn babes"* in Christ (I Peter 2:2). It is not merely chance that Jesus uses the terminology of "being born again" as He speaks to Nicodemus in John 3. Paul refers to his "son" in the ministry. There is an obvious link to a relationship being mentioned. Those whom we lead to Christ are likened to our spiritual offspring. Just as we would not neglect our natural children, so also we must not neglect those whom God has committed to our care.

There are some truths that must be learned in the context of a mentoring (discipling) relationship. The new convert is to be taught and nurtured along in his faith by a more mature Christian. If we Christians neglect our responsibility to the next generation, we will continue to reproduce carnal, struggling Christians in our churches. As mature Christians, we have an obligation to teach to others what we have learned.

The Discipleship Program

How To Start a Discipleship Program

1. Choose a discipleship director. It may be beneficial to have the soulwinning director also be the discipleship director. He will be the one with the most contact with new believers and new church members. This gives him a jump-start on knowing who needs to be discipled.

2. Choose your curriculum.

3. Train your adult Bible class leaders in how to use the discipleship session (explained in The Discipleship Session section). They should then choose key couples from their class to train. Then these key couples can be used to train others. Singles' classes would train key singles and then use those key singles to disciple other singles.

4. Introduce this new ministry to your church family through announcements, bulletin inserts, and a time set aside in a Sunday night service to explain and excite the members. You may also choose to do a 3–5 minute video with testimonies and information.

5. Enroll new believers and members who may need the discipleship training. The discipleship director should teach the adult Bible class leaders how to have a discipleship secretary in their classes and encourage the class leaders to consistently enroll new class members into the discipleship program.

6. Pair disciples with disciplers. "Disciples" would be the new believers—the ones being trained. "Disciplers" would be the key couples or singles that have already been trained

and would be the trainers or the ones discipling the new believers.

7. Select a room at the church that would accommodate your disciples and disciplers. It is very helpful for this room to be well lit, at a comfortable temperature, and have tables and chairs set up for groups of two and four.

8. All new members and new converts for the week should be contacted by a Sunday school teacher or the class secretary and encouraged to enroll in discipleship. Not all will enroll, but many will.

Note: Many church planters will take a core group of new believers through *Daily in the Word* (discussed later in the chapter) on Wednesday night. The use of the mid-week service allows an initial group to be discipled and then, a few of the folks from that group may be chosen to begin serving in the Discipleship Ministry with those who become Christians in the ensuing months and years.

How to Maintain a Discipleship Program

1. The discipleship director should keep accurate and up-to-date records of who is in discipleship, who is training whom, who is on what lesson, and who is ready to graduate into the regular Wednesday night service. At the end of the discipleship session, each discipler should turn in a discipleship report stating this information for the discipleship director (see CD 3.1). There are many computer programs that will help keep these important records. Lancaster Baptist Church uses Shelby Systems.

2. The discipleship director is responsible for:

   • Making sure the room is ready

   • Having light refreshments ready (trays of cookies, coffee, and pitchers of ice water or lemonade)

- Distributing the sign-in sheets that record the names of the disciple and discipler and what lesson they complete that night. He should collect these at the end of the discipleship session.

- Distributing the *Daily in the Word* curriculum to the discipler. There should be a teacher's guide and a student (disciple) workbook. This is done at the start of a new Christian's discipleship. The disciple and the discipler keep their books throughout the weeks it takes to finish. These are **not** distributed and collected weekly.

As we organize the discipleship program, it will become more effective. The following pages contain our discipleship handbook. They will give you a glimpse into the heartbeat of the *Daily in the Word* discipleship program that is in place at Lancaster Baptist Church.

The Discipleship Ministry

Dear Friend,

I want to welcome you to the Discipleship Ministry! I am thrilled that you have decided to become a part of this ministry. I pray that the Lord will use you to calm the nerves of and to encourage these new Christians who may be nervous about taking this next (and needy) step in their Christian walk.

It is a privilege to be able to serve the Lord in any way or fashion here. As you serve in this ministry, I would like you to keep in mind what the Bible says in Colossians 3:23–24: "And whatsoever ye do, do it heartily, as to the Lord, and not unto men; Knowing that of the Lord ye shall receive the reward of the inheritance: for ye serve the Lord Christ." Always be mindful that your service is unto the Lord and whatever we do for Him should be our best.

The thought of a "commitment to excellence" comes to my mind when I read those verses. As servants of God, our attitude toward the Lord's work should be on a different level of excellence because of Whom we are serving—the Lord. As a part of this ministry, you have the opportunity to train the next generation of Christian leaders—let us make sure we are reproducing excellence as a standard for Christian living.

Finally, let me express how excited I am that the Lord has led you to serve in this ministry. May the Lord bless you because of your faithfulness in this area of service, and allow you the opportunity to see countless numbers of disciples you have trained faithfully following the Lord.

Your friend,

Pastor

Who can be discipled?

Discipleship is a process for those who are already saved. Primarily, our Discipleship Ministry is designed to take new believers through a systematic study of the basics of the Christian life. Those who are discipled should have a desire to grow to maturity and should be faithfully attending at least one service a week.

In addition to new Christians, there are also new church members or those who have been saved for years but have never systematically studied the basics of the Christian walk. These same believers may have never been challenged to multiply other Christian disciples. This missing element may be the motivation to help more established Christians go through a discipling ministry along with the newer converts.

What are biblical goals for discipleship?

A biblical study of discipleship reveals that there are at least eight primary steps (or stages) in which the new convert will be encouraged to take. These steps should be learned by all of the disciplers (or else we will have the blind leading the blind).

1. A disciple must first be a believer. (John 3:16)

2. A disciple is in the Word of God every day. (John 8:31)

3. A disciple is in prayer to God every day. (Luke 11:1)

4. A disciple and discipler meet together every week. (John 13:35)

5. A disciple is in a local church that makes disciples. (Ephesians 4:11–12)

6. A disciple is faithfully obedient to the Word of God. (Luke 14:33)

7. A disciple leads people to Christ and disciples them. (John 15:8)

8.   A disciple has disciples who make disciples. (John 15:16)

Each of these steps is built upon the previous one. We have established a goal to take a lost person in our community to the point where he is not only saved, but is also involved in the multiplication of disciples.

What is the strategy used in discipling?

Our goal is established. We desire to be a ministry that produces committed followers of Christ who, in turn, reach others with the life-changing message of the Gospel. However, before a goal can become a reality, a biblical strategy must be developed to help us reach the goal.

As we endeavor to take a new believer through the remaining steps of discipleship, there are several key ingredients that are crucial to the new disciple's development. First, the discipler must be right relationally. This concept includes several aspects. Of course, the discipler must be correct relationally with the Lord if he desires spiritual growth in his disciple. In addition, he must cultivate a right relationship with the new convert that yields a trusting friendship. Our disciplers understand that there will be a commitment of time and energy for this key ingredient to be successful.

The second ingredient involves some essential qualities in the discipler. It is not enough to simply want to disciple someone. Our team of disciplers must believe in the importance of discipleship. They must believe that it is based upon a biblical mandate that has been given to the Church. Our disciplers must be willing to personally get involved in the life of another and be willing to patiently train the next generation of church leaders. Our disciplers understand that in a position of influence, there is a greater responsibility to be consistent in their walk with Christ.

The third key ingredient involves the proper relational procedures between a discipler and his disciple. The disciple must become a priority and may even require some sacrifice on behalf of a discipler. These times together are not simply to go over sections in a book, nor are they times only to sit and fellowship. There must be a balance between these two thoughts, as our disciplers seek to impact a life for eternity. In this type of relationship, a discipler has the awesome opportunity to demonstrate how the Christian life is to be lived. In the times spent together studying the Word of God, the discipler is involved in fellowship, answering questions, counseling, encouraging, teaching, correcting, making application, and giving "spiritual" homework.

The final key ingredient is a proper organizational procedure. If discipleship is not important enough to organize, it will not be important enough to emphasize. We believe that the Sunday school (or adult Bible class ministry) is the church organized. Therefore, we organize the outreach and discipleship through these classes. New converts are paired together with disciplers from their adult Bible class. Each class has its own discipleship secretary assisting each class leader in keeping the importance of discipleship before his class.

Given below are some final thoughts to consider as your ministry seeks to develop a biblical strategy for discipleship.

1. Disciple in such a way that when you are finished, your disciple can go on to disciple someone else.

2. Rather than simply teaching rules, teach doctrine and Bible principles, and strive to be a godly example.

3. Teach your disciple to become dependent on the Word of God, not on you, your church, or any other personality.

4. Teach your disciple to hear, read, study, memorize, and meditate on the Word of God.

5. Explain the importance of the Word of God for practical daily living.

6. Pray *with* and *for* your disciple.

7. Remember that your disciple will disciple others the way you disciple him.

8. Remember that discipleship will never replace soulwinning.

9. Teach the principle early on that spiritual strength can never be attained apart from the Word of God.

10. Preach the importance of discipleship to everyone.

What type of curriculum is used?

According to the Great Commission, local churches have the dual responsibility of reaching and teaching. To some extent, every church is involved with these directives. However, there are some churches that have tried to raise the standard for each one of these responsibilities. We have chosen to aggressively pursue both priorities at the same time. We desire to impact our valley with the Gospel of Christ, while simultaneously training those whom we reach.

In our Discipleship Ministry, we use a curriculum called *Daily in the Word*. This curriculum is being used not only to develop committed followers of Christ, but also to develop followers of Christ who reproduce more followers of Christ. In short, it is the fulfillment of Paul's instruction to Timothy in II Timothy 2:2, *"And the things that thou hast heard of me among many witnesses, the same commit thou to faithful men, who shall be able to teach others also."*

This curriculum has three primary goals to be accomplished in the life of each disciple. The first goal is that these new believers would be in the Word of God every day. The second is that these believers would be equipped for the ministry. This is the responsibility of the church leadership according to Ephesians 4:11-12. It is from this group of disciples that we look for our future laborers. This curriculum is part of our response to the Lord's prayer request: *"Pray ye therefore the Lord of the harvest, that he will send forth labourers into his harvest"* (Matthew 9:38).

Finally, this curriculum has been designed with the intent of seeing the multiplication of disciplers. To "ground" a believer to the point of being able to answer tough questions is not the same as "discipling" that believer. Our goal should be to help new believers fully understand, embrace, and pass on the foundational principles of the truth of God's Word. To order *Daily in the Word,* call *Striving Together Publications* at 800-201-7748 or visit the website at www.strivingtogether.com.

The Discipleship Session

1. Disciplers and disciples should meet at a set time every week for about 1 to 1½ hours. Lancaster Baptist Church holds discipleship on Wednesday nights during our midweek prayer service. There are many benefits to this:

   - It helps the new believer to form a habit of being in church on Wednesday nights.

   - Convenient childcare is already provided for the church service.

   - It assists our families in not having to take another night away from the home.

2. Remember the discipleship session is an informal time. It may get loud as your discipleship program grows! This is a happy, joyous time for these new believers, and there will be much talking between the disciple and his discipler. This multiplies as you grow and add more groups! This is a blessing and a good thing!

3. At the beginning of the discipleship session, the discipleship director should welcome everyone, give announcements that would be made in church, and open with prayer.

4. After prayer, one-on-one discipleship should take place between the already paired disciples and disciplers. (Remember the adult Bible class leader pairs up these groups.) With the couples, the husband should do the

teaching. The wife should enter into discussion times if she feels she has something to add, maybe something she feels would help the other wife.

5. The discipleship director should come back to the discipleship room and announce the beginning of the invitation in the main service. This should give the disciplers time to wrap up and dismiss about the same time as the main service would end.

What happens when I complete discipleship?

Upon completion of the last lesson of the program, the new Christian graduates knowing that he has taken a major spiritual step forward. He has spent five to six months (more or less depending on prior knowledge and the pace of his discipler) in an in-depth training program that will affect the remainder of his Christian journey.

Realizing the commitment it takes to finish, we endeavor to give "honor to whom honor is due." When one of our new Christians (or any new Christian who is using our curriculum) finishes, we present them a "*Daily in the Word* Laymen's Diploma" from West Coast Baptist College to commemorate this milestone. We then seek to provide opportunities for these people to serve and be involved in the future discipling of others. (For additional information on this ministry curriculum, or the West Coast Baptist College diplomas, contact *Striving Together Publications*.)

CHAPTER FOUR

Adult Bible Classes

*"Teaching them to observe all things
whatsoever I have commanded you:
and, lo, I am with you alway..."*
Matthew 28:20

One of the central components of a strong, growing church is a solid Sunday school program. Whether nine years old or ninety years old, all human beings have a strong desire to *belong* somewhere, to "fit in." Most Baptist churches are structured in such a way that the place to "belong" is in the Sunday school class. A healthy adult Bible class has proven to be the best way to involve people in small group fellowship that meets the individual spiritual needs and benefits the health of the church as a whole.

Adult Bible classes, in particular, have a vital role in the growth of the church. They are critical in the teaching of God's Word, the caring for spiritual needs, the nurturing of the entire church body, and evangelizing the lost world. A successful adult Bible class will provide a wonderful entry point to the church. Most visitors hesitate to leave their pews during hand-shaking time to meet new people or even stand to their feet and introduce themselves when the pastor calls for first-time visitors. Yet with the smaller, more relaxed atmosphere of a Bible class, visitors are given the opportunity to be noticed and welcomed informally by those around them.

The Adult Department Director

It is wise to have a director who oversees the entire adult department. This person should reflect the pastor's vision for the care and education of the adults enrolled in Sunday school. He will oversee attendance records and assist the class leaders with everything from the class name, signage, and visitation cards to the classroom assignments and curriculum. He is also responsible for staffing, training, and leading all teachers and workers in the adult Bible class department.

The Class Leader

Perhaps the most important people in the adult department are the class leaders or teachers. The adult Bible class leader will represent the Lord before the members of the class and, therefore, should be chosen wisely with much prayer. In addition, the adult Bible class leader should assure the class of the heart of the pastor for each of them and must be someone who understands the heart and the philosophy of the pastor. The class leader should have the spiritual gift of teaching and must be able to study God's Word, teach it with clarity, and apply it to the lives of those in his class. The Bible lesson taught each Sunday morning is the single most important aspect of the adult class. Nothing will keep a Christian faithful in attendance like a well-prepared, practical Bible lesson.

The teachers of adult Bible classes provide a multiplicity of leadership to support the pastors of the church. These teachers should be available to their class for counseling, answering Bible questions, and to help with other spiritual needs as they arise.

Many new Christians may hesitate to schedule an appointment with the pastor over a minor issue, but they will gladly ask a question of their teacher after class one day. Thus, it is important that the chosen Bible teachers be mature, proven members of your church. They should display and encourage loyalty to the pastor and should not hesitate to deflect a potential problem or question to his authority.

Generally speaking, but not always, the adult Bible teacher should either be at the same stage of life as his class or one who has recently passed out of that age bracket. The class members must be able to create a bond with the teacher through a commonality.

One goal of the teacher should be to encourage those in his class to get to know one another on a more personal level. Even the largest churches seem close-knit when they have a thriving adult Bible class ministry, and indeed they are. While walking into a large auditorium filled with people may seem overwhelming, stepping into a smaller classroom filled with people one's own age is far less intimidating. College-aged adults are now fellowshipping with others their age, and newlyweds suddenly find themselves surrounded by more young couples encountering the same challenges they have. As this happens, friendships develop and lives are enriched.

The Curriculum

The curriculum of an adult Bible class is vital to its growth both numerically and spiritually. People will not continue attending a Bible class for the donuts and coffee, but they will attend faithfully if they are growing and receiving Bible lessons that are relevant to today and to their situations. Class members will thrive in a setting that affords them the opportunity to discover Bible truths that will change the way they react in the "real world"—on the job, at home, and in personal relationships. Many times we write our own curriculum, but when we seek outside publications, we are very careful to ensure that they are doctrinally sound and currently relevant.

Concerning curriculums, we divide our year into four quarters. For two of the quarters, the education director provides a unified curriculum, which means all the classes church-wide are learning the same lesson on the same Sunday. The lessons are adapted to the various age levels. For the other two quarters, the adult Bible class leaders are encouraged to choose a series that they feel would benefit their LifeStage. For instance, a singles' class leader may teach a series on "dating." This would not apply to couples' classes. The couples' classes may have a series on "rearing children," and this would not apply to the Student Ministries classes. All class leaders must have their series approved by the education director.

The time of the year also influences what would be taught in the classes. The first quarter lessons are built around the new theme for the year. Special days on the church calendar may guide the direction of lessons. Six to eight weeks before a stewardship banquet, giving would be taught. During the weeks before Open House and Harvest Month, lessons on reaching out to the community and neighbors could be taught. Class leaders may also teach on soulwinning during those weeks.

Fellowship

An added advantage to having smaller adult classes is that it provides more opportunities for outreach and fellowship times. In addition to church family fellowship, many Bible classes are able to meet monthly for outside activities. These activities vary greatly, depending on the age and needs of the class, but can be anything from dinner at someone's house, to paintball, to bowling, etc. Be creative in your activities and do not be afraid to try new things!

Class Divisions

The benefit of having a variety of adult Bible classes is that each class can reach people with specific needs. For example, the need to have a Single Ladies' Department is becoming more and more prevalent in our society. These classes can tailor to the needs of all types of women, whether single, divorced, or widowed. The needs of a single, career woman are far different from those of a stay-at-home wife or even a working mother. Those needs should be recognized and brought up during the Sunday school hour. The lessons in these classes should be directly applicable to the member's life and be something she can put into practice daily.

One of the most essential aspects of an adult Bible class is that it provides accountability among its members. In a class of 20 or 30, it is easy to notice who is missing each week and express concern for them. We all need personal contact and interaction with others. If a person feels that he will be missed or needed when gone, he may be less likely to miss church services. This truth also applies to visitors. When someone visits your church for the first time and goes unrecognized, he feels unwelcome and will probably not return. On the other hand, if that person is greeted warmly inside the classroom and enrolled into an adult Bible class the first week he is there, he will immediately begin to feel like part of the church family.

This accountability also applies to the Christian's personal walk with the Lord. When someone becomes active in a Bible class, he instantly has 20 or 30 other people praying for him and pulling for him to succeed. He might obtain an accountability partner from this Bible class, someone who can ask him consistently how his daily prayer and devotional life are going. Being accountable to another brother in Christ is imperative in the life of a new Christian.

Care Groups

In addition to the accountability and encouragement one receives from his class, each member is also brought under the ministry of a care group leader, a mature Christian in his class who can maintain constant communication with him. This can be through visits, phone calls, and even letters. Every person needs to know that someone cares about him, and the care group is a wonderful way to accomplish this.

When calling or writing, the care group leader should remind his members of special activities or projects at the church, ask them often if they have any prayer requests, and just be there for support when a group member is struggling. The pastoral staff cannot contact every member of the church to discover his burdens each week, and they rely heavily on care group leaders for support in this area. The care group leader should be very careful to let the teacher and pastoral staff know of any potential problems or serious illnesses.

The care group is generally an unseen, but very significant and influential, branch of church ministry, and it is vitally important that the care group leaders have a healthy and growing relationship with the Lord.

Care groups are just one aspect of an adult Bible class' structure. An adult Bible class may also have interior and exterior greeters, fellowship leaders, hospitality leaders, and discipleship leaders.

The following guidelines outline the different ministries that take place within the adult Bible class program. The next page shows the welcome letter that is sent to all who volunteer to serve in class leadership. They should receive the letter with the LifeStages Leader's Handbook, which is shown in the several pages following the letter.

Adult Bible Class Ministry

Dear Team Member,

I want to welcome you to the LifeStages Leadership Team. First of all, I personally count it a joy that you are a part of the adult Bible classes, and it is a tremendous blessing to serve with you in this ministry.

Second, I believe God has blessed the adult Bible classes. I am convinced God would want us to do so much more in reaching other adults with the Gospel of Christ, caring for needs that arise in their lives, helping to disciple people who have a desire to have a strong walk with the Lord, and providing a place where Christians can develop lasting relationships. As our church grows, these objectives are being met through the adult Bible classes now more than ever.

Finally, for all this to happen, I realize I cannot achieve these goals on my own, and it would not be fair not to allow others to serve in these areas. It is my desire that you will open your heart as I share with you some of the vision God has given to me for our department. Thank you again for being a part of the adult Bible class team!

Your friend,

Pastor

LifeStages

t h e   p e r f e c t   f i t

The Adult Bible Class Ministry
of Lancaster Baptist Church

Leader's Manual

A Word from Pastor Chappell

The Sunday school is a big deal! It is big because the Sunday school is the reaching, teaching, winning, and caring arm of the church. It is "the church organized, to fulfill the purpose of the church."

I am thankful to God for you and for the opportunity He has given us to labor together in developing committed disciples of Jesus Christ. The Antelope Valley is still bursting with people who need Jesus. I believe He has called us to reach them and share with them His purpose for their lives.

My desire is to put into your hands the tools necessary to fulfill this awesome mission. I trust that each of us will walk with God closely, prepare diligently, and love people passionately. If we will, I know we can bear much "fruit that remains" in the coming days.

Pastor

Purposes of an Adult Bible Class

An Adult Class Inspires:

- by providing an environment that is warm and friendly.

- by inviting prospects to our worship services.

- by sharing the Gospel with class visitors and prospects.

An Adult Class Includes:

- by enrolling people into the class.

- by creating an atmosphere where people feel accepted.

- by providing fellowship through the class and care groups.

An Adult Class Instructs:

- by teaching God's Word weekly.

- by involving members in the discipleship program.

• by the model of the teacher and class leaders.

An Adult Class Involves:

- • by assigning weekly responsibilities to growing members.

- • by encouraging involvement in weekly church ministry.

- • by participating in church-wide outreach opportunities.

An Adult Class Impacts:

- • by enrolling members in T.E.A.M. Soulwinning.

- • by identifying and inviting prospects for the class.

- • by visiting in the homes of visitors and prospects.

The Missions of the Adult Bible Class

Our mission is clearly described by the Acts 2:41–42 pattern...

> *Then they that gladly received his word were baptized: and the same day there were added unto them about three thousand souls. And they continued stedfastly in the apostles' doctrine and fellowship, and in breaking of bread, and in prayers.*

Our Mission Is Evangelization.

- • Defined: To win people to Jesus Christ

- • Described: "*Then they that gladly received his word were baptized...*"

- • Delegated: To every class member

Our Mission Is Edification.

- • Defined: To build people up in the knowledge of Christ

- • Described: "*And they continued stedfastly in the apostles' doctrine...*"

- Delegated: To the class leader and discipleship leaders

Our Mission Is Exhortation.

- Defined: To minister to people within the body of Christ
- Described: "*...fellowship, and in breaking of bread, and in prayers.*"
- Delegated: To the class leader and care group leaders

The Structure of the Overall Adult Sunday School

(CD 4.1)

The Structure of the Individual Adult Bible Class

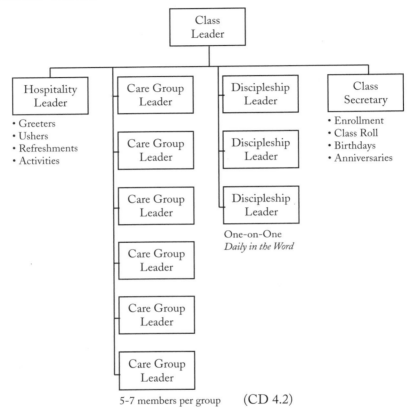

5-7 members per group   (CD 4.2)

The Structure of the LifeStages

Student Ministries Division

- Junior High Department
    - 7th–8th grade boys
    - 7th–8th grade girls

- Senior High Department
    - 9th grade
    - 10th grade
    - 11th–12th grade

- College & Career Department
    Years 1 & 2 out of high school
    Years 3 & 4 out of high school

Adult Ministries Division

- Singles' Department (ages 24–49)
    Ladies 20-29   Coed 24-34   Men 35–49
    Ladies 30-39   Coed 35-49
    Ladies 40-49

- Couples' Department (ages 20–49)
    Couples 20–29
    Couples 25–34
    Couples 30–39
    Couples 35–44
    Couples 40–49

- Median and Senior Adult Department (ages 50 and up)
    Couples 50+   Ladies 50+   General 60+

Outreach of the Adult Bible Class

Assimilation: Leading people from V to E to M

- as·sim·i·late *verb*

- To integrate somebody into a larger group so that differences are minimized or eliminated

- To incorporate digested food materials into the cells and tissues of the body

Visitor **Enrollee** **Member**

1. Stranger	4. Class Visitor	7. Baptized
2. Prospect	5. Enrolled in Class	8. Discipled
3. Worship Visitor	6. In Care Group	9. In Ministry

(CD 4.3)

55

What happens when a

1. Prospect Card
2. Church Visitor Card
3. Class Visitor Card is filled out?

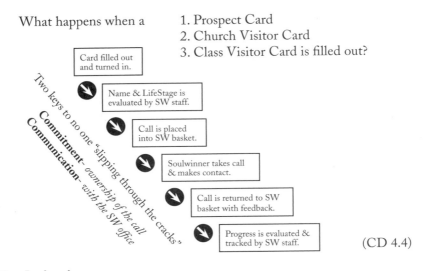

(CD 4.4)

Soulwinning

Strategic visitation through every adult class

- Every participant in T.E.A.M. Soulwinning will be assigned to a soulwinning team. The teams include:

  - Each adult Bible class
  - Children's Sunday school
  - Student Ministry
  - Bus Ministry
  - Spanish Ministry

- Each soulwinner is matched with a partner from his or her same soulwinning team.

- Every Tuesday morning, Tuesday evening, and Saturday morning, a soulwinning basket is available for each team upon dismissal (where calls are distributed).

- Each soulwinning basket contains the following types of contacts:

  - Church visitors (from worship services)
  - Class visitors
  - Class absentees

- Class prospects
- New move-ins
- Doorknocking maps

Enrollment into the Adult Bible Class

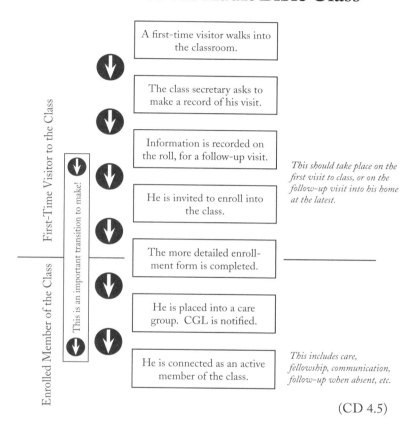

(CD 4.5)

The Role of the Class Leader

Definition:

The adult Bible class leader provides spiritual leadership for the members of his class as an extension of the ministry of the pastor.

Description:

The adult Bible class leader should possess:

- a sincere love for people.

- a passion to reach people for Jesus Christ.

- loyalty to the pastor and church ministry.

- the gifts of teaching and administration.

Duties:

1. Study and prepare for each week's lesson. Curriculum is selected quarterly with the education pastor.

2. Enroll people in the class and place them into care groups.

3. Witness for Christ regularly and carry out the Great Commission: win, baptize, and teach. Participate in weekly T.E.A.M. soulwinning.

4. Love, care, and minister to members and non-members.

5. Lead members to grow through personal, family, and church worship.

6. Support and communicate the work of the church.

7. Organize monthly class activities.

8. Delegate weekly class responsibilities to leaders within the class. Meet monthly or quarterly with these leaders.

9. Encourage new members to participate in discipleship.

10. Pray faithfully for members, visitors, and prospects.

11. Contact every absentee every week through a call or visit.

12. See that the classroom is set up properly.

13. Attend the weekly teachers' meeting.

14. Communicate members' spiritual or physical needs to the education pastor.

The Role of the Care Group Leader

Definition:

The care group leader helps his or her class leader to create an atmosphere of belonging within the class by fellowshipping with, contacting, and caring for the assigned members of the class.

Description:

The care group leader should possess:

- a sincere love for people.

- a passion to reach people for Jesus Christ.

- loyalty to the pastor and church ministry.

- the gifts of exhortation and mercy-showing.

Duties:

1. Help to make class visitors feel welcomed. Direct them to the class secretary to place their name on the roll sheet.

2. Look for and be informed of spiritual or physical needs within the care group. Always communicate these needs to the class leader.

3. Schedule times at least once each quarter for fellowship with the care group members in your home or another location.

4. Contact every absentee every week through a call or visit.

5. Send an encouraging note or card to every member of the care group at least once a quarter.

6. Witness for Christ regularly and carry out the Great Commission: win, baptize, and teach. Participate in weekly T.E.A.M. soulwinning.

7. Love, care, and minister to members and non-members.

8. Support and communicate the work of the church.

9. Assist the class leader with monthly class activities.

10. Pray faithfully for the members of the care group.

11. Provide meals through other members of the care group when needed due to illness, hospitalization, a new baby, etc.

12. Attend training clinics and class leadership meetings.

The Role of the Discipleship Leader

Definition:

The discipleship leader enters into a one-on-one relationship with a new believer or a new member to guide him through the *Daily in the Word* program and to provide a mature Christian friend for the purpose of mentoring.

Description:

The discipleship leader should possess:

- a sincere love for people and interest in their lives.

- a passion to reach and train people for Jesus Christ.

- loyalty to the pastor and church ministry.

- the gifts of teaching and exhortation.

- a working knowledge of the Bible and *Daily in the Word*.

Duties:

1. Meet weekly with your disciple(s), for the purposes of reviewing, covering new material, and answering questions.

2. Witness for Christ regularly and carry out the Great Commission: win, baptize, and teach. Participate in weekly T.E.A.M. soulwinning.

3. Speak to new class members about the ministry of discipleship.

4. Lead members to grow through personal, family, and church worship.

5. Support and communicate the work of the church.

6. Pray faithfully for current and former disciples.

7. Contact absent disciples through a call or visit.

8. Attend training clinics and class leadership meetings.

9. Be aware of spiritual needs or struggles in the life of disciples. Always communicate these needs to the class leader.

The Role of the Hospitality Leader

Definition:

The hospitality leader helps to create a friendly atmosphere as people arrive to class through overseeing the greeting, refreshments, and ushering. The hospitality leader may also assist with class activities. The hospitality leader's responsibilities may be divided between more than one member.

Description:

The hospitality leader should possess:

- a sincere love for people and a personable disposition.

- a passion to reach people for Jesus Christ.

- loyalty to the pastor and church ministry.

- the gifts of exhortation and administration.

Duties:

1. Have at least one person at each entrance of the classroom to shake hands, welcome people, and distribute the class bulletin.

2. Delegate the weekly responsibility to have refreshments provided and set up. Members can provide them on a rotating basis, or collections can be taken for refreshments to be purchased.

3. Have at least two ushers prepared to collect the offering and place it outside the classroom door for the church ushers to collect.

4. Take a count of the class attendance and write it on a note for the church ushers to record when they collect the class offering.

5. Help with sign-up sheets and collect money for class activities. Get direction from the class leader for the depositing of the money that is collected.

The Role of the Class Secretary

Definition:

The class secretary provides organizational support to the class leader. The class secretary would assist with all record keeping, bulletin production, and birthday/anniversary greetings and should be available before and after class to assist the class leader.

Description:

The class secretary should possess:

• a sincere love for people and interest in their lives.

• a passion to reach people for Jesus Christ.

• loyalty to the pastor and church ministry.

- the gifts of administration and helps.

Duties:

1. Make sure the class roll is ready each Sunday. The Sunday school secretary distributes the class rolls.

2. As members arrive, check their name on the roll.

3. Look for visitors, introduce yourself, welcome them to the class, and ask them if you can make a record of their attendance. Record every local visitor's name, address, and phone number.

4. Distribute the care group leaders' blank reports to them at the beginning of each class time.

5. Collect the care group leaders' completed reports at the conclusion of each class time.

6. Have enrollment forms available, and explain to visitors and non-enrolled attendees that we would love to have them enroll in the class, which means they are placed into a care group and their birthdays and anniversary will be recognized.

7. Keep class member information current, including children's names and birthdays, addresses, telephone numbers, e-mails, etc.

8. Assist the class leader in sending birthday cards to members and their children and anniversary cards to couples.

Commitment of the Adult Bible Class Leaders

Adult Bible Class Leader's Covenant

Recognizing the responsibility that comes with leading an adult Bible class, I covenant together with the pastor and leaders of my church in the following areas:

A COVENANT TO REACHING UP:

1. I will walk closely with Jesus Christ on a daily basis and seek Him in prayer for my own life as well as for the lives of my students.

2. I will prepare my weekly lesson with diligence by spending time during the week in study.

3. I will vocalize my support and loyalty to the pastor and overall ministry of the church.

A COVENANT TO REACHING OUT:

4. I will participate in a weekly organized soulwinning time and encourage my class leaders and members to be involved also.

5. I will be responsible for the distribution of calls from my soulwinning basket at each weekly meeting. I will have a representative from my class at the meetings I am unable to attend.

6. I will seek to enroll every local class visitor into my class. I will see that every local visitor receives a visit each week.

7. I will contact every class absentee every week through either a telephone call or a personal visit. I will use the mail in addition to these contacts when appropriate.

A COVENANT TO REACHING IN:

8. I will seek to enroll new members into the *Daily in the Word* discipleship program and will monitor their progress as they complete the program.

9. I will, in the event that a member has a disagreement with the ministry, bring it to the attention of the pastoral staff and refuse to allow gossip with other class members.

10. I will see that the spiritual and physical needs of the class members are met and will coordinate the care group efforts

in meeting those needs. I will inform the pastoral staff of any serious spiritual or physical needs of class members.

11. I will inform the pastoral staff of any major decisions being considered by class members, including marriage, ministry, moving away, etc.

If I have a question about the leadership of my class or if I am ever unable to fulfill this covenant, I will approach the education pastor, where I can expect to be received in a Christ-honoring way.

Signed: _____   Dated: _____

How to Build an Adult Bible Class

Determine the Target for Your Class

The church as a whole seeks to reach the community as a whole, and ultimately the world. But the adult Bible class has a narrower target in mind. This is the reason for the LifeStage guidelines.

Develop an Identity and Spirit for Your Class.

A. Design a class logo.

B. Utilize a class sign.

C. Print a class outline and bulletin.

D. Create a positive atmosphere in the classroom through cleanliness and décor.

E. Distribute class business cards to your members.

Devote Yourself to Meeting the Needs of Your Class Members.

A. Love your class.

B. Be available to your class. Have an open heart, an open home, and an open Bible.

C. Meet the needs of your class.

   1. The need for acceptance

   2. The need for accountability

   3. The need for activities (fellowship)

   4. How do you know the needs of your class?

      a. Through spending time with them
      b. Through asking questions
      c. Through observation
      d. Through prayer
      e. Through the Holy Spirit's prompting

Discipline Your Procedures to Include Weekly Enrollment.

A. The philosophy of enrollment (V to E to M)

B. The candidates for enrollment—every visitor!

C. The process of enrollment

   1. Designate a class secretary.

   2. Record visitor names to your class rolls.

   3. Distribute enrollment cards.

Designate Servant Leaders Within Your Class.

A. Hospitality Leaders

B. Care Group Leaders

C. Discipleship Leaders

D. Class Secretary

Decide on the Dates for Class Leader Meetings.

A. Weekly meeting with adult division leader and class leaders

B. Monthly meeting with hospitality, care group, and discipleship leaders

- At this meeting, you may distribute supplies, rotate care groups, assign new converts for discipleship, and plan upcoming class activities.

Design Your Class Schedule for Growth.

A. Evangelistic music

B. Enthusiastic announcements

C. Quality Bible lessons

1. Study your lesson throughout the week.

2. Support your main points with cross-references.

3. Define Bible words.

4. Move from literal context to personal application.

5. Avoid excessive references to your own life experiences.

6. Use biblical illustrations.

Direct Your Class to Develop a Heart for God.

A. Through church attendance

B. Through a personal time with God each day

Direct Your Class to Support the Pastor and Church Program.

A. Direct them to love the pastor.

B. Direct them to be loyal to the overall church program.

Delight in the Work of Visitation.

A. Visit in person.

1. Visit every visitor within a week.

2. Visit absentees.

3. Visit new prospects.

B. Visit by phone.

C. Visit through the mail (e.g. birthday cards).

Depend on the Lord through Prayer.

A. Class prayer

B. Personal prayer

Class Signage

The adult class leader is responsible to purchase a 2' x 3' sign from a local banner company. The sign should include information such as:

- Class name

- Time class meets

- Class leader's name

- Class artwork

- Class tag (theme or motto)

- Class verse

CHAPTER FIVE

Adult Ministry Activities & Events

*"And they continued stedfastly in the apostles' doctrine
and fellowship, and in breaking of bread, and in prayers."*
Acts 2:42

The adult Bible classes will provide learning and fellowship for the adults in those classes; however, the adult Bible class should not become disconnected from the rest of the church family. It is important that the classes remain open and friendly within the church as a whole. To encourage fellowship between the classes and to encourage all adults in the church family to become involved and grow spiritually, Lancaster Baptist Church holds a variety of church-wide events. These events occur under the leadership of various ministry directors, are scheduled on our yearly calendar, and are carefully planned to meet the dual needs of spiritual growth and fellowship.

Men's Activities

The purpose of all men's activities and events is to foster leadership abilities and spiritual growth.

Men's Prayer

Held in the Main Auditorium on Saturdays at 9:00 A.M. and 5:00 P.M., this is a time for the men of the church to gather to pray for Sunday's services, the unsaved, and special requests. This time of prayer is announced regularly, and "pushed" at special times of the year such as the Saturday before Missions Conference, where men have the opportunity to pray with various missionaries. It is pushed the Saturday before Open House Sunday when the entire church family is invited to come to the 5:00 P.M. prayer meeting to pray for the special day.

Men's Prayer Breakfast

These are scheduled about twice a year on a Saturday morning at 8:30. This is another time to encourage the men to pray and be involved. Announcements are made regarding special days ahead, and the men enjoy a time of fellowship and prayer. The prayer breakfast is scheduled to dismiss in time for the men to attend the 9:30 A.M. soulwinning meeting.

Leadership BBQ

For a special time of learning and fellowship, Lancaster Baptist Church hosts a Men's Leadership BBQ. These are usually scheduled two to three times a year on a Friday evening. The men enjoy a great meal, such as steak and baked potato, as they fellowship with the other men in the church. A special guest speaker is scheduled who will encourage the men in the area of leadership. Also, a good book on leadership or other character-building principles is given to every man who attends. To encourage attendance, sign-up sheets are sent around and announcements are made in the adult Bible classes. Announcements are also made during the church services and in the bulletin. This evening is very beneficial to your church and the growth of your church families; therefore, if your church can cover the cost of the meal, it should.

Men & Boys' Campout

Occasionally it is beneficial to get away from daily routines and responsibilities to allow your mind and spirit to be refreshed. Lancaster Baptist Church has an annual Men & Boys' Campout for the men and boys to have a little fun and fellowship, but more importantly, to have an intense time of strong Bible preaching and training. It is effective to have a dynamic guest speaker who will "let 'er rip" and train the men in areas of leadership in the home, on the job, and for the Lord.

You will need to plan for the practical side of camping such as campsites, what individuals need to bring on their own (such as tents, sleeping bags, etc.), and what the church can provide (the church may want to provide one or more of the meals). You will also need to plan for the spiritual side of the campout such as an area large enough for all the men and boys to gather for the preaching. And, of course, everyone should bring his Bible.

You will probably want to provide somewhat of a schedule for the campout. It adds to the fun to have activities such as a fishing contest, hiking areas, and a shooting range. Also, meal times and "lights out" times should be established to keep the campout going in a unified direction.

When men and boys get out in the wilderness, they are sure to have a good time, but it is important to remember that the main emphasis of the campout is to establish a closer relationship with the Lord. The main focus should be the preaching and the decisions that the men make that will strengthen their homes and their relationships with the Lord that will in turn strengthen the church.

Ladies' Activities

Activities and events for ladies provide the fun and fellowship that a lady desires while encouraging faithfulness and spiritual growth at the same time. Lancaster Baptist Church has a Ladies' Ministries director to plan activities and encourage the ladies of the church.

Weekly Activities

LADIES' BIBLE STUDY—TUESDAYS, 8:00–9:15 A.M.

The Ladies' Bible Study at Lancaster Baptist Church provides a weekly time of fellowship and learning. It is convenient for the ladies if it is held during school hours. This provides childcare for older children. Nurseries for the younger children may be provided also. Ladies' Bible Study is suspended during the summer months.

The Ladies' Ministries director oversees the schedule and speaks at the Bible study. Below you will see an approximate schedule.

- Refreshments
- Welcome, Prayer, and Song
- Bible Memory Verse
- Missionary Update
- Prayer List and Prayer
- Bible Lesson
- Dismissal

LADIES' SOULWINNING—TUESDAYS, 9:30 A.M.–12:00 P.M.

Lancaster Baptist Church encourages ladies to attend a dedicated soulwinning time. Satan discourages them; therefore, it is helpful to make a time that is as convenient as possible for young mothers. Ladies' soulwinning is scheduled immediately following the Ladies' Bible Study so they only have to bring the children out once.

This soulwinning meeting is led by the soulwinning director. All ladies should be paired with someone from their adult Bible class and should use maps and follow-ups from their class baskets.

All baskets and materials should be set up as directed in the Soulwinning Ministry Chapter (Chapter One).

The meeting usually ends by 10:00 A.M. The ladies would then have from 10:00 until 12:00 to knock doors and make follow-ups.

STRENGTH & BEAUTY—TUESDAYS, 12:30–2:30 P.M.

The world is full of diets and gyms that worship the creation instead of the Creator. Under the leadership of the Ladies' Ministries director, any ladies in the church may sign up and attend this teaching session. Strength & Beauty assists and teaches the proper biblical prospective on diet and health. The ladies receive a diet plan, weekly accountability, and a lunch that follows the Strength & Beauty diet plan. There is a one-time charge that covers the 12-week plan. These 12-week plans can repeat. Returning members can sign up again, and new ladies can join as well.

Annual Events

LADIES' NIGHT OUT

Ladies' Night Out is held three to four times a year and is like a "mini" retreat. Different themes each time will promote fun and participation. Friday evenings are a good time to schedule this event, especially during the school year. Childcare may be provided. There is a good meal, fun games and skits, singing, and a special speaker. Ladies' Night Out is another great tool to encourage fellowship and spiritual growth.

MOTHER/DAUGHTER/FRIEND TEA

Held on a spring Saturday, this event is an exciting time for mothers and daughters! The Tea is a semi-formal event in that many will "dress up" and dress alike. There will be a luncheon with specialty foods and, of course, tea! The social aspect is wonderful in that mothers get to spend some special time just with their daughters, and those who do not have a daughter can have a great time of fellowship with a friend. The ladies are also encouraged to use this time as an evangelistic outreach and bring an unsaved friend, neighbor, or co-worker. After the meal, there is a fun time of skits and a game or two. The most important part of the Tea is the special speaker. It will benefit the ladies greatly to hear a lady who has succeeded in the home and for the Lord. The Mother/Daughter/Friend Tea is an extra event that is designed to encourage the ladies in their walk with the Lord.

LADIES' RETREAT

The Ladies' Retreat is a three-day event that takes place in the autumn. The focus is mainly a time of learning through the many various sessions that are held. There are several fun times, such as skits, games, crafts, gifts, nice dinners, and time for shopping. Below is a general schedule of what may take place during a one-night away retreat.

Thursday:

8:00 A.M.	Tables open for the ladies to pick up their retreat bags which include a notebook of session outlines and any other goodies and giveaways that you may wish to include.
9:00 A.M.	Opening session (combined)
10:00 A.M.	Break (During each break, some kind of treat or giveaway is distributed.)
10:15 A.M.	Split sessions (The split sessions can be named to support your main theme.)
11:00 A.M.	Break
11:15 A.M.	Split sessions
12:00 noon	Lunch (Meals should be covered under the price of the retreat.)
1:00 P.M.	Split sessions
1:45 P.M.	Dismiss to get dressed for dinner/banquet
4:30 P.M.	Arrive at dinner/banquet for informal picture-taking and hors d' oeuvres
5:00 P.M.	Prayer and Dinner
6:30 P.M.	Skit, game, songs

7:00 P.M.	Guest speaker
8:30 P.M.	Dismissal

Friday:

7:30 A.M.	Breakfast
8:30 A.M.	Combined session
10:00 A.M.	Dismiss to head to hotel (Sack lunches or fast food certificates can be given out to cover lunch.)
	The time from dismissal until hotel check-in and dinner is free time for the ladies to get lunch, travel to the hotel, and shop.
3:00 P.M.	Hotel check-in
5:00 P.M.	Dinner and evening session at the hotel (If your group is too large for a restaurant, nice hotels have conference rooms that can be rented. The conference room is convenient because the evening session and Saturday morning sessions can also be held there.)
9:00 P.M.	Dismissal (This is early enough to allow the ladies to go out for coffee or dessert, and some ladies will enjoy a time of fellowship or games.)

Saturday:

8:00 A.M.	Breakfast in the conference room
9:00 A.M.	Session
10:00 A.M.	Break
10:15 A.M.	Session
11:15 A.M.	Break
11:30 A.M.	Closing session
12:30 P.M.	Dismissal

This is a basic schedule that can be adapted to fit any church size, schedule, budget, and need. Our Ladies' Retreat varies yearly depending on the activities we incorporate. Skits, games, or giveaways can be inserted at any time. Themes and decorations change. Dinners can be formal or informal. Travel times may vary depending on the location of the hotel. Depending on the cost, you may choose to be at the hotel for both nights. However you choose to schedule the retreat, it is an effective tool to get the ladies away from responsibilities and distractions and to teach, challenge, and encourage them. This should be a refreshing time for all the ladies who attend.

Couples' Activities

Central in the foundation of the church is the family; therefore, it is wise to invest time and effort into building it. Having activities and events for couples is a highly effective tool to educate, encourage, and equip the husband and wife for the life-long task of leading and loving their family.

Couples' Retreat

A two-day event held in February at a nice hotel (away from the kids). There can be a theme, and the price should cover the hotel and meals (dinner and breakfast). Below is a general schedule that can be altered to fit the needs of your church.

Friday:

2:00 P.M.	Hotel check-in
3:00 P.M.	Opening session in conference room at hotel
4:00 P.M.	Split sessions
5:00 P.M.	Dinner
7:00 P.M.	Evening session—guest speaker
9:00 P.M.	Approximate dismissal

Saturday:

8:00 A.M.	Breakfast
9:00 A.M.	Combined session
9:45 A.M.	Break
10:00 A.M.	Combined session
10:45 A.M.	Break

11:00 A.M. Closing session
12:00 noon Dismissal

Fall Day Trip

The Adult Ministry coordinates a church-wide day trip for couples to Lake Arrowhead, which is up in the mountains of our area. The fall foliage is beautiful at this time of the year, and there are great shops and restaurants in this area. The day trip is an informal time of fellowship that encourages the various couples' classes to form friendships with the couples in their class. Sign-ups are distributed in the adult Bible classes during the weeks before the trip, and childcare is provided through either the Adult Ministry director's office or through individual adult Bible classes.

To adapt this type of an activity to your church, plan the following:

- Beautiful scenery within two hours of the church

- Quaint shopping

- Good restaurants

- Reasonable cost

- Transportation

- Childcare

College & Career Activities

The College & Career Ministry includes single adults ages 18–23. This is the age group that sees the sharpest decline in church involvement. Many students who are faithfully involved in the youth group find themselves lost in a "no man's land" after graduation. They struggle to "fit in." They no longer belong in the Youth Ministry, yet they do not feel like a single adult either. This causes many students to quit attending church altogether.

To create a smooth transition into adulthood, Lancaster Baptist Church created the Student Ministries LifeStage (further explained in the LifeStages Handbook in the Adult Bible Class Chapter and the Student Ministries Chapter). Student Ministries span the years of junior high, senior high, and college. The Student Ministries pastor is the director of Student Ministries. (If the groups become too large, additional group pastors can be added to specific age groups.)

As teenagers progress through the youth group, their sense of belonging is greatly affected by the youth group, youth activities, and youth pastor. The transition from junior to senior high feels comfortable because they are still under the guidance of the youth pastor. The transition from senior high to the College & Career Ministry becomes just as smooth because they retain the same Student Ministries pastor's leadership. Thus, they stay connected, and the drop-off rate declines after high school.

The College & Career Department is organized much the same as the junior high and senior high youth groups. It includes Sunday school classes, activities, and a team of leaders who know them and provide counseling and accountability.

Single students remain in this ministry until they become 24 years of age. At that time, they advance to the Singles' Department.

College & Career Winter Sequester

The Student Ministries director plans a time every winter for the College & Career singles to get away for a time of fellowship and learning from the Word of God. To create an exciting sequester, a fun activity (such as a great shopping mall or a fun amusement park) could be included in the schedule.

The main focus of the sequester is growing in the Lord. A nice hotel with a conference room makes it convenient to hold sessions and meals. The price of the sequester should cover the hotel, meals, and activities. Below is a basic schedule that can be altered to fit the needs of any church.

Friday:

8:00 A.M.	Meet at church and depart for activity
11:00 A.M.	Activity
4:00 P.M.	Hotel check-in
5:00 P.M.	Dinner
7:00 P.M.	Evening session
9:00 P.M.	Dismissal

Saturday:

8:00 A.M.	Breakfast
9:00 A.M.	Combined session
10:00 A.M.	Break
10:15 A.M.	Split session
11:00 A.M.	Break
11:15 A.M.	Combined session
12:00 noon	Break
12:15 P.M.	Closing session
1:00 P.M.	Dismissal

The sequester can have a theme, decorations, notebook with session outlines, giveaways, skits, and games.

Singles' Ministries

The Singles' Ministries includes single adults ages 24 and up. (Since this is a totally different ministry than the Student Ministries, it would normally have a different director than the Student Ministries.) As this ministry grows it can be broken down into smaller groups of similar LifeStage. For example, different classes could be established for various age groups such as:

- 24–35
- 35–45
- 45 +

The Singles' Department would incorporate singles from different walks of life. Singles who have never been married, divorced singles, widows, and widowers would all belong in this ministry. They will have different spiritual and social needs than the singles in the Student Ministries department. For the most part, these singles will be more established in their lives and in their desire for a relationship with the Lord. They probably have careers and homes; therefore, they will have different needs, which can be met through an active Singles' Ministry.

The Singles' Ministries would schedule monthly activities, have multiple Sunday school classes, and have a director who would be available for counseling and encouragement.

Singles' Summer Sequester

The Singles' Summer Sequester is a two-day event coordinated by the Singles' Ministries director. It would flow similarly to the other sequesters and retreats explained in this chapter. The purpose of any sequester is to promote developing a heart for God while simultaneously encouraging fun and fellowship. Generally, it is best to plan a sequester such as this on a Friday and Saturday due to the job situations of the members. Class members can be encouraged to attend a soulwinning meeting earlier in the week.

Keenagers' Ministry

The Keenagers' Ministry is designed to be a "youth group" for the "young at heart" even though they may be "up in years"! It can include fellowships and activities that will encourage this unique generation to stay active and involved. Most in this group will be retired, many will have lost a mate, and most will have children who are busy with their own lives, thus, leaving a group of people who are prone to become lonely and disconnected. The Keenagers' Ministry is used to love and focus on these people. Through monthly activities, annual trips, and opportunities for service, this generation will feel needed and connected to the church family. Below are listed some suggested activities:

- Los Angeles Arboretum
- Trip to Solvang
- Ripley's Believe it or Not! Odditorium
- Holyland Museum
- Fort MacArthur Military Museum
- Getty Center
- LaBrea Tar Pits
- Huntington Library and Botanical Gardens
- Los Angeles Maritime Museum
- Petersen Automotive Museum
- Planes of Fame Air Museum
- Ronald Reagan Presidential Library and Museum
- Richard Nixon Presidential Library and Museum

Christian Living Discipleship Classes

These rotating classes are taught quarterly and repeat annually. Adults may sign up for these classes through their adult Bible classes or at the Information Center. Brochures about these classes can also be offered at the Information Center. These classes meet on Wednesday nights.

Marriage

This class includes principles on how to develop and maintain a marriage that would be pleasing to the Lord.

Child Rearing

This class includes practical, biblical lessons for rearing godly children in this ungodly age.

Financial Planning

This class includes planning a budget, following a budget, biblical giving, and planning for the future.

Recovery

This class includes lessons developed to bring a person back from devastation in marriage, relationships, temptation, guilt, and anger teaching him how to leave these in the past and to encourage him to begin a fresh walk with the Lord.

CHAPTER SIX

Church Membership

"Then they that gladly received his word were baptized:
and the same day there were added unto them about three thousand
souls. And they continued stedfastly in the apostles' doctrine and
fellowship, and in breaking of bread, and in prayers...And all that
believed were together, and had all things common...And the
Lord added to the church daily such as should be saved."
Acts 2:41,42,44,47b

According to Acts 2, Christ instituted the New Testament church to be the center of the spiritual and social activity of a Christian. Oftentimes, Christians today desire a career, a social life, and a spiritual life—all as separate aspects of their lives. This type of compartmentalizing removes the authority of Christ in the "secular" areas. Active church membership meshes the spiritual, social, and daily activities of our lives.

How does someone totally unfamiliar with the church get to the point where he desires to become a member? Consider these three steps:

1. **Interfacing**—This involves any means by which someone would become aware of the church. An individual may receive a church brochure, see a billboard, or notice an advertisement. A neighbor or co-worker who is already a member of the church may invite him. A soulwinner may knock on his door. These would all be methods of interfacing with those in our community.

2. **Bonding**—With the first visit to the church, bonding begins to occur. The first-time visitor is greeted warmly at the entrance of the church by several smiling, happy greeters. The bonding continues as he shakes hands and meets people. Attending an adult Bible class or a service gives him a glimpse of the church. With every interaction, he begins to feel accepted. This is the point where he begins to desire membership.

3. **Ownership**—Once the individual decides to become a member or trust Christ as his Saviour, he will feel an ownership. He will go from saying, "I visited that church," or "I went to that church," to "This is **my** church!"

Church membership is more than a list of names. But, what does it mean to become a member of the church? Church membership is a two-fold responsibility.

The Church's Responsibility

When a person chooses membership, he becomes a part of the church family. The church family naturally provides a higher level of support for a member as opposed to a non-member. The new member does get placed on a mailing list so that he will receive informative letters, brochures, and the monthly newsletter, but he is also added to the pastor's personal prayer list and is assigned a deacon who will visit him and care for him during times of hardship. Special support for baby showers, weddings, and funerals is provided as well.

The Member's Responsibility

The benefits of a strong, loving church family are yoked with the responsibilities of the member. He should be committed to spiritual growth, be accountable, and should follow the biblical pattern of Christian living established in the New Testament.

Joining the Church

The deacons of Lancaster Baptist Church assist with the membership by counseling prospective members and hearing their testimonies. The church employs the following three methods for adding new members:

1. **Baptism or re-baptism**—When a new believer is baptized, he becomes a member of the church. When a person is already saved but was baptized in a church of different faith, he is encouraged to be re-baptized to identify with our church and its doctrine.

2. **Transfer**—A person can become a member by transferring his membership from a church of like faith. He would give a statement of his salvation and baptism to the deacon.

3. **Statement**—Occasionally a person provides testimony that he was saved and baptized at a church of like faith, but extenuating circumstances prevent Lancaster Baptist from contacting the previous church. (The previous church may have closed, and there are no records of membership.)

In the cases of a membership transfer or statement, the church family votes to receive the new members.

Membership Follow-Up

Every new member receives follow-up and instruction regarding the purpose and vision of Lancaster Baptist Church. This is done in three steps.

Deacon Visit

The deacon assigned to the new member will visit him during the week after he becomes a member. The deacon introduces himself as the new member's deacon. The new member can call him with prayer requests and inform him of emergencies and deaths. The deacon also presents and explains the "New Member's Packet." This packet might include:

- A booklet describing the beliefs and operational guidelines of the church

- A brief statement of doctrine and philosophy (see CD 6.1 for sample)

- The financial policy of the church (see CD 6.2 for sample)

- A booklet explaining the relationship between the church member and the pastor

- A one-year Bible reading schedule

- A church calendar

- A tithe envelope

New Members' Brunch

The membership office plans the brunch, contacts the new members, and confirms that they will be present. The brunch is a great time for the pastor and the new members to become acquainted. After the meal, the pastor explains the purpose of the church. Briefly, the purpose of Lancaster Baptist Church is to:

- Inspire people to develop a heart for God

- Include people in a loving church family

- Instruct people from God's Word

- Involve people in a biblically correct and culturally sensitive ministry

- Impact people in the Antelope Valley and the world with the Gospel of Christ

After the purpose of the church is explained, the pastor presents the vision for the future of the church. The new members' sense of ownership is heightened when they know where the church is headed. It is beneficial to inform them of new building projects and various goals for the ministries.

New Members' Reception

One Sunday night about every six weeks, the church family meets all the new members at the New Members' Reception. The reception takes place after the Sunday night service. It is simple in nature—there is cake, coffee, and other beverages. The membership office plans this event, contacts the new members, and gets commitments from those who will attend. The membership office also makes sure the new members receive nametags at the beginning of the service so they can be easily recognized as a new member. It is helpful to know in advance which new members will be in the service so that nametags can be made and an accurate list of names can be given to the pastor. At the end of the service, the pastor informs the church family that there will be a New Members' Reception and invites them to attend. He then announces the names of the new members and has them line up at the front of the auditorium. This allows the church family to see the new members and begin to get acquainted with them. After the closing prayer, everyone is dismissed to the reception, and a host or hostess escorts the new members to the reception area.

"Welcome Aboard" Booklet

Our "Welcome Aboard" booklet, which includes what we believe and our purpose, is given to people who are interested in becoming a member of the church. (See CD 6.3 to view this booklet.)

PART TWO

Getting Started:
Every Member a Minister

CHAPTER SEVEN

Ministry Involvement Night

"And he gave some, apostles; and some, prophets; and some, evangelists;
and some, pastors and teachers; For the perfecting of the saints, for the
work of the ministry, for the edifying of the body of Christ."
Ephesians 4:11–12

Nothing is more rewarding than watching a new believer pass through the waters of baptism, complete the discipleship program, and begin attending church faithfully. As that new Christian continues to grow and begins to express a desire to become more involved in the church, you are overwhelmed with a sense of awe at God's work in his life. But suddenly, you are presented with a dilemma—for what area of service is he best suited? How *does* one become involved in the ministry?

A great way to involve more workers for the ministry of your church is by having a Ministry Involvement Night. This can be done on a Sunday or Wednesday evening, when the entire service is dedicated to helping members find their place in the church. (To view a sample cue card for Ministry Involvement Night, see CD 7.1.) Remember, there is not one "right" way to conduct a night such as this, but the following are some helpful hints to having a successful Ministry Involvement Night:

1. Plan this event when the church is not in a "peak time" (e.g., Christmas or Easter), so that there is time for adequate preparation by the church staff. Lancaster Baptist Church holds this event in the autumn in conjunction with the Soulwinning Kick-off Night.

2. Incorporate an energizing theme each year that will streamline the entire evening. Examples: "Get Plugged In!" or "You Are God's Gift to the Church; It's Time to Get Unwrapped!"

3. Ministry Involvement Night can be held during an evening service, but if it takes place on a different evening, encourage all members to attend the service, even if they are already involved in a ministry.

4. Perform a skit or short humorous play that somehow parallels ministry involvement. Keep the skit theme a secret until that night. This will help create some curiosity as you promote the night.

5. Preach a Bible message about spiritual gifts and compel every member of your church to serve the Lord in ministry.

6. Consider having testimonies from people who currently serve in ministry sharing the blessings of serving.

7. Share the vision of changed lives, emphasizing that we can invest our labors into eternal rewards.

8. After the service, have a room set up with display tables for each ministry. This gives members a chance to quickly gain an overview of each department by walking around.

9. Post experienced workers from each ministry at the designated tables and allow members to ask them questions about their department.

10. Urge each member to take information from at least one ministry in which he might like to be involved.

11. Have a spiritual gifts testing area set up where members can take the Spiritual Gifts Test to see what ministry would best suit them. This area should have knowledgeable workers, tables, chairs, Spiritual Gifts Test booklets (see CD 7.2 and end of chapter), pencils, and flyers that list the different ministries they can choose.

12. Designate a place on each table where members can sign up to be contacted about possible ministry opportunities. You can also pass out a flyer in the service wih a list of ministries where members can check off areas of interest. The back of the flyer can have a place where members mark if they have experience in a certain field (see CD 7.3 and 7.4 for front and back of flyer).

13. Schedule a follow-up interview with each prospect before placing him into a ministry and ask permission to perform a background check of those working with children.

At the same time, the following are a few reminders of what to be careful *not* to do when conducting a Ministry Involvement Night:

1. Do not allow someone to serve in a Children's Ministry without having performed a thorough background check and interview.

2. Do not ask anybody to be in a certain department just because there is a shortage of workers.

3. Do not encourage someone to be involved who has not yet completed the church's discipleship program or has not proven himself by attending church faithfully for at least six months.

4. Do not put a new Christian into a ministry where he will be the main teacher, speaker, etc.

5. Do not allow a new member to serve in several ministries at once just because he is willing. This will lead to burnout, frustration, and resentment.

6. Do not place false guilt upon someone who seeks a different ministry or someone who asks to be removed from a ministry for a season.

The real spiritual battle begins once a person enters a position of service. It is vital that the church leadership team is committed to nurturing, training, and equipping these new servants for Christ. Periodic training and follow-up is vital to make sure this new servant enjoys long-term fruit and personal reward in ministry.

In addition to these suggestions, included in this chapter is an example of a booklet that could be given to members at Ministry Involvement Night.

YOU ARE GOD'S GIFT TO THE CHURCH...

AND IT'S TIME TO

GET UNWRAPPED!

Ministry Involvement Night
Lancaster Baptist Church

Ministry Involvement Night

Dear Friend,

I am thrilled that you have chosen to be a part of our annual Ministry Involvement Night! It is our prayer that tonight's program and presentations will convey to you that serving Christ in local church ministry is a joy, a privilege, a responsibility, and a source of fulfillment.

Lancaster Baptist Church is a body made up of many different parts that Jesus Christ has fashioned together into one church, and He is our Head. The Bible teaches that He adds to His body as He sees fit. When He brought you and me to Lancaster Baptist Church, He knew what He was doing! The Bible also teaches that God wants to use each member of that body in a unique way in His work.

So, approach tonight with an open heart and mind. First, be open to the fact that God has gifted you to serve Him. Second, be open to the possibility that there is a job to be done that "has your name on it"— something God has in mind just for you. Finally, be open to making a commitment to serve Jesus Christ genuinely and faithfully, from your heart.

Should you have any questions, or if there is any way we can assist you as you "get unwrapped," please do not hesitate to let us know. One of the responsibilities of your pastoral staff is to equip "the saints for the work of the ministry." I count it a great joy to serve our Saviour along side of you.

Your friend,

Pastor

The Steps of a Serving Christian

Step One: Christ

Before one may genuinely enter ministry, he or she must have a personal growing relationship with Jesus Christ. This is the foundation upon which all true ministry is built. Jesus explained to us in John 15:4–5, *"...the branch cannot bear fruit of itself, except it abide in the vine; no more can ye, except ye abide in me. I am the vine, ye are the branches..."*

Step Two: Church

For Christians to serve the Lord in their church, they must be a part of their church. The members of Lancaster Baptist Church are simply Christians who have been scripturally baptized and have banded together in carrying out the cause of Christ. When Paul and Barnabas were sent, the Bible indicates that they were a part of the church in Antioch (Acts 13:1–2).

Step Three: Consistent

One who has difficulty carrying out the basics of the Christian life may not be ready for the commitment necessary for ministry involvement. Consistency in our Bible reading, prayer time, and church attendance serve as indicators that we might be ready to go to another level in our service to Christ. I Corinthians 4:2 says, *"Moreover it is required in stewards, that a man be found faithful."*

Step Four: Consider

The Bible teaches us that God adds members to the church. We are fit together like a body, and every member serves a vital function (I Corinthians 12). A Christian who enjoys serving in ministry is one who has discovered his spiritual gift and has prayerfully considered which ministry opportunity might be the right one in which to exercise that gift.

Step Five: Counsel

When someone feels ready to become involved or when a pastor feels that a Christian is exhibiting growth, an interview-type appointment should be held. At this time, the new servant and one of the pastors may discuss his spiritual gift, areas of ministry which might be suitable, and the requirements of a particular field of ministry (Ephesians 4:11–16).

Step Six: Commit

When a growing Christian has discovered an area of ministry where he would fit, has met with a pastor, and is ready to jump in with both feet, a commitment must be made. This commitment may include preparation times or participation in training meetings and will include personal soulwinning and practical guidelines for distinctive Christian living. We are challenged with the commitment of the first-century Christians in Acts 2:42–47.

Step Seven: Commence

Once folks "get their feet wet" in ministry, they begin to see that the little things they are doing are making a difference in the lives of others. Whether it is singing a song, telling a story, or sharing a testimony, it is thrilling to know that they are being used for God's glory (I Peter 4:10–11). Challenges come, but the spiritual rewards of serving outweigh the price that is paid. People's lives are forever changed because you entered ministry!

Step Eight: Continue

Beginning is one thing, but continuing is another. The Devil loses a battle when someone begins to exercise his or her spiritual gift for God's glory. Now, instead of trying to prevent him from serving, the Devil attempts to render him ineffective in his service. His strategies include unmet expectations, the failures of people, and service in the flesh. This is why maintaining a walk with Christ is vital (Ephesians 6:10–18).

The Need for Leadership Requirements

As you read the following pages, you will further understand the heart behind what we call "The Leadership Requirements." They are not just a list of rules; they are not meant to be enforced with a "legalistic" or "holier-than-thou" attitude—and they are not meant to define "spirituality." Our heart in this matter is simply that our lives would be consistent with the Bible both inside and out, and that our leaders in ministry would be pure vessels, fit for the Master's use!

Many today emphasize our freedom as Christians. Freedom does not mean the absence of constraints or moral absolutes. Suppose a skydiver at 10,000 feet announces to the rest of the group, "I am not using a parachute this time. I want freedom!" The fact is that a skydiver is subject to a greater law than that of wearing a parachute—the law of gravity. But when one chooses the "constraint" of the parachute, he is free to enjoy the exhilaration of skydiving. God's moral laws act the same way—they restrain, but they are absolutely necessary to enjoy the exhilaration of real freedom. Romans 6:18 explains, "Being then made free from sin, ye became the servants of righteousness."

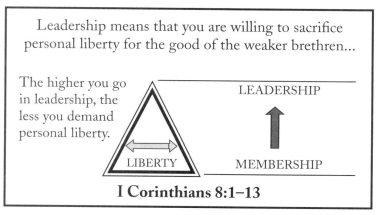

Leadership means that you are willing to sacrifice personal liberty for the good of the weaker brethren...

The higher you go in leadership, the less you demand personal liberty.

LEADERSHIP

LIBERTY

MEMBERSHIP

I Corinthians 8:1–13

(CD 7.5)

28 Principles in Developing Biblical Standards

By Dr. R.B. Ouellette

1. The Principle of Vision: The eye affects the mind, and the mind affects the body.

2. The Principle of Representation: I represent Christ in everything I do and say.

3. The Principle of Fellowship: God commands us to fellowship with other believers.

4. The Principle of Holiness: Because I belong to God, I must be holy.

5. The Principle of Light and Darkness: Christians have nothing in common with the world.

6. The Principle of the Weaker Brother: My actions will influence others.

7. The Principle of Replacement: Wrong must be replaced by right.

8. The Principle of Affections: I must make the eternal more important than the earthly.

9. The Principle of Association: Wrong associations lead to wrong behavior.

10. The Principle of Priorities: Jesus should be Number One.

11. The Principle of Doubtful Things: When in doubt—don't! (If it is doubtful, it is dirty.)

12. The Principle of Temptation: I must avoid temptation, not just sin.

13. The Principle of Purity: It is God's will for me to be pure.

14. The Principle of Authority: I should follow God-ordained authority.

15. The Principle of Feelings: I must live by the Bible, not by feelings.

16. The Principle of Imitation: I am to imitate Jesus.

17. The Principle of Weights: I must lay aside weights as well as sin.

18. The Principle of Excellence: God wants me to do my best.

19. The Principle of Readiness: We should be ready and able to explain our beliefs.

20. The Principle of Concentration: Do not look back. Do not look around. Do not look down.

21. The Principle of Preparedness: I must always be ready for Jesus to return.

22. The Principle of Generosity: It is godly to give.

23. The Principle of Enslavement: A Christian should be controlled by God.

24. The Principle of Minding your Own Business: I must mind my own business.

25. The Principle of Worry: God wants me to pray instead of worry.

26. The Principle of Defilement: A little defiles a lot.

27. The Principle of Yieldedness: I must yield my will to God.

28. The Principle of Discipleship: I am to make disciples.

Note: Dr. R. B. Ouellette is the pastor of First Baptist Church in Bridgeport, Michigan, and a speaker at regional *Striving Together* Conferences.

Examples of Leadership Requirements in the Workplace

The Aerospace Industry

"SKUNK WORKS PRIDE" FROM *LADC STAR**, APRIL 28, 1995

I was a little surprised by the questions I received prior to the recent visit of Dan Tellep and Norm Augustine relative to Skunk Works dress code. The visit was on a Friday, and concern was expressed that this would conflict with "casual Friday."

First, let me say that Skunk Works does not have a formal dress code other than clothing must be suitable and appropriate to the work environment. We do not expect those working in the factory to wear ties or expensive garments that could be ruined by fuel or oil.

It is also recognized that some manufacturing areas are not environmentally controlled, and clothing must be appropriate for the temperatures encountered and the personal protection required for the specific job. Similarly, the white-collar staff is expected to dress in a manner consistent with the professional organization that we are. That does not mean a coat and tie or a dress is always required, unless you expect to have some contact with our customers or others outside the company.

Second, "casual Friday" is not a Skunk Works policy. To the best of my recollection, "casual Friday" started as a once-a-month activity on the F-117 program in conjunction with purging files of classified holdings and evolved to the every Friday format during preparation to move from Burbank to Palmdale. Others seemed to find it popular and adopted it.

I am concerned that many of our employees have extended "casual Friday" beyond its original intent. I see many people wearing clothes that would be more appropriate for mowing the lawn on Saturday morning or picnicking at the beach or park.

Pride

It is here that I introduce the word "pride." Clearly, if one must ask if he or she is appropriately dressed for a visit by the corporate chairman, then perhaps we have gone too far in "casualness" and lost perspective of the appropriate time to so dress.

I would suggest that professionalism goes beyond just our daily business transactions and includes the manner in which we present ourselves. Appropriate dress is a measure of respect that we hold for ourselves, each other, and our Skunk Works organizations. The pride we have in ourselves and in our organization should result in never wondering if our clothing is appropriate.

It is not my desire to have a formal dress code. To avoid the necessity for one, I urge each of you to consider what you wear to work to ensure its appropriateness. Hint: jeans, sweats, and tennis shoes are not "business casual" in my judgment. Slacks, sports shirts, sweaters, and comfortable shoes may be appropriate for much of our work. Coats and ties for men and dresses or attractive pant suits for women are always appropriate in presenting a business image to our customers and the outside world.

If we dress appropriately, I see no reason that our day-to-day apparel cannot be less formal. I believe that "casual Friday" may be an inappropriate reduction in our professionalism.

Accordingly, I request that the concept of "casual Friday" be dropped in favor of appropriate dress for every day. We all take great pride in our facilities and organization. Let us show it in the way we dress.

Copied from Lockheed Martin Corporation

Corporate America

THE FOLLOWING ARTICLE APPEARED IN THE MAY 2002 ISSUE OF *AMERICAN DEMOGRAPHICS*.

Unless you work for one of the handful of surviving Internet start-ups, wearing vintage Pumas and a Def Leppard T-shirt to work may no longer cut the mustard. According to the "American Industry Dress Code Survey," a national poll of 201 senior executives at companies with over $500 million in annual revenue, more than half of large businesses (56 percent) maintain a business attire policy—that means a suit and tie for the gents and a suit or dress for the ladies. What's more, the study, conducted by the New York City-based Men's Apparel Alliance between November and December 2001, reveals that of those companies with a business dress code, 19 percent have reinstituted their policy within the past year. Think this reeks of the Old Boys' Club seeking revenge upon the minions? Perhaps, but the companies have their reasons. Respondents in the survey predict that a switch from a casual to a professional business dress code could result in an average 3.6 percent productivity gain for their company. Says James Ammeen, president of the Men's Apparel Alliance, "The executives surveyed believe a professional image can translate into improved work ethics and growth in overall productivity."

An Article from a Christian Periodical

The business world knows it. The professional world knows it. The manufacturing world knows it. *The only way to achieve excellence in service or products is by establishing and maintaining high worker standards.* If a company does not have high worker standards, we would be fearful of using its products or services. Now the Sunday school must learn it. If you want your Sunday school to achieve excellence, you must have high worker standards.

Worker standards state the personal and spiritual qualifications of the people who teach in your Sunday school. They define what a person should *be* as a teacher. A job description, on the other hand, defines what a person should *do* as a teacher.

Your leadership requirements should at least address the following:

1. Church Membership

A wise pastor and superintendent will require that all Sunday school teachers be members of the church. Such a practice creates needed accountability and helps reduce the risk of someone working against the church in practice or doctrine.

2. Regular Attendance
   Every Sunday school teacher should faithfully attend all regular services of the church. People's schedules are busy, but when a teacher habitually misses services, problems can develop. What will the teacher's students think when they never see him in the Sunday evening service? What is the teacher missing out on in his own spiritual life and fellowship when he skips services? We must insist on regular attendance.

3. Doctrinal Correctness
   It is essential that every teacher agree with the church's doctrinal statement. A teacher can do great harm if he teaches contrary to what the church teaches.

4. Cooperative Spirit
   Excellence in Sunday school comes when all the people pull in the same direction. When a person seems to be continually at odds with church leadership, he is probably not a good candidate for a teacher.

5. Separation To The Lord
   A holy life is a pre-requisite for effective service for Christ. A person characterized by worldliness presents a wrong model to his students and brings reproach to the Sunday school and the church in the community.

You may want to include additional items and you may want to be more specific in each area, but you should at least cover these five categories in your leadership requirements.

About Spiritual Gifts

What Is a Spiritual Gift?

When you accepted Christ, you not only got saved—you were given something very special from God. You were given an ability—a giftedness to serve God in a unique way. God's plan for your life is that you would meet a specific need in the church family and He has gifted *you* in a special way to meet that need. Notice what the Bible says…

> *As every man hath received the gift, even so minister the same one to another, as good stewards of the manifold grace of God.* I Peter 4:10

Do I Have a Spiritual Gift?

If you have trusted Christ—yes, you do have a spiritual gift! Even if you do not know what it is or do not feel particularly gifted in a specific area, the Bible teaches that you **do** have a special gift that you can use to serve God. And, believe it or not, your gift is vital to the work of God in our church family; otherwise God would not have placed you here (I Corinthians 12:18–24).

God's Word teaches that, as a member of this church family (this *body*), you are important to His work in this place. He has appointed you a gift and a purpose for being here—and you will greatly enjoy discovering and using that gift for His purpose!

How Do I Find Out What My Gift Is?

Glad you asked! Tonight you will be taught what the spiritual gifts are from the Bible, and you can take a simple test that will help you discover what your spiritual gift is and how you can best use it to serve the Lord. Simple hint: it is something that you already enjoy doing—and feel like you can do well!

What Is the Purpose of a Spiritual Gift?

What should I do with it? You should discover it, develop it, and use it! Look at what the Bible says,

> *Wherefore I put thee in remembrance that thou stir up the gift of God, which is in thee by the putting on of my hands.* II Timothy 1:6

> *As every man hath received the gift, even so minister the same one to another, as good stewards of the manifold grace of God.* I Peter 4:10

God wants you to be a good steward of His gift to you! The best way to do that is to begin now discovering, developing, and using your gift to serve the Lord and His church. The great result of using your gift is that the entire church family ministers to each other and to the community! That is the way the church is supposed to work!

What are the Spiritual Gifts?

This will be more carefully explained if you make an appointment with a staff ministry leader. But in a quick survey, here is what the Bible says,

> *Having then gifts differing according to the grace that is given to us, whether prophecy, let us prophesy according to the proportion of faith; Or ministry, let us wait on our ministering: or he that teacheth, on teaching; Or he that exhorteth, on exhortation: he that giveth, let him do it with simplicity; he that ruleth, with diligence; he that sheweth mercy, with cheerfulness.* Romans 12:6–8

The spiritual gifts, which are permanent causes for edification, can be summarized in this way...

Prophecy—the ability and desire to preach God's Word

Ministry/Helps—the ability and desire to serve and help God's people

Teaching—the ability and desire to teach God's truth

Exhortation—the ability and desire to encourage others in their faith

Giving—the ability and desire to give to God's work and God's people

Ruling/Administration—the ability and desire to lead and administrate part of God's work

Mercy—the ability and desire to feel the pain of others and help them during trials

Conclusion

Would you like to find our what your gift is? Are you interested in serving God in the way He has gifted you to serve? It is a great day in any Christian's life when he discovers God's purpose for placing him in a church family and then begin to fulfill that purpose! Let us help you begin this journey soon!

Spiritual Gifts Test

The Spiritual Gifts Test is available after the service in the area where the various ministry tables are displayed. Below is a sample of the Spiritual Gifts Test.

On the pages to follow, you will find various questions which are designed to aid in discovering how God has uniquely gifted you for His work. Using a scale of one to five, five being the strongest, answer each question. Be sure to answer all of the questions, and wait until you have completed each question to score your test.

1. I am always looking for practical ways to help.
    1   2   3   4   5

2. I enjoy public speaking and teaching.
   1   2   3   4   5

3. I find it easy to motivate people to do the right thing.
   1   2   3   4   5

4. I am a take-charge person who can usually bring order out of chaos.
   1   2   3   4   5

5. I am very sensitive to the emotional state of others.
   1   2   3   4   5

6. I am able to discern wise investments so as to have more to give.
   1   2   3   4   5

7. When people are in my home, I like to wait on them "hand and foot."
   1   2   3   4   5

8. People often tell me that I helped them understand things better.
   1   2   3   4   5

9. I am always uplifting those who are around me.
   1   2   3   4   5

10. I can organize people and delegate easily.
    1   2   3   4   5

11. I am an easy mark for stray animals, especially if they are hurt.
    1   2   3   4   5

12. I have a desire to give quietly without public notice.
    1   2   3   4   5

13. I often stop to help motorists in trouble (if not dangerous).

    1   2   3   4   5

14. I prefer systematic Bible teaching as opposed to a series of unrelated topics.

    1   2   3   4   5

15. When people ask my advice, I suggest a definite course of action.

    1   2   3   4   5

16. I enjoy a team effort more than doing the work myself.

    1   2   3   4   5

17. People in emotional distress often come to me for comfort.

    1   2   3   4   5

18. I am motivated to give unto the Lord at His prompting, not man's.

    1   2   3   4   5

19. I sometimes get irritated when others do not jump in to help.

    1   2   3   4   5

20. I find it easy to illustrate spiritual truths and make them clear.

    1   2   3   4   5

21. I tend to be optimistic—always giving hope.

    1   2   3   4   5

22. People who talk about problems but never take action irritate me.

    1   2   3   4   5

23. I am sometimes accused of being too soft on sin.

    1   2   3   4   5

24. I have a desire to give gifts that are of high quality.
    1   2   3   4   5

25. I find it almost impossible to say no to others.
    1   2   3   4   5

26. Disorganized messages (with no outline) irritate me.
    1   2   3   4   5

27. Even in failure, I see the potential in people.
    1   2   3   4   5

28. I am a goal-oriented person.
    1   2   3   4   5

29. I am reluctant to confront people; I do not want to hurt them.
    1   2   3   4   5

30. I have a tendency to test faithfulness by how people handle funds.
    1   2   3   4   5

31. I prefer a "behind the scenes" role. I am not an "up front" person.
    1   2   3   4   5

32. I get upset with people who use verses out of context.
    1   2   3   4   5

33. I am able to encourage others, even when I am suffering.
    1   2   3   4   5

34. I am "pushy" and demanding—driving people to the limit.
    1   2   3   4   5

35. I love ministering to the sick, to the poor, and to the handicapped.
    1   2   3   4   5

36. It is important to be involved in meeting the church's financial need.
    1   2   3   4   5

37. I find it difficult to delegate; it is usually easier to do the job myself.
    1   2   3   4   5

38. People tease me about being a "bookworm."
    1   2   3   4   5

39. People tease me about being a "cheerleader."
    1   2   3   4   5

40. Some say projects are more important to me than people are.
    1   2   3   4   5

41. Others tell me that I am a good listener.
    1   2   3   4   5

42. It is important to consult with my spouse to determine how much to give to a project or ministry.
    1   2   3   4   5

Spiritual Gifts Test Answer Key

Directions: Transfer the number you circled to the blank beside the corresponding question. Add the totals up in each column. The highest possible score in one column would be 35. For example, if you answered question one by circling the "5", you would record that answer as follows: (1._5_)

1._____	2._____	3._____
7._____	8._____	9._____
13._____	14._____	15._____
19._____	20._____	21._____
25._____	26._____	27._____
31._____	32._____	33._____
37._____	38._____	39._____

Totals: _____   _____   _____

   Helps   Teaching   Encouragement

4._____	5._____	6._____
10._____	11._____	12._____
16._____	17._____	18._____
22._____	23._____	24._____
28._____	29._____	30._____
34._____	35._____	36._____
40._____	41._____	42._____

Totals: _____   _____   _____

   Administration Mercy   Giving

(CD 7.2)

CHAPTER EIGHT

Hospitality Ministry

"Distributing to the necessity of saints;
given to hospitality."
Romans 12:13

Visiting a church for the very first time can be one of the most scary, insecure, and intimidating experiences a non-Christian can experience. Everybody has a different paradigm of church that is formed from a combination of life experiences—both good and bad. For an unsaved person to step onto your church property, he must overcome a variety of hesitations and concerns—and it must be our goal as faithful ministers to understand those concerns, and seek to alleviate them to the best of our ability. This is not compromise—it is simply compassion and consideration. Having sensitivity to the lost involves understanding where they are coming from and how the Devil will fight and attempt to "keep them away" from the preaching of the Gospel.

The Hospitality Ministry on your church campus could be a wonderful tool to help people immediately feel welcome, comfortable, and at home in this "foreign" environment. Recognize that when a first-time visitor drives into your parking lot, they are usually at a loss for: where to park, where to go first, where they fit in the best, where the kids go, etc. Regardless of the size of your church or campus, this confusion will be a reality. Yet, the more space or buildings you have on your campus, the more this confusion can build, and the more you should labor to "offset" it.

The responsibility of the Hospitality Ministry Team is to greet and welcome everyone that comes onto the campus on Sunday mornings. This team is to keep a special watchful eye for those who are first-time visitors or new-comers. They work diligently to greet guests, introduce themselves, and then to direct or host the guests to various locations—nurseries, children's classes, adult classes, and services. Each of these team members is equipped with an outgoing personality, a joyful spirit, and a keen understanding of the service schedule and class locations.

The Hospitality Ministry can transform a visitor's paradigm of your church from a cold, uninviting campus to a warm, inviting environment where he is accepted *as he is*. It is the Hospitality Ministry Team (or lack thereof) that gives visitors the first impression of your church.

The Hospitality Ministry is not a difficult area in which to serve. It makes a great "starter" ministry for newer Christians who wish to become more involved in church, because they do not have to be extremely knowledgeable in the Bible to participate. The Hospitality Ministry Team's function is three-fold: to direct, to inform, and to be friendly. In short, the Hospitality Ministry Team member shows visitors where to go, tells them which classes would be best for the entire family, and offers a warm smile with a friendly word to first-time visitors and faithful members alike. He helps visitors with any questions and makes them feel at ease by acknowledging them and seeking to meet their needs.

The members of the Hospitality Ministry Team should be some of the most outgoing, friendly, caring people in your church family. They should be people who have a warm smile and the ability to put someone at ease.

Finally, the Hospitality Ministry Team could wear carnations or nametags to denote their hosting role, and they should be equipped with campus guides, ministry information, and welcome cards thanking first-time visitors for coming.

The guidelines that follow give a general summary of the Hospitality Ministry Team member's role in ministry and offers practical suggestions on how to be more effective in that role.

Hospitality Ministry

Dear Friend,

I want to welcome you to the Hospitality Ministry Team! It is a privilege to be able to serve the Lord here in any way or fashion. Through this area of service, I pray that you will grow spiritually as you meet the needs of others.

As you serve in this ministry I would like you to keep in mind Colossians 3:23–24, "And whatsoever ye do, do it heartily, as to the Lord, and not unto men; Knowing that of the Lord ye shall receive the reward of the inheritance: for ye serve the Lord Christ." As you serve the Lord in the Hospitality Ministry Team, be mindful that your service is unto the Lord and whatever we do for Him should be our best.

The thought of "commitment to excellence" comes to my mind when I read those verses. As servants of God, our attitude toward the Lord's work should be on a different level of excellence because of who we are serving—the Lord.

Finally, let me express how excited I am that the Lord has led you to serve in this ministry, and may the Lord bless you because of your faithfulness in this area of service.

Your friend,

Pastor

Purpose

Give Direction

When guests who have never been here before enter our facility, they feel totally inadequate, not knowing what to do and where to go. It is our responsibility to put these people at ease as soon as they approach our property. Tell them where the Main Auditorium is, where to take their children, and how to find the class that will best meet their needs.

Be Informative

Know where classes are and answer any general questions they may have concerning the schedule for that Sunday. This will leave a helpful, caring, and professional impression upon them.

Be Friendly

People can sense and know when they are accepted and wanted. Being friendly should be the greatest quality we demonstrate in this ministry. A warm handshake and friendly smile will leave a lasting impression on everyone you greet.

Vision Statement

The mission of the Hospitality Ministry Team is to make a positive impression on those who arrive on our property and to offer our assistance in helping them feel informed and comfortable as they visit our church.

Characteristics

1. A Hospitality Ministry Team member is one who is spiritually prepared to meet and greet church members and guests as they enter our church facility.

2. A Hospitality Ministry Team member is one who will be faithful in this area of the ministry.

3. A Hospitality Ministry Team member is one who will have a professional attitude as he is ministering.

4. A Hospitality Ministry Team member is one who is friendly.

5. A Hospitality Ministry Team member is one who is very personable (get the visitor's name and use it!).

6. A Hospitality Ministry Team member is one who looks sharp (hair is neatly combed, breath not offensive, etc.).

7. A Hospitality Ministry Team member is one who is dependable. Someone said, "The greatest ability is dependability."

8. A Hospitality Ministry Team member is one who is enthusiastic about meeting and greeting people as they enter our property.

9. A Hospitality Ministry Team member is one who is sensitive to people who need help.

10. A Hospitality Ministry Team member is one who is always punctual.

Practical Procedures

1. Hospitality Ministry Team members should arrive at church 20 minutes before the service starts for prayer and a brief meeting. (For a two-service schedule, a crew would greet before each service.)

2. Any special information needed for that day will be discussed at this time.

3. Work stations will be assigned at this meeting.

4. Leave your Sunday school class ten minutes early and report to your station.

5. Remain at your station until five minutes after the service starts unless otherwise needed.

6. At the close of the service, designated men should be stationed at the perimeter doors. Their responsibility is to say to each person, "Thank you for coming, and we will see you tonight."

7. If, by any chance, you will not be present for any Sunday, please contact your Hospitality Ministry Team leader at least 24 hours in advance.

CHAPTER NINE

Parking Lot Ministry

"Let all things be done decently and in order."
I Corinthians 14:40

Another vital yet often overlooked branch of ministry in the church is the Parking Lot Ministry. When all is running smoothly, few members notice the men who direct the flow of traffic week after week; safety within the parking lot may be taken for granted. However, a growing church with a disorganized parking lot will frustrate members and visitors alike. Church visitors may feel so intimidated searching for a parking space in a large lot that they decide it is not worth the trouble and simply leave.

On the other hand, a well-organized parking team wearing brightly colored vests or matching shirts and directing traffic with uniform hand signals makes a positive first impression. Visitors may feel secure in knowing that since your church appears organized on the outside, it will be so on the inside as well. This feeling increases when a friendly parking director introduces himself and guides them to a parking space reserved just for visitors near the front of the lot. As the visitors exit their car and walk up to the church, the stage is set for a wonderful first visit.

Depending on the size and needs of your church, the Parking Lot Ministry can accomplish several tasks.

1. It can direct traffic before the church service begins to maximize use of the parking area you have.

2. It can guide visitors and special guests to parking reserved specifically for them.

3. It can give visitors directions as to where to go once inside the church building.

4. It can provide security as one or two members of the Parking Lot Ministry patrol the parking lot during the service. (This should be done on a rotating schedule so that members of the Parking Lot Ministry hear the preaching as well.)

5. It can provide direction to overflow parking on special days or at peak times.

6. It can provide valet parking for guests, elderly, and handicapped attendees.

7. It can guide existing traffic after the service reducing the risk of accident or injury.

Regardless of the duties the Parking Lot Ministry Team members perform, they should have a specific plan and purpose to follow. There should be a coordinator for this ministry who is directly accountable to a staff member of the church. The coordinator, together with the staff director, should plan periodic meetings and keep all team members up to date on any changes in policy, etc. Good communication is essential for the safety of both the Parking Lot Ministry Team and the people they are directing.

The Parking Lot Ministry can be a great ministry opportunity for newer Christians who do not yet have enough Bible knowledge to help with a Sunday school class, but who have a desire to be involved. Each new team member, whether he is a faithful church member or recently saved, should be trained and shown exactly what is expected of him as a member of the Parking Lot Ministry Team. These essentials include learning uniform hand signals, arm gestures, and the particular route each car is to travel to arrive safely at its destination. Guidelines, beginning on the next page, can be especially helpful for reference and review of the policies and procedures of the Parking Lot Ministry.

Parking Lot Ministry

Dear Friend,

I want to welcome you to the Parking Lot Ministry! It is a privilege to be able to serve the Lord here in any way or fashion. Through this area of service, I pray that you will grow spiritually as you meet the needs of others.

As you serve in this ministry I would like you to keep in mind Colossians 3:23–24, "And whatsoever ye do, do it heartily, as to the Lord, and not unto men; Knowing that of the Lord ye shall receive the reward of the inheritance: for ye serve the Lord Christ." As you serve the Lord in the Parking Lot Ministry, be mindful that your service is unto the Lord and whatever we do for Him should be our best.

The thought of "commitment to excellence" comes to my mind when I read those verses. As servants of God, our attitude toward the Lord's work should be on a different level of excellence because of who we are serving—the Lord.

Finally, let me express how excited I am that the Lord has led you to serve in this ministry, and may the Lord bless you because of your faithfulness in this area of service.

Your friend,

Pastor

Purpose Statement

The purpose of the Parking Lot Ministry is to ensure a smoothly operating and organized parking lot. Our parking ministry exists to:

A. Provide a Safe Environment in the Parking Lots
   First and foremost for any facility is the safety of those who use the facility. If the Parking Lot Ministry Team does its job correctly, then drivers and pedestrians are going to feel safe from harm and injury. Proper procedures will help us to have the safest facility possible.

B. Create a Positive First Impression for Our Guests
   First impressions are always the most valuable. When someone visits our church, we want him to feel loved and welcomed when the day is done. A Parking Lot Ministry Team member will be the first person that they will see at church. Therefore, make a Christ-honoring impact.

   1. Be friendly.
      Be friendly to those you see. Have a smile and a good attitude. You may not know the person, but still be friendly and show that you are glad to see him. Remember: every car carries souls that Christ died on the cross to save.

   2. Be courteous.
      Give each person the idea that you are there to assist him.

   3. Be helpful.
      You are there to help those coming in to get to the proper parking place. People will ask questions, so have a ready answer for them.

C. Coordinate a Smooth Flow of Traffic
   Traffic must move in quickly and efficiently, so that people get to classes and church on time and do not feel that

127

the parking lot causes them to be late. The needs of our church are changing constantly in this area, and we must stay a step ahead of the flow of traffic. Our positions and routes in the parking lot will change from time to time, so we must remain flexible as needs arise.

Pertinent Information

A. Campus Layout

Know where the various buildings are located on the church property. Study the maps of the campus and the classrooms that are listed in the church's visitors' guide so you can direct people from their cars to their destinations.

B. Dress Code

We must be recognizable as parking lot attendants, so everyone will wear an orange vest that distinguishes him as a member of the Parking Lot Ministry Team.

C. Shuttle Routes

From the far reaches of the parking lot there will be shuttle transportation. There are definite pick-up points for this shuttle. When the shuttle is crossing traffic, it shall always have the right of way. Stop the flow of traffic for the shuttle and then resume the flow after it passes. This will allow the shuttle to move as many people as possible.

D. Emergencies

Our desire is that we would have no emergencies. However, we are prepared if the need should arise. There are police officers here at all times for any medical emergency or any theft or vandalism that occurs on the property.

E. Reserved Parking

There will always be reserved parking spaces for the handicapped. These spaces are permanently marked near the front of the Main Auditorium, as well as along the sides of the North Auditorium. There are also spaces for the elderly, single moms, and visitors on any given Sunday. On special service days (e.g., Dedication Sunday, Resurrection Sunday, Open House Sunday), you will be informed of who will have reserved parking and where it will be located.

F. Bus Arrivals

The Bus Ministry has buses that run at specified times each Sunday. The buses arrive from the main entrance and proceed to their designated locations to unload. Upon their arrival, you will direct them to the proper place. The buses will receive priority when entering the parking lot, just as a shuttle would.

G. Personal Schedule

On a regular Sunday, the Parking Lot Ministry Team should arrive at least a half hour before the first service is scheduled to begin. During the Sunday school hour, leave your class about 15 minutes early to direct traffic for the second service.

Professionalism

The Parking Lot Ministry could be the most vital ministry you will serve in here at our church because of its visibility. We want the first impression of our members and visitors alike to be that we strive for excellence in every aspect of every ministry. This brings glory to our Saviour and lifts up His name!

The parking lot plan that we have designed and selected for this ministry is the most effective at expediting parking and traffic flow, which is our key objective, provided safety has been fully addressed. Learn the plan so that you can be called upon to work at any station within the parking lot.

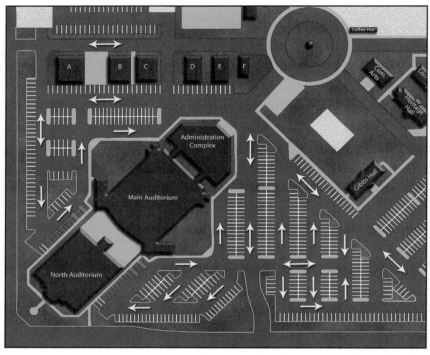

(Lancaster Baptist Church's flow of traffic)

CHAPTER TEN

Receptionist Ministry

"Whether therefore ye eat, or drink, or whatsoever
ye do, do all to the glory of God."
I Corinthians 10:31

In the early days at Lancaster Baptist Church, not one person held a "salaried" position. We moved to Lancaster with the promise of support from several like-minded churches and began with faith in the Lord to provide for the needs.

During those days, I would knock on five hundred doors per week in our community, endeavoring to win souls and invite people to visit Lancaster Baptist Church. Because I have never personally appreciated calling a church and hearing an answering machine, I began to enlist different ladies in the church who would come and serve as receptionists. There were always two ladies at the church at any given time—one to answer the phones and do light secretarial work and the other to assist in various projects, such as calling through the white pages and inviting people to church, folding church bulletins and preparing Sunday school rolls.

The early staff meetings of our church primarily consisted of a time of training when I would teach the receptionists protocol regarding answering the phone and greeting those who visited the church.

It has always been our desire to convey a welcoming, professional image, both in the physical environment of the church and in our personal contact with people who visit, who call, and who see our website.

To this day, there are several volunteer receptionists who serve at Lancaster Baptist Church. I believe that a staff-run church is a staff-ruined church. It should never be our desire to have every position as a paid position, and the folks who are on paid staff are there simply to help equip the saints for the work of the ministry.

Having a receptionist to answer phones and to direct visitors during the week and on Sundays shows the community that your church operates in a professional manner and pays attention to details. Nothing is more frustrating than for a potential church visitor to call a church for more information, only to leave messages on an answering machine that never seems to be checked. An answering machine of any kind is a poor first impression for a church. On the other hand, a cheerful, friendly voice on the other end of the line can brighten anyone's day and show him that his call is important.

Under the direction of a paid staff member, a team of volunteer receptionists can be developed. Older teen girls, college-age singles, wives who do not work outside the home, and retired ladies can be involved to assemble this team. Many church ladies would love the chance to serve in this ministry. All volunteers need to be thoroughly trained in several areas—how to answer phones professionally, how to answer questions that may arise, how the campus is laid out during the workday, and how to use the receptionist's notebook and extensions list.

Although the receptionist may have more responsibilities than answering the phone, that task in itself will prove invaluable for your church. The receptionist can answer basic questions about childcare, service times, etc., giving the secretaries more time to do other tasks. Callers are also relieved when they can talk to someone rather than leaving a message or calling back at a later time. In fact, many people prefer not to leave messages, and their inquiries would go unanswered without a receptionist. When a call is urgent, she can help direct a need to the right person.

The receptionist can also direct mail, receive packages, and take messages for those out of the office. Having a specific person to sign for important items and deliver messages will eliminate much confusion in the everyday affairs of a church. If a staff member has a question about a phone message, he can go straight to the receptionist. It is also helpful to have the receptionist positioned in such a way that she is the first person visitors see when they arrive at your church. Rather than having those people wander around the church offices, she can notify the proper staff member of their arrival and direct them to the appropriate location.

While a deep, philosophical understanding of the Scriptures is certainly not required to answer phones and deliver messages, discretion is an important quality in a receptionist. She will be aware of confidential information from time to time, where privacy must be respected (Proverbs 15:2). She will also take important messages that must be given *directly* to the person for whom it was intended. Other times, the receptionist may need discernment to handle an upset caller or a caller who is probing for too much information.

Each receptionist should also be knowledgeable about the church to answer inquiries about specific ministries and to transfer phone calls to the proper staff member. To help with these questions, your church may want to compile a receptionist handbook with a complete list of the staff and their responsibilities, extension numbers, and other important information. An example of information you may want to have available begins on the next page.

The Receptionist Ministry

Dear Friend,

I want to welcome you to the Receptionist Ministry! It is a privilege to be able to serve the Lord here in any way or fashion. Through this area of service, I pray that you will grow spiritually as you meet the needs of others.

As you serve in this ministry I would like you to keep in mind Colossians 3:23–24, "And whatsoever ye do, do it heartily, as to the Lord, and not unto men; Knowing that of the Lord ye shall receive the reward of the inheritance: for ye serve the Lord Christ." As you serve the Lord in the Receptionist Ministry, be mindful that your service is unto the Lord and whatever we do for Him should be our best.

The thought of "commitment to excellence" comes to my mind when I read those verses. As servants of God, our attitude toward the Lord's work should be on a different level of excellence because of who we are serving—the Lord.

Finally, let me express how excited I am that the Lord has led you to serve in this ministry, and may the Lord bless you because of your faithfulness in this area of service.

Your friend,

Pastor

Job Description:

A. Answer the church telephone in a friendly, efficient manner.

   1. You are often the very first contact a person may have with our church. How you handle a call can encourage or discourage a person from visiting our church.
   2. Be happy and pleasant!

B. Handle incoming and outgoing packages.

   1. Accept deliveries and log packages into the shipping log (see CD 10.1).
   2. Give outgoing mail to the mail carrier.
   3. Accept incoming mail and inform the appropriate staff member.

C. Greet lobby visitors.

D. Update the lobby marquee.

E. Keep the desk clean.

F. Help keep the lobby tidy.

Job Requirements:

A. Servant's heart

B. Sweet spirit

C. Faithful to church services

D. Understanding of the phone system

E. Knowledge of staff responsibilities

F. Adherence to the church leadership requirements

Numbers at the Desk:

A. Name and extensions of each staff member

B. Classroom/Nursery extensions

C. Important numbers

It would be helpful to include this section not only in the receptionist handbook, but also on a card that is easily accessible to the receptionist.

Using the Phones:

Be sure to include specific instructions on how to answer the phone properly, how to transfer a call, how to send a call to voice mail, etc., depending on your telephone system.

Start Up Procedures:

At the beginning of the day:

A. Clean off the desk.

B. Begin answering the phones by 8 A.M.

C. Change the lobby marquee accordingly.

At the beginning of your shift:

A. If you are the second shift, ask the receptionist on the first shift if there is anything you should know:

1. Who is here?
2. Who is not here?
3. Is there anything else I need to be aware of?

B. Check the lobby marquee.

End of the Day Procedures:

At the end of your shift:

A. Take all remaining messages which have not been voice mailed or e-mailed upstairs to a secretary (or ask a secretary to come down and get them).

B. Tidy up the desk.

C. Communicate with your replacement anything she needs to know.

At the end of the day:

A. Put all notebooks, reference cards, etc., in a drawer.

B. Tidy the desk.

C. Empty the trash can.

Daily Procedures:

A. Dress modestly and professionally.

B. Be on time.

C. Be cheerful and helpful.

D. Use a normal voice—not too breathy or soft-spoken.

E. Do not answer questions for a staff member. This includes doctrinal and procedural questions. Do not answer any questions that you wonder about. If in doubt—don't! Do not let someone push you into saying anything you do not want to say.

F. It is okay to say, "I don't know," or "I'm just a volunteer."

G. Do not answer questions from reporters, lawyers, or questions regarding our attendance, facilities, etc.

H. If someone is not here (whether they are away from their desk, have gone on an errand, or are gone for the day), simply say, "I am sorry he/she is not available, would you like to speak with his secretary?" or, "Would you like his/her voice mail?" You do not need to say, "She went to run some errands," or, "He is out of town for the day." The caller really does not need to know that. If you are asked further questions, transfer the call to the appropriate secretary.

I.   Do not say, "I will have him return your call." You cannot promise that. You can promise to get a message to him. Only promise what you can do.

J.   Never assume someone is here and available. Say, "Let me see if he is available."

K. Callers requesting phone numbers and/or addresses of church members should be referred to a secretary.

L.   You will periodically hear things that should not be repeated. Please keep these things between you and the Lord.

M. Remember, please do not counsel over the phone. You really do not have time, and you may end up on a subject you really do not want to discuss. Please refer them to the appropriate secretary.

N. You may answer questions regarding service times, upcoming events, and childcare.

O. Use proper names for intercom—Miss Smith, Mrs. Brown, Dr. Jones, etc.

P.   Answer the phone before the third ring.

Q. Choose your words carefully. Do not promise anything we can't deliver.

R.   Scheduling—Please notify your coordinator as soon as possible if you will not be able to work on your scheduled day.

Handling Incoming Mail:

A. When the mail arrives, please notify the proper secretary, and she will come down to get the mail.

B. Please do not let non-staff members sort through the mail.

Activity Log:

A. There is a notebook in your drawer entitled "Activity Log." It contains a page on each of the major upcoming events. After reading the information on a given activity, you should be able to answer general questions regarding the activity.

B. If there is an upcoming event that is not covered in the log, please let a secretary know so a form can be completed.

Lobby Marquee:

The lobby marquee needs to be changed daily, sometimes twice. Please check the schedule at the beginning of your shift and make any necessary changes.

Shipping Log:

A. There is a notebook in your drawer entitled "Shipping Log" (see CD 10.1).

B. It is vital that you record each shipment we receive.

C. When UPS comes, count the boxes he is delivering BEFORE you sign your name. Make sure you are signing for the correct number of boxes.

D. Log each box into the book. Include who it was shipped from and where you put it.

E. For boxes that are addressed to a specific person, leave a message telling him that he has a box in the lobby and request that he comes down to get it.

F. Boxes that are not addressed to a specific person need to be opened by a staff member to determine where they are to go.

Greeting Visitors:

A. Treat each visitor as you would like to be treated. Smile and be friendly. Make each visitor feel welcome.

B. Always acknowledge a visitor. Stop what you are doing and say, "Hello, how may I help you?" If the visitor is a pastor, stand and greet him.

C. Go out of your way to help guests.

D. If the visitor has an appointment, announce his arrival to the appropriate secretary.

E. If the person does not have an appointment, discreetly call for assistance. If the person is seeking financial or spiritual help, call for a pastor.

Directing Calls:

See below for an example of a call directory you might use for your church. Be sure to include the subject of the call, who would take that call, and how they can be reached.

Subject	Person Responsible	Send the call to...
Advertising	*John Doe*	*ext. 145*
Bible Questions	*Jack Jones*	*ext. 124*

Taking a Message:

A. We would rather that you write down too much information than too little.

B. Take complete and accurate messages.

C. Ask for the correct spelling of the caller's name.

D. Ask for the company name.

E. Always get his phone number, even if the caller says, "He already has my number." Never assume.

F. Record the date and time of the call. This is vital.

G. Record the nature of the call. Be as informative as possible.

H. Always put your name or initials at the bottom of the message in case we have any questions.

Handling Calls:

A. Childcare Referrals
You may give out the names and phone numbers of the following members who provide childcare in their homes. (See example)

Name	Location	Phone	Licensed
Sally Smith	*Lancaster*	*555-1234*	*Yes*

B. Church Service Schedule
You may give out general information regarding church activities and service times. Below is a list of our weekly church services.

Sunday		Wednesday	
8:15 A.M.	Sunday School	7:00 P.M.	Bible Study
9:30 A.M.	Sunday School/Worship Service	7:00 P.M.	Discipleship
11:00 A.M.	Sunday School/Worship Service		
5:30 P.M.	Evening Service		

C. Collect Calls

1. Only accept collect calls from staff members.
2. Do not accept collect calls from prisons.

3. You may accept collect calls from workers out on church activities, (e.g., the bus driver on a youth activity or a chaperone on a children's activity).

D. Dialing Out

1. Please limit your personal calls to only those that are necessary.

2. No long distance calls, please.

E. Giving Directions
You may give directions, but if you are unsure about them, please transfer the call to a secretary.

F. Doctrinal Questions

1. Do not answer doctrinal questions. Refer them to a pastor.

2. Periodically someone will call asking directions to our church or our service times, then start asking doctrinal questions. Please do not answer them; say, "Why don't I transfer you to one of our pastors who can better answer that question?"

G. Calls from Missionaries

1. The assistant pastor coordinates our Missions Ministry. Most calls from missionaries should be directed to his office.

2. If a missionary that we support calls asking for a pastoral staff member, send the call to the appropriate office.

3. If a missionary calls whose name you do not recognize or who says he is interested in presenting his work at our church, the call goes to the head of the Missions Ministry for screening.

H. Prayer Requests
Refer callers with prayer requests directly to the secretary in charge of the prayer page.

I. Calls Regarding the Christian School
Please refer questions regarding our Christian school to the school receptionist. If you must give out information, you may say the following:

"Our school offers [Kindergarten] through [12th] grade and is [for our faithful members only]." Even if you know tuition information, do not give it out.

J. Wedding Information
We do not rent out our facilities for weddings or other such events to those other than our members. All wedding questions can be referred to the wedding secretary.

Upset Callers:

Periodically, you will receive a call from someone who is upset. Please remember the following:

A. You are not here to be cursed at. If someone speaks to you in this way, either put them on hold and get a pastor, or just hang up.

B. The Bible says that a soft answer turneth away wrath. Be friendly and use a soft voice.

C. Take a complete, accurate message and pass it on to the correct department. Do not make promises that we cannot keep. For example, if someone is upset that we knocked on his door, first attempt to transfer the call to the Soulwinning Department. If you must take a message, get his name and complete address. Tell him that you will pass it on to the Outreach Department with a request that we do not knock on that door again. Do not say, "We will never knock on your door again." We cannot promise that.

D. Log the call into the log so that we can refer back to the call if it becomes necessary (see CD 10.2).

CHAPTER ELEVEN

Choir & Orchestra Ministry

"Praise ye the Lord. Sing unto the Lord a new song,
and his praise in the congregation of saints."
Psalm 149:1

The Music Ministry is to the preacher and preaching service what John the Baptist was to Jesus—the forerunner, the team that says, "prepare ye the way for the Word of the Lord." While the preaching of the Word of God should be preeminent in a church service, music has been divinely ordained and chosen by God to be a tool that invites His power and presence into our lives. Music is a mode of communication that prepares our hearts, softens our spirits, and makes us ready to hear and respond to God's truth. In this light, it should be given a high priority in the local church. God's instructions are clearly defined in His Word:

> *Sing unto him a new song...For the word of the Lord is*
> *right; and all his works are done in truth.*
> Psalm 33:3-4

It is a good thing to give thanks unto the Lord, and to sing praises unto thy name, O most High. Psalm 92:1

O sing unto the Lord a new song; for he hath done marvelous things: his right hand, and his holy arm, hath gotten him the victory. Psalm 98:1

I will sing unto the Lord as long as I live: I will sing praise to my God while I have my being. Psalm 104:33

God not only commands us to sing, but He instructs us to come into His presence with singing. He tells us that our music should be glad, joyful, and even "loud!" God's commands and instructions for our music are plentious and clear in His Word. He tells us in Psalm 100:2–4:

Serve the Lord with gladness: come before his presence with singing. Know ye that the Lord he is God: it is he that hath made us, and not we ourselves; we are his people, and the sheep of his pasture. Enter into his gates with thanksgiving, and into his courts with praise: be thankful unto him, and bless his name.

The music portion of a church service truly sets the spiritual "backdrop" upon which the message will be delivered. Music always sets a "spiritual" context in any situation. Never is that context more important and vital than just before the preaching of the Word of God. God makes it clear in His Word that Christ-honoring music truly "moves Him into action" in the hearts of people. When God's people give themselves to sincere singing "as unto the Lord," they are truly opening their hearts and lives to Him in a way that invites Him to work within. In the truest sense, what happens at the altar at the end of the message begins during the song service.

The cornerstone of the church Music Ministry is the Sunday morning choir and orchestra. This core team of people will present the first "note" people hear in their worship of God each

Sunday, and from this team will flow all other vocal ensembles and instrumental specials. The building, training, nurturing, and oversight of this team should be a priority simply because music is a priority with God. As you strive to build an effective choir and orchestra, God will bless your efforts, multiply your team, and increase your influence for His glory.

Many churches approach the Music Ministry with a scarcity mentality. In other words, they bemoan what they do not have and what they cannot do, rather than doing the best they can with what God has provided in the way of talent and tools. Rather than looking constantly at what you cannot do, determine that you will be the best steward with the people and resources that God has given to you. Choose to build with what you have. In time, God will add to your ministry, increase your team, and provide you with greater resources.

In addition to this, there is a movement in our world to approach the church service as an entertainment venue rather than a true time of worship and spiritual growth. There is an attempt to be "seeker-sensitive" rather than "Saviour-sensitive," to minimize God's truth, and to simply connect with people on a surface level. Many churches conduct services that would seem more like a late night talk show or nightclub than a time of worship. This slippery slope of contemporary music has led many churches to bring in any and all kinds of worldly music in an attempt to "connect" with unchurched people.

The problem with this approach is that it goes directly against God's command that we should not be *"conformed to this world"* (Romans 12:2). This "unholy" approach also contradicts the very nature of God's holiness. The contemporary Christian music movement has reduced God and His truth to nothing more than a secular rock concert, and the Christian walk to nothing more than a flesh walk.

The church service is not entertainment, and it is not about pleasing people—it is about pleasing God. Our goal should not be to mimic our culture but to obey the Word of God. Our desire in the Music Ministry should not be to please our desires, but to honor the Lord. Our Music Ministry should be built upon a spirit of surrender and submission to God, not upon a self-centered "I want my MTV" attitude.

Is it possible to resist the cultural norms and to build a truly spiritual Music Ministry? Is it possible to maintain conservative, Christ-honoring music and still reach people? One look on the face of a lost person walking the aisle after they have truly experienced a Christ-centered service will answer that question. One glimpse of a joyful choir and orchestra corporately serving God with a spirit of surrender will make it abundantly clear. God still blesses those who worship Him—His way!

Building an effective choir and orchestra team is not hard, but it does take time and diligence. This is a part of ministry that requires constant oversight, coordination, development, and patience. As you read through the following pages you will see the tools used to enlist, commit, and build God's people into an effective choir and orchestra. Please realize as you launch into this journey, that you must commit to years of development, and realize that it is God who truly "builds" the church. He will add to your team as He sees fit. He simply requires of us that we be good stewards of what He has entrusted to us.

Do not minimize the vital role that your song service will play in the overall spiritual growth and development of your church family. With every passing week, give your whole heart and effort to using music that pleases God and engages His people in worship from the heart. Invest your time and energy into building musical skills and approach your Sunday services with a desire to honor the Lord with excellence. God will bless your hunger to "do things right," to constantly improve and to be more effective in Music Ministry.

Above all, as you grow this part of your church, it is vital that you keep "a heart for God" in first place. The Music Ministry can tend to attract talented people who seek self-gratification. God cannot bless a ministry with this focus. He will not share His glory. For Sunday's music to have any spiritual impact whatsoever, those singing, playing, and leading must do so with hearts of surrendered humility before God. They must yield their talents and their whole hearts to God's Holy Spirit. The singers and players must be sincere, Holy Spirit filled Christians—vessels fit for the master's use. They must not be performers. They must be servants. To the extent that we are self-centered in Music Ministry (whether in musical style, song choice, etc.), we hinder and prevent God's divine power from using our service.

At the end of the day, those who serve in the Music Ministry must desire that their music be powerful in its spiritual impact. We must hunger that God would use our songs to influence true spiritual transformation in the hearts of people! Without this, our music is nothing more than entertainment—or worse, just noise. Yet, God can do great things through a Music Ministry made up of yielded hearts and consecrated lives. May God grant you wisdom and blessing as you seek to build a stronger more effective choir and orchestra.

Starting and Leading a Choir

Volumes could be written about how to start, build, and lead the church choir. Hopefully these brief thoughts will serve to get you started in the right direction.

Starting a Choir

1. **Be willing to start small and grow gradually.** There are two primary goals in starting a choir. First, the church services are enhanced by the special music. Second, the choir is a wonderful opportunity to involve people in serving the Lord. In the early days of your choir, you may opt to include every willing voice, regardless of vocal ability. On the other hand, you could opt to start with a small ensemble of people who can at least carry a tune

and learn a harmony part. Both are valid in God's grand scheme of things, although the latter might be a little more pleasant to the human ear. You might consider blending the two approaches by having an ensemble that presents your Sunday morning music, and a larger choir (open to anyone) that sings only on Sunday evening.

Whatever the case, be willing to start somewhere and to grow in God's timing. Do not be afraid to pace the growth of your team—perhaps you will have the choir sing only once per month at first. This could be a positive! Promote it in the bulletin—"Don't miss the choir next Sunday morning!" This sort of gradual approach to both choir and orchestra will give your team time to learn music and to prepare, and it will help the entire church family anticipate something new!

2. **Search out and learn fresh music.** While there is nothing wrong with singing straight from the hymnal to begin with, at some point it is important that you commit both money and time toward finding and purchasing fresh choral arrangements of good songs. These arrangements could be great hymns arranged conservatively, new songs that honor the Lord, or strong older songs that carry a great message. Keeping fresh copies of music in the hands of your choir will keep them growing, improving, and loving what they do! Finding this music will take time and effort on the part of the music director—much like preparing the Sunday morning message requires time in the study for the pastor.

3. **Constantly build your singing repertoire.** Very few choirs have the budget or the skill to learn new music for every service. For years here at Lancaster Baptist Church, our choir has consistently built a rotating repertoire of music. In the early days, the choir would have repeated a song 8–10 times a year, but gradually the repertoire

grew, and the rotation became less predictable. Having a dependable repertoire takes years, but it also allows plenty of time in practice for learning new music.

4. **Grow your choir through deliberate personal enlistment.** There is really only one way to grow a choir—personally ask people to get involved. The music director should make a concerted effort, on a regular basis, to peruse the church directory, jot down names, and personally talk to potential new choir members. The choir is a fantastic bonding ministry for new church members. It is a great way to get someone "connected" in ministry, and you will be surprised how quickly the choir will increase if you consistently ask individuals to get involved. Be sure not to pressure or guilt someone who chooses not to join, but do not ever be hesitant to ask.

5. **Personally meet with every new choir member.** Becoming a part of the choir at LBC involves a personal commitment. That commitment is outlined later in this chapter. Each new choir member must agree to faithful attendance, leadership requirements, and other important factors. It is vital that the music director have a personal appointment to share the heart and reasons for this commitment prior to a person joining the choir. Do not be afraid to "raise the bar" in this commitment arena. Serving Christ requires faithfulness and steadfastness, and your church family will rise to the challenge if it is delivered with a transparent heart and biblical reason.

6. **Constantly nurture the choir with encouragement and growth.** We live in a busy culture. Christians want to make their service for God truly count, because our lives are busy. To keep people faithful in the choir, you must make the investment worth it! In other words, if you are not getting anything done in choir practice, people will quickly lose interest. Learning music, growing in musical

skill, and sharing spiritual encouragement are vital ways to keeping the choir alive with forward progress.

7. **Recognize that 70-80% of your choir will be there.** This may sound like compromise, but it is not—it is merely reality. Across the board, no matter the church or religious group, volunteer choirs generally have 70-80% participation at any one setting. This simply means that whether a practice, a service, a music training seminar, or a special event—you will probably have 70-80% of your total team there at any one time. Why is this important to know? First, it will keep you from getting frustrated over those who are absent. Generally these absences are for legitimate needs—work, family sickness, out of town travel, or even other ministry commitments. Second, it will help you target a number as you grow the choir. If your goal is to have 80 people singing in a service, you will need to have a choir enrollment of at least 100. Third, it will help you to educate the choir as to the importance of faithfulness and accountability. Finally, it will probably just encourage you to know that your church is not the only one dealing with this challenge.

Leading the Choir

1. **Lead in loving music and nurturing God's vision in your own heart.** The music director must make a conscious choice to love music, to learn music, and to capture God's vision for the Music Ministry. This is monumental! The man leading the choir and orchestra must be able to do so with heartfelt vision and with skill. Vision is contagious, and the entire team will either capture or lose their vision, based on that of the leader. As the music director, decide that you will ignite your heart with a passion to understand and fulfill the pastor and God's vision for your Music Ministry.

Regardless of your musical background up to this point, it is vital that you commit yourself to "owning the mantle" that you have been given. Give yourself to learning and growing in a technical understanding of music. Find books to read, classes to take, mentors to learn from, seminars to attend—do whatever you can to increase your own skill and the skill of your team. Whether or not you consider yourself a good "music conductor"—do everything within your power to become one for God's glory!

2. **Lead by being an enthusiastic example of a joyful Christian.** The Music Ministry should be fun! Serving God should be an enjoyable experience, and there is no greater way to keep your choir faithful and growing than to help people have a "great time" while they are serving God. While choir practice ought to be a focused time of preparation and hard work, it ought to also have some laughs, some testimonies, and some light-hearted interjections! Historically, our choir practices at LBC have been a mixture of all of the above. We generally do not derail the entire train, but several times each practice there is a good laugh—generally at the director for doing something musically stupid! Be able to laugh at yourself, have a great time with God's people, and genuinely enjoy serving God in the Music Ministry. If choir practice is drudgery for the music director, it will be drudgery for everyone!

3. **Lead in soulwinning.** America needs music directors who will turn off their stereos, put away the headphones, and actually get out and witness to someone. As a music director, you will have a whole team of people following your cue in this area. Music Ministry tends to lend itself toward an "exclusive mentality." In other words, music people can often, unintentionally come across as arrogant,

high minded, and unwilling to truly serve in other areas. Nothing will bring a sincere, down-to-earth approach to your Music Ministry faster than a team that will be involved in soulwinning. At LBC, soulwinning is a requirement for all choir members, and it has always been a priority for our pastoral staff. As the music director, refuse to be the kind of guy that waltzes in on Sunday, waves your arms, and forgets people the rest of the week. Ask God to help you break the mold, to make a difference in someone's life personally. Ask Him to give you fruit that will remain through your soulwinning.

4. **Lead in supporting the vision of the church.** Too often we ask, "How can the church support the Music Ministry?" This is the wrong question. The right question is, "How can the Music Ministry better support the whole church?" Although unintentionally, music participants can often get tunnel vision and think only of their ministry. This is a mistake, especially in Music Ministry. The Music Ministry on Sunday morning, to some extent, sets the context for all other ministries of the church all week long! It ought to be the vision of the music director to own the pastor's vision for the entire church and then to influence that corporate vision through the Music Ministry.

   The choir and orchestra should never allow even the smallest of items to become a wedge of division in ministry. The entire Music Ministry should be "on fire" with the vision and passion of the church as a whole, and not in any way feel "apart" from it. This kind of passion and commitment will again flow from leadership. The music director must work at maintaining the vision for the "big picture" of ministry. This will minimize disagreements over song selection, room usage, music schedule changes, pastoral "veto," and any other minor thing that could become a "burr under the saddle." The pastor's vision must be your vision. Anything less is nothing more than a self-centered lack of surrender—and God will not bless this kind of leadership.

Tracking the Choir

1. **Take regular attendance and recognize faithfulness.** This can usually be done with the help of a meek-spirited volunteer. This person should be meek-spirited because you do not want the attendance taker becoming the self-appointed "rebuker" of God's people. Perhaps you could have a section leader that takes attendance at each practice. However you choose to do this, take weekly attendance and uplift faithfulness and accountability. The spirit of taking attendance is not so you can cast judgment or harshly confront someone who is not being faithful. It is so you can reward faithfulness and lovingly encourage those who struggle. At LBC there is a master choir attendance roster for the entire year, and those who are the most faithful every month are recognized in the monthly newsletter. In addition to this, something special is done periodically for those who have stayed faithful over long periods of time.

2. **Review attendance for inconsistencies.** From time to time, someone may enter the choir ministry and then fail to maintain the commitment that was agreed upon. How you handle this in your Music Ministry will either lower the bar of commitment for everyone, or maintain the direction that God has set. As your choir and orchestra grow, it is important to review the attendance for those on your team who are missing more than you expected. This increase in absences should be a red flag to your pastoral heart. It may be that this person is going through a trial, carrying a heavy burden, or experiencing some discouragement that you can help with. In this case, you would want to be aware, to encourage, and to pray with

this person. It may be that this person was enlisted in another ministry without telling you. In this case you would want to talk to the ministry leader, get the story straight, and keep your "big picture" heart for the whole ministry. Keep a right spirit, and be thankful that your loss is another ministry's gain!

3. **Periodically contact absentees.** A weekly absentee letter will lose its impact. A "once a year" absentee letter will do the same. Choose to periodically contact absentees by letter, phone call, or personal touch in some way. This will help you maintain touch without seeming "overbearing." It will show that you care, especially when you find out that someone is dealing with a trial you knew nothing about.

4. **Lovingly confront problems or negligence.** On rare occasions, you may discover that someone is just slacking off in their choir participation for no good reason. "Not" to confront this behavior is to condone it. To "slam dunk" a person in this case would be "lording over" God's heritage. You must learn how to lovingly yet directly confront this person and ask him to "renew" his commitment or perhaps give him an opportunity to "step down." Do not allow someone to feel "trapped" in ministry as though he can never "get out." Yet, remain concerned for someone who was once moving forward in service who starts moving backward. Any kind of confrontation goes better "over lunch," and remember that the goal of your confrontation is restoration, not condemnation. You are confronting this person to help restore them to service, not to condemn them for failure.

Encouraging and Supporting the Choir

1. **Thank them for their sacrifice.** Every time you step in front of your choir you should be humbled that these wonderful people would give their time, their talents, and their hard work to sit under your leadership and to serve God. They do not owe you their service, and they certainly do not have to be involved. Be sure to frequently and to sincerely thank those who labor so hard to make the Music Ministry possible.

2. **Reward them for their labor.** When you come through a particularly busy season of ministry or through a big event—take a break. Go a week or two without choir practice. Give your team a chance to recoup, catch their breath, and re-energize their hearts for future service. From time to time, shorten choir practice, share testimonies, or maybe have a potluck fellowship. Whenever you get an encouraging note about the Music Ministry, share it with the choir. Let them know that their labor is well worth it!

3. **Pray for them and love them through trials.** As the music director, you can assist your pastor and bless your church family by truly being a "pastor" to your team. Ask God to help you love and care for people. Someone on your team right now is going through a difficult trial. Do you know about it? Are you doing anything to be a blessing to him? Write letters of encouragement every week to everyone that the Lord lays on your heart. Take discouraged Christians to lunch, pray for the members of your choir who are under burdens, and generally reach out to encourage and edify those within your reach. You cannot possibly know of every single need, but you can make a big difference by simply seeing your role as that of a "pastoral influence."

4. **Stay in touch with them.** Communication is so vital in ministry. At LBC, we send out a monthly music schedule and ministry newsletter, weekly updates for orchestra, and regular thank you notes and notes of encouragement. In addition to this, everyone on the music schedule every month receives several mailings, updates, and memos regarding service details and potential changes. The more clearly you communicate, the more effectively your team will serve. (See CD 11.1–11.3 for an annual music schedule, Music Ministry newsletter, and a music reminder card.)

Organizing the Choir

1. **Create music filing and preparation systems.** When you commit yourself to building the choir ministry, you will soon find a need for storage space and volunteer help. For years at LBC, faithful volunteers have arrived early to prepare music, stayed late to store music, and given time during the week to file and organize the music library and supplies. This volunteer team makes Music Ministry possible. There are many different types of "systems" that could be put in place. The key is to find what works best for your own ministry and keep your library decently in order.

2. **Abide by copyright laws.** Except for out-of-print music, be sure to purchase copies of music rather than photocopying them. This is often a short cut and a quick savings, but it is wrong. It may take years to build the library you desire, and it may mean you grow slower in your use of new music. It may mean that you share music rather than have one copy for each individual. In rare occasions, when asked, publishers will even grant permission to photocopy for specific purposes. Determine to keep your Music Ministry on course legally as you grow.

3. **Maintain an accurate choir roster and mailing list.** This can be done by a paid secretary or a volunteer person—depending on your needs and budget. Every week some detail should be given to maintaining the choir roster for effective communication and tracking.

4. **Designate practice times, locations, and schedules.** Determining the best practice time for your choir may require some "trial and error." "What works" varies from church to church across the nation. At LBC, the choir practices Sunday evenings from 4:30–5:30 P.M. In addition to this, there are weekly warm-up times 15 minutes before the services, and seasonal (Christmas and Easter) rehearsals for 4–6 hours on Saturday afternoon.

   The orchestra practices from 5–6 P.M. on Saturday evenings just before the Saturday evening sound check at 6 P.M. In addition to this, they rehearse (often in sectionals) during choir rehearsal on Sundays. One of the reasons we keep our primary choir practice shorter than many churches is that we also ask our choir members to be involved in an organized soulwinning time each week. Over the years, God has blessed this focus.

5. **Set up childcare for the choir members.** As your choir grows you are going to find a need for nursery and childcare for your choir members. One suggestion would be to host children's choirs for the older children at the same time the adult choir meets. For the younger children, you will need to enlist a team of faithful volunteers or set up a rotating schedule for your own choir members to take turns in the nursery. At LBC, we have done both over the years. Currently, we have a faithful team of non-choir members who have made it their ministry to work in the nursery during choir practice.

(See CD 11.4 for sample service cue cards.)

Starting and Leading an Orchestra

Many of the thoughts on leading the orchestra would be exactly as listed in the choir section; yet an orchestra, in many ways, is a unique ministry. Below are some brief thoughts that apply to the church orchestra.

1. **Recognize the value of additional instruments.** Scripture has many illustrations of using a multiplicity of instruments in the worship of God. In some ways, each new instrument adds a new dimension, a new sound, a new quality to your church service. With every added instrument, your music can communicate and connect in new or different ways. The key is that the sound be appropriate for the musical style and setting—that it actually contributes to and enhances what is being sung or played. Just as it is possible to bring in modern instruments to mimic the same "grunge" sounds of our pop culture, a natural instrument played poorly can emit some of the most "unworshipful" sounds known to man!

2. **Decide your orchestral philosophy.** What will the purpose of your church orchestra be? Are you simply trying to fill the room with sound during congregational singing? Are you trying to fully accompany the choir and ensemble specials? Will they play every week? Will they play in all the services? If you are simply trying to accompany congregational singing, strive to find orchestral arrangements for the actual instruments you have.

   Every instrument is different, and not every instrument should play every part of every song. This would be like getting into your car and turning on every knob, pushing every button, and engaging every possible function all at once. Rather than a driveable vehicle, you would have a chaotic mass of noise and movement—and you would likely damage your car and your hearing!

160

When a group of orchestral instrumentalists just starts "winging from the hip" (every man doing that which is right in his own eyes) during a song service, the result is much the same—chaotic disorder. For this reason, we chose to begin our orchestra with a commitment to using music arranged for each instrument. Every instrument plays only what is arranged for them to play—like a true team. This gives not only order and design, but also an incredibly beautiful sound as each instrument complements the other, rather than competing with the other.

The LBC orchestra plays only orchestral arrangements, and each instrument plays only when the arrangement calls for it.

3. **Finding the right music.** The logical question from point two is "where can I find orchestral arrangements and how much do they cost?" Fortunately, there are several acceptable solutions. Most music publishers today are releasing fully arranged orchestrations with every newly published piece of music. These orchestrations range in price from $25 to $300 depending on how many songs are being purchased, etc. Many of the arrangers understand the limitations and abilities of a volunteer church orchestra, and most of the orchestrations are within reach of an intermediate player. Bear in mind that you may need to alter arrangements from the publisher to fit the context of your church service.

4. **Be willing to start small and build.** Most churches never start an orchestra simply because of "who they do not have." Our church orchestra started with a bulletin announcement asking for those who could play an orchestra instrument "with skill." At the very first orchestra practice, there were twelve players with greatly varying skill levels—most of them had not touched their instrument since they were in high school. Yet, God took that twelve and multiplied them over the years. At first the orchestra only played on

Sunday evenings, once a month. As the repertoire grew, they began to play every Sunday night, and then eventually every Sunday morning.

5. **Keep God first and skill second.** At LBC, the priority has always been on serving with a pure heart for God. As you grow your Music Ministry, you will be tempted to compromise in this area because of someone's skills. Eventually someone will visit your church with incredible skill in some needed area. Quite often, this type of person worships their skill and not God. In other words, they will attend any church in order to "do their thing" for God. Our approach with this type of person is to always tell them the Music Ministry requirements and the doctrine of the church right up front. When a musician chooses a church based upon a doctrinal position, regardless of ministry opportunities, you can be sure God will soon give you peace to place them into the Music Ministry. Be willing to lose a very "skilled" visitor to preserve a heart for God in your Music Ministry. You may grow more slowly, but you will grow more healthily!

   At the same time, please do not minimize skill and improvement! The church orchestra is a specialized place of ministry—not everybody is ready or qualified for it. There is nothing pleasant nor worshipful about a sloppy, off-key song service. If you have a lot of beginner instrumentalists, consider allowing them to play only during practice or only on Sunday evenings, until their skill level reaches a point where you feel they are ready to play more frequently. Every time a new instrumentalist enters the LBC orchestra, they wait to play in a service until the orchestra director feels they are ready.

6. **Have a philosophy to "contribute" not "detract."** If you are using additional instruments currently—are they adding or detracting from the musical message? Our philosophy

162

in starting our orchestra was "to contribute positively" to the music. Whenever we run into an arrangement or a particular portion of music that cannot be delivered with skill or that does not have a Christ-honoring quality—we simply omit that part. There have been hundreds of times over the years that a particular player or even whole instrumental sections left off portions of an arrangement that were too difficult or that did not enhance the message to the glory of God. From your very first practice, labor to create a flexible spirit among your team. No one should "wear his feelings on his shoulders." Every player should be able to accept their limitations and fit into his place with a good spirit.

7. **Consider having parts played on keyboard.** Most current orchestrations ship with a full string reduction that could be played by an intermediate pianist on a keyboard with a pleasant string sound. You will be amazed how these string parts, even played by a keyboardist, will add to your service. For years, prior to having a string section in our orchestra, all the string parts were played from the keyboard. Thankfully, there are many other parts you may choose to fill in with keyboard—chimes, brass, bass, or even occasional solo lines. Before you give up on using a part that you do not have an instrument for, consider this route.

8. **Set a separate orchestra rehearsal time.** It is important for the orchestra to grow together as a group. Find out the most convenient time for your crew to be faithful, and begin practicing. If the Lord has given you someone with a greater understanding of instrumental music than you, ask him to help develop the team.

9. **Create separate orchestra files.** The cardinal rule of orchestra ministry is that no one ever uses "the master" copy of music. When you purchase an orchestration, we

would recommend that you stamp the master copies with a red stamp that says "master." After you make a copy for your orchestra, make a back-up copy for future use, and then lock the master in a vault where it can only be retrieved in an emergency! Over time, this orchestration will go out of print and your master copy will be the only way you can obtain replacements.

10. **Enlist volunteers to help with preparation.** At LBC, willing volunteers make the orchestra possible. From childcare, to set up, to music preparation, to filing— volunteers coordinate the entire Music Ministry.

11. **Pray for additional parts.** Perhaps the greatest way to build your orchestra, aside from just starting one, is to pray for additional players. God will answer your prayer, one player at a time, and will probably grow your group faster than you would have anticipated. Consider having a weekly prayer time during orchestra practice when you pray for the services as well as for additional players.

The Choir & Orchestra Ministry

Dear Friend,

Welcome to the Choir and Orchestra Ministry of Lancaster Baptist Church. Each week, thousands of people gather together to hear and participate in honoring the Lord through song with our choir and orchestra. This is no small responsibility!

As you join this team, I ask and encourage you to see your task as something that only God can enable you to do. Commit yourself to serving Him with a pure heart, and serve Him with gladness each week.

As you learn this ministry and grow in God's grace, do not ever forget that your influence is being felt powerfully each week. What could become commonplace to you (singing and serving) must be fresh, spirit-filled, and empowered by God every week.

Do not ever get tired of preparing the way each week for the preaching of the Word of God. Every time a soul walks the aisle or a decision is made at the altar, please know that you had a part in it! May God bless you as you serve Him!

Your friend,

Pastor

Attributes of a Fantastic Choir & Orchestra Member

Faithfulness

As a choir member, it is vitally important that you regard your position in high esteem. If you are teaching a class, the chances are very slim that you would be absent without communicating with the Sunday school director so that someone else could teach in your place. For some reason, when it comes to choir, we often feel like we would not be missed. You need to realize that your part in the choir is extremely vital and it must be filled every time the choir is rehearsing or singing. As you grow in your ability to sing and in your understanding of what a choir member is, your presence at every practice and every service will become increasingly more important.

Undoubtedly, there will be times that you will be required to miss practice or miss a service due to sickness, work requirements, or other unforeseen obstacles. It will be helpful for you to communicate with the music director ahead of time. Just determine now as you join the choir that you will be faithful to all practices and services.

A Great Attitude

As we practice during a normal musical year, undoubtedly we will sing songs that do not perfectly suit your taste. Since we all have such varied tastes in music, it is important that we keep a good attitude toward every song and every rehearsal. The best choir members are those who consistently pour their hearts into every song that is sung, recognizing and appreciating it for the truth that it represents. Do your best in every practice and every service to keep a sweet spirit and a godly attitude toward everything that takes place. This will make choir fun for you and fun for those around you.

A Desire to Improve Musically

Our choir is filled with people from many various musical backgrounds. You may be a person with no musical education at all. In fact, the only thing you have ever played might be the radio! On the other hand, you may be very well versed in sight reading and in choral experience. Wherever you may fall in the spectrum of musical ability, please do not feel alone. There are a host of other people in the choir who are probably just like you. We simply ask that you have a willingness to grow and to go forward from wherever you may be in your musical ability. It may be learning how to sight read music, learning how to count notes, learning how to sing harmony, or memorizing music. Participate wholeheartedly in whatever we may be working on at a given time with a desire to grow and improve as a vocalist and musician. We should want our music to be as effective as it can possibly be. As we grow in skill and ask for God's power, our music will become more effective with each passing week. By the way, do not ever feel intimidated or belittled if you do not know the meaning of a note or a musical term; none of us did when we first began.

A Heart to Serve

The Music Ministry is a unique part of the church. At times, it tends to attract people who have a desire to be on stage performing in front of others. This is not the philosophy of our Music Ministry. At our church, musicians, singers, players, and participants are all servants. We are here for one purpose—that is to serve the Lord in our church. Every time we stand to sing, we are not merely performing—we are serving. Every time we stand before our church family to sing, we are representing the Lord, and we are setting a context in which the Holy Spirit of God will work through the preaching of His Word.

Above all, we need the power of God's Holy Spirit. We do not need showmanship or perfectionism; we do not need proud or haughty spirits. We simply need humble hearts to communicate

Bible truth in a musical way. As we strive individually to have servants' hearts as an entire Music Ministry, God will bless and use us far beyond our expectations.

A Mind to Work

Though choir will be great fun, and though we spend a lot of time laughing, we also spend a lot of time working, especially as we approach more crucial times in our musical year, such as preparation for Christmas and Easter. I ask that you come to every practice with a mind to work hard and to pour your concentration and your wholehearted participation into every song that we sing. Please work diligently at looking at the music, studying your part, and memorizing the words for every piece that we learn. It is very easy to fall into the trap of talking and visiting with people around you while we are not going over your particular part. I simply ask that you do your part to help maintain continuity and concentration throughout the entire practice. This will help us to become a better choir in the months and years ahead.

General Procedures

    A. Little things that mean a lot:

        1. Holding music—hold it low enough to see the director and music. If you are sharing music, the person closest to the center should hold it.

        2. Walking in—move quickly and fill the rows from the center.

        3. Watching the director—keep your eyes fixed and be responsive to his leadership.

        4. Caring for music—be mindful that in the course of a year, our church will invest $50 to $100 for your music; please take care of it.

        5. Facial expression—be pleasant and be consistent with the message of the song.

6. No gum—this is extremely distracting.
7. Do not look at others when mistakes are made.
8. Promptness—be early; you will otherwise miss warming up and important announcements.
9. Posture—stand straight but not rigid, facing the director, and lean slightly forward.
10. Stay on pitch—nervousness causes your pitch to go sharp; tiredness and not concentrating causes your pitch to go flat.
11. Bring pencils and highlighters.
12. Understand and read over text.

B. Dynamic marks:

1. p—softly (emotional)
2. m—medium
3. f—loud, dynamic (Forte)
4. Accelerando—gradual increase in speed
5. A tempo—in time
6. Crescendo/Decrescendo—to increase/decrease in volume of sound
7. Birds eye or breath mark—these marks notate when to hold or pause

C. Platform guidelines:

1. Walk briskly but smoothly to your place.
2. Hold your belongings in the hand opposite the congregation.
3. Do not carry a lot of paraphernalia into the service with you.
4. When the director is in place, all eyes should be on him.
5. Do not talk, look funny, or call attention to yourself in any way.
6. Keep your eyes focused on who is at the pulpit at all times.

Orchestra Commitment

lowing commitment sheet is handed out to all new rchestra members. It details the commitment required to s... these ministries. Prior to entering the choir or orchestra, all new members meet with the music director to cover these aspects of ministry and fill out a questionnaire (see CD 11.5).

As a part of the Lancaster Baptist Church choir/orchestra…

1. **I will hold my place of service in high regard**—I realize I serve Christ and His church in this position of service and will hold this as a privilege and a responsibility not to be treated lightly.

2. **I will fill my place of service faithfully**—I commit to being in my place for all practices and services unless providentially hindered. When possible, I will make the music secretary aware of absences before they happen.

3. **I will avoid the "they will never miss me" mentality**—I will understand that I am a part of a team of people who work together for a common cause. The team needs me to be in position and growing with them at every opportunity. When I am missing, part of the team is missing, and the whole team suffers as a result.

4. **I will structure my schedule not to interfere with my choir commitment**—I understand that weekly I will have opportunities to miss practice and services, even for potentially good things. Unless I have spoken with the choir director, I will structure my schedule so that my commitment to choir is faithfully fulfilled.

5. **I will give 100% of my mental and vocal effort during practice time**—I understand that practice times are critical times of growth, preparation, and team building. Without strong concentration and vocal effort, I will hurt the team and weaken the effectiveness of our ministry together.

When practicing I will work, concentrate, and devote myself to growing and learning with the rest of the team.

6. **I will be on time for services and practices**—Except for providential hindrance, I will be in my place on time and ready to sing for every weekly service and practice time.

7. **I will faithfully participate in occasional special rehearsals**—I understand that in the course of a year the choir will meet for special times of rehearsal and preparation for special musicals and events. I agree to be in my place during these times and to do everything within my power to arrange my schedule to accommodate these practices.

8. **I will faithfully prepare on my own time with any special rehearsal tapes/CDs**—I will get my tape/CD early, learn the music with the rest of the team, and do my best to support these special times of advance preparation.

9. **I will be a faithful example of a godly church member and Christ-like christian**—I understand that my place in the choir is one of visible leadership. Thus, I will agree to the church leadership requirements; I will support the overall ministry of the church, and I will strive to be a godly testimony within and without the walls of my church.

10. **I will be right with God and fully dependent upon his power each time I sing**—I realize that our services are not performances or shows; they are times of worship and service to God. Realizing I cannot serve from impure motives in my own strength, I will sing for God's glory, being right with Him and depending upon Him to do the work through me.

I willingly, freely, and wholeheartedly agree to the above commitment and am ready to begin serving in the Music Ministry.

Signed _____ Date _____

(CD 11.6)

CHAPTER TWELVE

Usher Ministry

"For a day in thy courts is better than a thousand.
I had rather be a doorkeeper in the house of my God,
than to dwell in the tents of wickedness."
Psalm 84:10

Our God is a God of order. From the 365¼ days it takes the earth to revolve around the sun to the bird's natural instinct to fly south for the winter months, God has even the smallest details of creation arranged with logical precision. In Ecclesiastes 3:1, Solomon says, *"To every thing there is a season, and a time to every purpose under the heaven."* Throughout the Old Testament, the Lord shows us the importance of organization through naming each of the animals, forming the tribes of Israel, and giving precise instructions to Solomon for building the temple.

The role of the usher in helping to maintain order in a church service cannot be underestimated. It is vital that the ushers be men of spiritual integrity, and that they possess a servant's heart. When Christ was about to feed 5,000 people, he did not have them form a single-file line and organize themselves. Instead, Luke 9:14–17 tells us that Christ delegated this job to the first "ushers:"

> ...he said to his disciples, Make them sit down by fifties in a company. And they did so, and made them all sit down. Then he took the five loaves and the two fishes, and looking up to heaven, he blessed them, and brake, and gave to the disciples to set before the multitude. And they did eat, and were all filled: and there was taken up fragments that remained to them twelve baskets.

The "ushers" in the above verses were responsible for not only arranging the people in an orderly manner (companies of fifty), but also for distributing the food and collecting the leftovers. Ushers in modern churches have similar obligations. They assist with the seating and filling of the auditorium and also make arrangements for those with special needs. People who have trouble walking need to be seated as close to the doorway as possible; those who are hard of hearing should be seated near the front; wheelchairs should be at the end of an open aisle; and the list goes on and on.

Ushers are also in charge of distributing bulletins and special announcements as people enter the auditorium. If there is a special handout to be distributed during or after the service, ushers must do this as well. Some churches have the ushers collect and count the offering, or this may be done by the deacons. Ushers should be friendly, courteous, and knowledgeable about the church's Sunday school classes and campus directions to assist visitors. Above all else, ushers must be willing to work as a unit and be servants for Christ's sake. III John 9–12 tells us of two men in the same church who had differing views of their positions as workers:

> I wrote unto the church: but Diotrephes, who loveth to have the preeminence among them, receiveth us not. Wherefore, if I come, I will remember his deeds which he doeth, prating against us with malicious words: and not content therewith, neither doth he himself receive the brethren, and forbiddeth them that would, and

casteth them out of the church...Demetrius hath good report of all men, and of the truth itself: yea, and we also bear record...

Diotrephes fell into sin because he wanted "to have the preeminence..." There is a danger of this happening in the Usher Ministry because ushers are at the forefront of the entire church service. Yet an usher must never seek to be exalted; he should not wish to be recognized above any other servant in the church. Many times, the endless duties and menial tasks an usher must perform will go unnamed, but each servant can rest assured that his "*labour is not in vain in the Lord.*" (I Corinthians 15:58) A Christ-honoring usher possesses the spirit of Demetrius. People can easily identify him as a person who is kind, is gracious, and possesses a servant's heart.

Maintaining the Usher Ministry

Organize

The Usher Ministry should be organized and maintained by the senior pastor or an assistant pastor. He should assign a head usher and approve all ushers serving in this ministry.

Enlist

At every Ministry Involvement Night, the Usher Ministry should have a display table and recruit new ushers. New members transferring from another church of like faith can also be enlisted as ushers if they are deemed spiritually ready.

Train

Have a regular time of training for the ushers. Practice taking an offering, handling the doors, etc. The ushers can be observed to correct problems during a training time. Also teach them how to deal with different types of people, review policies regarding emergencies and the collection and counting of offerings (some churches prefer for the deacons to count offerings).

Recognize and Honor

Holding an annual Ushers' Banquet is a great way to schedule consistent praise and gratitude for a job well done. The church can provide a special meal in which the ushers and their families are invited. The pastor can thank them for a productive year and challenge them to stay faithful in the upcoming year.

Fellowship

The head usher can plan periodic fellowships for the ushers and their families. They work hard as a team, and this activity will give them a chance to actually talk and get to know their teammates.

The next several pages are guidelines that we give to our ushers which lay the basic groundwork for the Usher Ministry.

Usher Ministry

Dear Friend,

I want to welcome you to the Usher Ministry! It is a privilege to be able to serve the Lord here in any way or fashion. Through this area of service, I pray that you will grow spiritually as you meet the needs of others.

As you serve in this ministry I would like you to keep in mind Colossians 3:23–24, "And whatsoever ye do, do it heartily, as to the Lord, and not unto men; Knowing that of the Lord ye shall receive the reward of the inheritance: for ye serve the Lord Christ." As you serve the Lord in the Usher Ministry, be mindful that your service is unto the Lord and whatever we do for Him should be our best.

The thought of "commitment to excellence" comes to my mind when I read those verses. As servants of God, our attitude toward the Lord's work should be on a different level of excellence because of who we are serving—the Lord.

Finally, let me express how excited I am that the Lord has led you to serve in this ministry, and may the Lord bless you because of your faithfulness in this area of service.

Your friend,

Pastor

As Christians, we are ambassadors for our Lord Jesus Christ. As ushers, we also represent our pastor and fellow church members. We are a part of the public relations of the church.

At each service, we expect God to work in people's hearts in a powerful way, drawing them to Christ. This work that he accomplishes often begins not with the ministry of the *preacher*, but with the ministry of the *usher*. God wants to use ushers as genuine "men of God" who are a part of His grand efforts to bring the lost to himself. Ushers have the opportunity either to *facilitate* these efforts, or to *frustrate* them depending on whether they understand and fulfill their ministry responsibilities or not.

An usher should dress with proper shirt and tie, and jackets which are provided. Shoes should be shined and hair neatly combed. Use breath mints, but do not chew gum. REMEMBER: "You only have one chance to make a good first impression."

Organizing the Usher Ministry

Responsibilities of the Head Usher

A head usher may be designated to assign positions and specific responsibilities to the other ushers. He would be in charge of usher meetings to update ushers on special events or changes in procedure.

Responsibilities of an Usher

    A. Pray—Personally, daily, and with the ushers before the service

    B. Welcome visitors and members

    C. Assemble visitor's packets (explained later in chapter)

    D. Assist with seating people

    E. Help deal with situations involving babies/children

    F. Sunday school count

G. Service count

H. Offering collection

I. Confront problem people with kindness

J. Help minimize distractions

K. Help with traffic flow in and out of auditorium

The Dress of an Usher

A. Dress attire (dress pants, dress shirt, tie, etc.)

B. Usher's jacket—provided by church (should all be same color so the ushers are readily distinguishable)

C. Name badge—brass plated (can be inscribed "Usher" or use individual names)

D. The church should provide an Usher's Closet where the usher's jackets are stored. This storage area can be used by the ushers to hang their personal suit jackets and store personal items if necessary.

Basic Timeline for a Service

A. Remain at your assigned station; do not get involved in conversations with other ushers or church members.

B. Make people feel welcome, especially visitors. Smile. Maintain good eye contact and a firm handshake (only shake a lady's hand when it is extended to you).

C. Escort visitors to the nurseries and classrooms; do not point the way.

D. Close the auditorium doors when the choir begins to enter the choir loft.

E. Seat people from front to back; know where the empty seats are.

F. Seat parents with small children and babies in the back of the auditorium. If a problem occurs with a baby, ask the parent to take the child to the nursery or lobby.

G. You are assigned to collect the offering. When collecting the offering, walk briskly to the front, walk upright, hold the offering plate as a book. When passing the plate, look down the main aisle, not at the people giving the offering.

H. Your position is the aisle way in which you receive the offering.

I. In case of an emergency, the usher in that area must stay calm. Help the person out of the auditorium as quickly as possible. The head usher will assist in all emergencies.

J. Move around as little as possible, so as to not draw attention to yourself.

K. Please keep your jackets on after the offering and find a seat in your area. You may be needed in case of an emergency, and your jacket will let people know that you are there to help.

Service Checklist

A. Do you have bulletins available?

B. Are visitor's cards available?

C. Are welcome packets ready?

D. Are offering plates available?

E. Are there special handouts today? If yes, when will they be given out?

F. Are there babies or small children in your section?

G. Did you pray for your section today?

Visitor's Packet

When the pastor welcomes and recognizes visitors, the ushers distribute a visitor's packet to each visitor or visiting family. This packet contains the following:

- Visitor Book (see CD 12.1)

- Sermon cassette or CD

- Response card—to be filled out by the visitor (see CD 12.2)

- Pen with church name—could have logo or yearly theme

Ministry Attendance Ushers

These ushers serve in the Sunday school area during Sunday school times.

RESPONSIBILITIES:

A. You are assigned to assist visitors in finding classrooms, to pick up Sunday school/Junior church offering, and to record the attendance for each class.

B. Your position is the classroom area.

C. Be in your area twenty minutes before the start of the service.

D. After you have recorded attendance and picked up the offering, take attendance information and offering to ushers in the Main Auditorium.

CHECKLIST

A. Do you have information guides available (see CD 12.3)?

B. Is there an offering bag available?

C. Are there attendance forms available?

D. Are there special handouts today?

E. Check your area for children that should be in their classrooms.

F. Did you pray for your area today?

Note: To protect the church and the ushers, any time an usher will be handling offerings, he should be paired with another usher. This promotes accountability and protection.

Lobby Responsibilities

A. Welcome people and give out bulletins.

B. Hold doors for handicapped and elderly.

C. Assist with lobby setup prior to service.

D. Assist with and minimize traffic flow in and out of the auditorium during the service.

Handicapped Seating

It is helpful to have reserved seating for people who have a handicap. The following are some special needs to consider:

A. Deaf and hearing impaired should have a section designated for them if your church is able to supply an interpreter.

B. Rows or parts of rows can be reserved for families who have a loved one in a wheel chair. These rows should be located in an area with plenty of room for wheelchair access.

C. Elderly or people with extremely poor eyesight can have a seat reserved toward the front to help them be able to see and to enjoy the service.

D. Members with leg/foot problems can be seated near the door.

Ushers should be sensitive to the physical needs of anyone attending the service. They should offer their assistance whenever it is needed.

CHAPTER THIRTEEN

Deacon Ministry

"For they that have used the office of a deacon well purchase to themselves a good degree, and great boldness in the faith which is in Christ Jesus."
I Timothy 3:13

Any pastor can attest to the fact that there is too much work to be done in a church by one man. When a pastor is called to a church, he is called to equip the saints for the work of the ministry.

This responsibility will be accomplished through preaching God's Word. There are so many day-to-day tasks that must be taken care of in the ministry that if the pastor had no help, he would neglect his greatest duty—making sure he is spiritually prepared to preach through study, prayer, and time alone with God.

For this reason, the early church leaders appointed godly men from out of the congregation to help them in the daily administration over the church's affairs.

Then the twelve called the multitude of the disciples unto them, and said, It is not reason that we should leave the word of God, and serve tables. Wherefore, brethren, look ye out among you seven men of honest report, full of the Holy Ghost and wisdom, whom we may appoint over this business. But we will give ourselves continually to prayer, and to the ministry of the word. Acts 6:2–4

The Nomination of the Deacons

I believe that Acts 6 outlines the selection of the first deacons of the church at Jerusalem. Several key phrases give us some insight as to how best to approach the nomination and election of deacons. First in verse three, the Bible says, *"…look ye out among you seven men of honest report, full of the Holy Ghost and wisdom, whom we may appoint over this business."* This would imply that these were men who were from among the congregation and proven in their testimony.

At Lancaster Baptist Church, the deacons are the nominating committee, and each November they begin praying about potential new nominations for deacons. Members of the congregation may suggest names to the deacons at any time throughout the year.

At a deacons' meeting in December, 3 x 5 cards are distributed on which each deacon may write down a few names for nomination. During the meeting, from those cards a master list is made by the pastor. At that point each of the deacons have their heads bowed and eyes closed for a season of prayer. With heads remaining bowed and eyes closed, the pastor reads each of the names of those who have been nominated. If a deacon is aware of any situation in one of the nominees' life that would hinder him from becoming a deacon, he may raise his hand to indicate a veto of the nomination. This process allows for complete confidentiality and abstinence of gossip about any particular man.

Once this process is concluded, the pastor should have some names from which he can begin interviewing potential deacons. Each of these nominees has a meeting with the pastor. At the meeting, several items are shared with the nominee.

First, the nominee is congratulated for being unanimously nominated for the office of deacon. Then, the Bible is opened to I Timothy 3, where each of the qualifications of a pastor and deacon are defined. A complete list of deacon responsibilities is shared with the nominee as well as an approximate amount of time to be invested, should they accept the nomination. Items shared with the nominee at this time are the monthly deacons' meetings, caring for widows, counting the offerings, attending Deacons' Orientation, the responsibility for the wives to set up for the Lord's Table, and the need for deacons to serve the Lord's Table. Many other items may be shared at this time as well.

After the qualifications and job description of the deacon are shared, the nominee is given at least a week to pray about accepting the nomination. Should he determine to accept the nomination, his name is placed on a ballot for the annual Victory Meeting of Lancaster Baptist Church. The church family is instructed that we do not vote on "the best two out of three," but that they should vote on each individual who has been nominated. Traditionally, as these men are presented with the unanimous recommendation of the pastor and deacons, they have been elected to serve along side the other deacons of Lancaster Baptist Church. The term of service is two years, at which time they may be re-elected to serve an additional two years.

Annual Deacon Events

There are two very special annual events for the deacons and their wives that we highly recommend. The first event is the annual Deacons' Orientation. This retreat provides a time for the pastor to nurture and encourage the deacons in their family lives, deacon responsibilities, and overall commitments to the Lord Jesus Christ. Typically, this retreat takes place in a hotel setting, somewhere away from the church. The church budget allows for some offsetting of the cost of the retreat, with the deacons also contributing to the payment for the retreat. Normally, we invite a guest speaker to bring the evening challenges and the pastor speaks on issues ranging from benevolence and meeting the needs of widows to communicating during a building program. Split sessions may be offered to the deacons' wives where they learn more about serving with their husbands in the Deacon Ministry. Often, it is helpful to choose a deacon who has served for many years, to speak on the subject of being an effective deacon. This training has become invaluable over the years, and has helped to develop a cohesive team spirit amongst the deacons of Lancaster Baptist Church.

Another annual event that has been a tremendous blessing amongst the deacons is the annual Christmas party. This party is more than simply a time for food and fellowship. It is a time of reflection on the past year of victories and faithfulness of God. For many years, Terrie and I have purchased a gift for each deacon and his wife. We delight in the opportunity to thank them for being a blessing to our church family throughout the year.

Meetings like these are vitally important in the heart and life of a church. In leadership training sessions over the years, I have often said we need to spend "more time growing grass than killing weeds." The relationship development aspects of these types of retreats and parties will go a long way when challenges come into the life of a church.

Under-Shepherd's Program

Another unique aspect of becoming a deacon of Lancaster Baptist Church is that each deacon is assigned a particular section of our city, in which dozens of our members live. This Under-Shepherd's Program is one in which each deacon is given a list of members who live in their particular area. The deacon is responsible to visit these members at a time of death, bereavement, or grave illness. Additionally, the birth dates of these families are shared with the deacon and his wife, who may send birthday cards to those within their area.

The hope of Lancaster Baptist Church is that, through the combined efforts of the deacons' Under-Shepherd's Program, the Pastoral Care Ministry and adult Bible class care groups, no one will be forgotten during a time of difficulty or sickness. The assignment of the Under-Shepherd area and names of members are given at the annual Deacons' Orientation and a large map is displayed to show each of the deacons his respective area for service.

Ministering to Widows

One of the primary functions of the early deacons was to minister to the needs of widows. At Lancaster Baptist Church, each deacon is given his "widows assignment" at the Deacons' Orientation. Typically, our deacons serve two or three widows throughout the year. This ministry may include things as simple as a phone call to give a word of encouragement—to major things like replacing water heaters, garbage disposals, and completing other household needs for the widows of our church. If the item of service needed for a widow is something that can be accomplished easily, the deacon will normally take care of it himself. If it requires professional labor, such as a certified plumber, the deacon will notify the church financial administrator and arrangements are made for the widow's need to be met. We believe that serving the widows in this fashion is honoring to the Lord and consistent with the principles found in Acts 6.

Altar Counseling

One of the primary ministries of the deacons at Lancaster Baptist Church is doing the work of counseling after each message is preached. At the Deacons' Orientation, training is often given to the deacons and their wives, showing them how to lead someone to Christ, how to explain baptism, or how to receive new members into the church. We believe the reception of new members into the church is one of the most vital aspects of the altar work being done in churches today. This is especially true for churches that do not have a membership course required before membership.

We believe churches today are often filled with members who are unsaved or unaware of the true beliefs of a Baptist church. Therefore, it is vital that a deacon be prepared to ask questions adequately at the membership interview time. The deacon asks about the salvation testimony of the membership candidate and if he is transferring membership into the church (it is vital in our situation that the candidate has been baptized in a church of like faith).

We believe that the ordinance of baptism must be ministered according to proper mode, order, and authority. The mode, of course, is immersion. The order is after salvation, and the authority for baptism is an authentic New Testament church. To promote doctrinal unity, we have required transfer members to be people who are saved members of a sister Baptist church of like faith.

Upon hearing the salvation and baptism testimony of the potential new member, the deacon then explains the doctrine of Lancaster Baptist Church and recommends that each new member consider attending a discipleship class of the church, so he might become more thoroughly acquainted with the doctrine and practice of Lancaster Baptist specifically. Once the candidate has spent this time with the deacon, his transfer of membership paper is given to the pastor at the earliest service possible and the new member is added to the church.

Within the first two weeks of their membership at Lancaster Baptist, all new members, whether by baptism or transfer of letter, will receive a New Members' Packet (see Chapter 6). This gives a more thorough explanation of the doctrine and practices of Lancaster Baptist Church. Many small pamphlets are included in this packet that give them knowledge of a variety of subjects, including our Baptist history, our stand on the Charismatic Movement, the purpose of our church, and the names and service areas of our staff members. We give each new member a copy of the church constitution in this packet as well.

In whatever area the deacon serves, he must remember that it is a God-ordained position, and that he is accountable for the way in which he serves. In I Timothy 3, God gives a list of requirements for deacons that is almost as extensive as the requirements for a pastor. The remaining pages of this chapter will explain in detail the requirements and expectations of a deacon in his service to the Lord.

The Deacon Ministry

Dear Friend,

I want to welcome you to the Deacon Ministry! It is a privilege to be able to serve the Lord here in any way or fashion. Through this area of service, I pray that you will grow spiritually as you meet the needs of others.

As you serve in this ministry I would like you to keep in mind Colossians 3:23–24, "And whatsoever ye do, do it heartily, as to the Lord, and not unto men; Knowing that of the Lord ye shall receive the reward of the inheritance: for ye serve the Lord Christ." As you serve the Lord in the Deacon Ministry, be mindful that your service is unto the Lord and whatever we do for Him should be our best.

The thought of "commitment to excellence" comes to my mind when I read those verses. As servants of God, our attitude toward the Lord's work should be on a different level of excellence because of who we are serving—the Lord.

Finally, let me express how excited I am that the Lord has led you to serve in this ministry, and may the Lord bless you because of your faithfulness in this area of service.

Your friend,

Pastor

Policies and Procedures

Lord's Table Preparation

I. Preparation for Lord's Table (I Corinthians 11:23–34)

    A. This is a sacred time and should be treated with the right spirit. (vs. 27)

    B. We should pray and have our hearts ready. (vv. 27–28) We should have the right heart not only when partaking of the Lord's Table but also during the set-up of the Lord's Table.

    C. The Lord's Table should be accomplished decently and in order. (I Corinthians 14:33, 40)

II. Procedures for Lord's Table

    A. Double check the schedule and know when you are scheduled for set-up or clean-up.

        1. Each team is made up of deacon's wives and is scheduled for three set-ups, three clean-ups, and six off-months per year. Make sure to plan accordingly.

        2. Each team has a team leader to help in reminding her team when they are scheduled.

    B. This is a sacred time and should be accomplished in the right heart and spirit. Have a place for your children. They should not be in the set-up room or helping with the Lord's Table.

    C. Lord's Table set-up should be accomplished in the proper place. Choose an appropriate, quiet, and private room.

    D. Any out-of-the-ordinary circumstances will be communicated from the deacon to the set-up team. Examples would be: services in which a greater attendance is expected or if extra juice is needed in certain areas of the auditorium.

E. Be sure to contact the supply team leader if supplies are getting low so more supplies can be ordered.

New Members' Receptions

A reception for the new members of the church is held every six to eight weeks. There are several aspects regarding preparation for this event which makes the New Members' Reception a blessing:

A. The New Members' Reception coordinator will call three deacon's wives and ask them to call two ladies who are newer members to help with serving the cake at the reception. As a courtesy to our members, these calls should be made at least one week prior to the event. The coordinator will oversee the purchasing of the cakes, punch, and supplies necessary for this reception.

B. All deacons and their wives and staff are encouraged to greet the new members at this reception. Please introduce yourself and spend some time in fellowship with them.

C. Following the New Members' Reception, the deacons who are not part of the counting team will need to help put the tables away and make sure the cakes are given away or stored in the church freezers.

Let us do our best to work together as a team and support one another in this endeavor throughout the new year as we welcome our new members!

Funeral Procedures (see Chapter 24)

A. Pastor (is notified by member, etc.)
The pastor will let the assistant pastor know what he wants done for the family.

B. Assistant Pastor

The assistant pastor will find out what the family wants to do and will inform the funeral assistant of details.

C. Funeral Assistant

This person will inform the deacon or care group leader what the pastor and the family want done and the approximate number of people to prepare for.

D. Deacon or Care Group Leader

1. There may be a situation where the family needs to have meals in their home.

2. If a room at the church is to be set up for the family before the funeral, make available coffee, ice water, and cookies, depending on the time of day.

3. If the family wants the reception at the church, the deacon and his wife or the care group leader and his wife (who are assigned to the family) will line up three ladies to help with set-up, two ladies to help serve, and three ladies to help clean-up.

4. The food coordinator will purchase supplies, cold cuts, and rolls. She will also call upon ladies to help with the salads, chips, dips, and extras.

5. If the food coordinator is not available to do the purchasing, the church clerk will give the deacon or the care group leader a check to do the shopping.

6. After the reception, it is very important that the kitchen is tidied and all food is either given to the family or put in the refrigerator.

7. If the family wants the reception at home, the deacon or care group leader will line up food to be taken to the home.

Deacon Committees

Although our church does not officially have functioning committees for the purpose of ministry operations, the deacons of the church will formulate the following committees for the purpose of serving the congregation and the pastor more effectively in the developing of the ministries and membership of this church. Listed below are the committees formed by the deacons of the church:

1. Building and Expansion Committee
2. Legal Committee
3. Finance Committee
4. Missions Committee
5. School Committee
6. Building and Safety Committee
7. College Committee
8. Discipline Committee

All deacons will attend a joint meeting each month on a designated Tuesday evening.

The Committee Work Of Deacons

Text: Acts 6:3

1. Committees are not a separate office. (The word "committee" is not a biblical word.)

2. Committees are created by the pastor based on perceived ministry needs.

3. Committees may be changed or members re-assigned from time to time.

4. Committee work is done on an assigned basis.

5. Committee work provides an opportunity to "serve" in a specific function for the purpose of allowing the pastor more time in prayer and study.

6. The pastor is a de facto member of all committees.

Philosophy

Relationships of the Deacon

Text: Acts 6:3

1. With the Lord—personal and daily

2. With the lost—reach them

3. With the pastor—a friend and leader

4. With staff—the staff reports to the pastor

5. With the bookkeeper—the bookkeeper reports to the financial administrator

6. With the church family—be an example; help them; be humble; love them.

7. With one another—be a team; work together; pray for each other.

8. With your wife—love her; be sensitive to her; lead her; communicate with her.

The Master's Principle of Servitude

Text: Isaiah 42:1–4; Mark 10:35–45; Galations 5:13; John 13:10–15

The word "leader or leaders" is seen only six times in the Bible. The term used most for leader is servant.

1. Dependence—Be dependent on the Lord.

2. Approval—Strive for God's approval, not man's (vs. 1).

3. Modesty—Do not brag (vs. 2).

4. Empathy—Have a sweet spirit toward everyone. Do not condemn. Do not be soft on sin (vs. 3).

5. Optimism—Guard against discouragement. Do not be pessimistic (vs. 4).

6. Be anointed—Acts 10:37–38

A Faithful Deacon

1. Prays for Pastor and church
2. Is daily a man of the Word of God
3. Displays a good, positive attitude
4. Is humble
5. Does not become bitter about serving (neither does his wife)
6. Is a soulwinner
7. Is loyal to God's Word, Pastor, and the church
8. Is a servant
9. Is not petty
10. Is confidential
11. Is faithful (leads his wife and family)
12. Does not compare
13. Communicates with Pastor
14. Loves his pastor and church
15. Ministers in the church
16. Administers his areas of responsibility

Serving as a Godly Deacon

Text: Acts 6:3–5
  I. Serve with integrity (I Timothy 3:8–13)

   A. Grave—serious-minded about the things of God
   B. Not double-tongued
   C. Not given to much wine
   D. Not greedy of filthy lucre—selling their product
   E. Holding to the faith

F. Pure conscience

G. Proven

H. Blameless

I. Godly in family life

II. Serve with indwelling (full of the Holy Ghost)

A. For service

B. For witnessing

III. Serve with insight

A. Dealing with others

B. Developing a heart of faithfulness (Proverbs 4:23)

IV. Serve with instruction (Acts 6:3)

A. Pastor gives instruction.

B. Deacons help deploy the instruction.

V. Serve with inspiration (Acts 6:5)

A. Walk in faith.

B. Talk in faith (Philippians 4:13).

C. Pray in faith.

Dealing with Rebellious or Sinful People

Leadership implies responsibility. Leadership means "to go before and show the way." Here are some scriptural principles from Proverbs chapter one for dealing with defiance.

1. The "simple" man is a follower.
2. The "fool" hates knowledge.
3. The "scorner" has nothing good to say and is malicious.
4. A "wise" man weighs things out.

I. The Purpose of Discipline

A. For their profit (Hebrews 12:10)

B. To restore a brother (Galatians 6:1–5; II Timothy 2:25; II Corinthians 7:9–11)

    C. To protect the assembly (II Thessalonians 3:6–7, 14–15; I Timothy 5:20–21)

    D. To remove the defilement of sin (Galatians 5:7–10)

    E. To deliver to Satan for the destruction of the flesh (I Corinthians 5:5)

II. The Process of Discipline

    A. Deal with it privately (Matthew 18:15–20).

    B. "Mark" the individual (Romans 16:17–18; Titus 3:9–10).

    C. Let them go (I Timothy 1:20).

    D. Remove yourself from them (I Timothy 6:1–5; II Timothy 2:16–19).

III. The Pursuit of Discipline

    A. Prayer (James 1:5)

    B. Patience

Devotion of Deacons

Areas of Commitment

I. Committed to Relationships

    A. With our Lord (Matthew 22:37; Jeremiah 9:23–24, 29:13; Psalm 27:4)

    B. With our spouse (Ephesians 5:25; I Peter 3:7)

    C. With our children (Ephesians 6:4; Deuteronomy 6; III John 1:4)

    D. With our pastor (Hebrews 13:17–18; I Thessalonians 5:12–13)

    E. With our church family (I Thessalonians 5:13–15; Romans 12:18–19)

II. Committed to Responsibilities

    A. Service (Acts 6:1)

    B. Daily needs of others (Acts 6:1–3)

C. Visit and pray for the sick (James 5:13–16)

D. Help serve the Lord's table (I Corinthians 11:24–34)

E. Assist our pastor in any way possible (I Thessalonians 5:12)

III. Committed to Role Modeling

A. Servant leadership (Matthew 20:25–28; John 12:26)

B. Christian character (I Timothy 3:8–13)

C. Soulwinning (Acts 6:8, 10; 8:5, 26–40; 21:8)

D. Positive attitude (Hebrews 3:13, 10:25)

E. Commitment to role modeling (Acts 6:5; I Corinthians 2:6,7; Colossians 4:5; Hebrews 11:6)

How to Handle Criticism

1. Consider the accuracy of criticism. Never reject your critic. There is usually some truth to every criticism.

2. Take it to the Lord. (And leave it there!)

3. Do not develop a persecution complex.

4. Remember: The majority of people are behind you.

5. Remember: The pastor is behind you.

6. Do not seek to get even.

7. Time is often the best healer.

8. You may need to go to your critic and endeavor to gain a brother.

9. Do not become a "sounding board" for someone criticizing the ministry.

10. Pray with the critic.

11. Shield the pastor from minor issues; inform him of "trends" or major criticism.

12. Do not allow your discouragement to be viewed by church members.

13. If you are discouraged over a legitimate problem, set up a meeting with Pastor—before a critic finds you!

Ministering to the Needy

The primary objective of the church is to fulfill our Lord's Great Commission: to win, baptize, and train people for Christ. However, in the process of carrying out this work, there are many other duties which the pastor and deacons face each week.

One such duty is to compassionately assist those who are in need of physical and financial assistance. The following paragraphs are designed to explain the mode of operation for ministry regarding the needy in and around this church.

Before entering the study of "How to Minister to the Needy," remember that we must never lose sight of a person's greatest need, the need of salvation through Jesus Christ.

Those Who Are of the Members of the Church

"As we have therefore opportunity, let us do good unto all men, especially unto them who are of the household of faith." Galatians 6:10

From time to time there are members who are going to request financial assistance from the church. Such requests are factored into the budget annually; however, great discernment must be used with the distribution of funds or help for the church family.

1. Be responsible stewards with the amount of budgeted funds for the needy within and without the church. I Corinthians 4:2 says, *"Moreover it is required in stewards, that a man be found faithful."* Remember to help as many people as possible rather than distributing funds to a "select few."

2. Analyze whether the financial need is due to poor financial management on the part of the member. A session on

budgeting may be required with one of the men of the church prior to helping the member financially.

3. Do not create a dependency on the church for a prolonged period, especially to those who are not actively seeking employment.

    II Thessalonians 3:10 says, *"For even when we were with you, this we commanded you, that if any would not work, neither should he eat."* The goal is to seek to help each member learn to depend on the Lord and have a mind to work.

    Philippians 4:5–7 says, *"Let your moderation be known unto all men. The Lord is at hand. Be careful for nothing; but in every thing by prayer and supplication with thanksgiving let your requests be made known unto God. And the peace of God, which passeth all understanding, shall keep your hearts and minds through Christ Jesus."*

4. Remember that those who are helped the most will often resent you at a later time for the help. In the long run, they will appreciate your prayer and godly counsel more than financial help. A child who is continuously "bailed out" by his parents will never truly learn how to provide for himself and will ultimately lose respect for his parents.

5. Active members take first priority. If a family who has faithfully supported the local church "hits hard times," they are not only a part of "God's family," but they are truly a part of the "Household of Faith" locally. Inactive members often come to the church only in time of need, and we must not foster and promote their crisis mentality.

6. Widows also should be treated with high priority and respect. Acts 6 implies that the early church ministered very conscientiously to the widows. Any need of a widow should be handled quickly and efficiently (see I Timothy 5:3–10).

7. Single mothers who have been abandoned by a husband must also be considered as a priority.

8. Concerning the actual procedures for helping the church member, the following guidelines are recommended.

    a. If the need is highly confidential or personally sensitive, it will be dealt with by the pastoral staff.

    b. If a member calls the pastor, and it is determined that a deacon can help, a deacon will be assigned as a temporary "case worker." Your ministry, in this capacity, should not be prolonged for more than one month without the pastor's knowledge, and your involvement should be reported on the Monthly Deacon Report Form (see CD 13.1).

    c. We do not pay for credit card bills or cable T.V. bills.

    d. We can help with housing and basic utility needs.

    e. We may also help with car needs.

    f. We do not give cash or checks made out to an individual. Checks will be written to the company involved, whether it be a utility company, car repair, etc.

    g. Any amount over $100 should be cleared by the pastor without the member's knowledge.

Non-Members or Travelers through the Area

The following are guidelines that should be used when assisting people who are destitute or needy and have no affiliation with the church.

1. Remember that, while these people have had difficult situations with their finances, they still are a soul for whom Jesus Christ shed His blood. Never give any assistance to such people without sharing with them the Gospel of Christ. NOTE: Sometimes people will say a prayer in hope of receiving assistance. While this decision may

not be for Christ, we must not judge a person's motive. This must be left between the individual and the Lord Himself. It is not our responsibility to save souls. It is our responsibility to preach the Word.

2. Single mothers and children should receive our attention and help in a priority sequence over an able-bodied man.

3. Persons who indulge in habits such as smoking, drinking, and drugs may receive limited food items or help with utility bills. However, we will not provide continual care for those who deny the biblical principles of stewardship in their everyday lives.

4. Food items or utility bill assistance of over $75 will not be provided for those couples who are living outside of wedlock. In dealing with such families, the plan of approach would be:

    a. Help them with their initial need. Set up a time of counseling with a deacon at which time salvation can be presented and then steps for recovery can be presented. In some cases this may mean that couples should be married if they intend to live together. Any couple who will follow the biblical steps to recovering spiritually and financially will qualify for continual help. NOTE: In essence, anyone who comes to our church may receive limited help the first time. However, no one will be continually helped who is living in violation to Scripture.

    b. Able-bodied men may also be helped with limited food items and other physical needs. No able-bodied man shall receive cash in any form. Also, we do not allow non-members to work for money or food. This could present a potential insurance liability problem.

5. No transient individual or family shall be housed on the church property. Also, no family shall be recommended to

live with a church family unless they have frequented the church services often enough to receive pastoral approval in this matter. Families may receive one night of lodging assistance from our church (in certain cases, up to three nights). One night of lodging assistance does not require the pastor's approval.

6. The deacons of the church shall be notified by ushers and, at times, pastoral staff members regarding the needs of visitors such as are herein described. Also, deacons should be sensitive toward the pastor after each service to help in the event that he is being "pressured" or "cornered" by anyone for assistance. Kind, gentle, loving, and firm intervention should take place on the part of pastoral staff or the deacons in the event of such an occurrence. This does not imply that the pastor has no sensitivity toward those in need; however, after the services, the pastor is greeting the flock and dealing with people. At times, there may be certain security risks involved with those who perhaps feel they did not get as much help as they needed.

7. In the event the person seeking assistance is obviously under the influence of alcohol or drugs, have two deacons work this particular case.

8. In the event that a woman is the sole requester of assistance, always have a deacon and deacon's wife, or in case a wife is not available, two deacons, to deal with this situation.

The guidelines that have been given in this outline are in no way all-conclusive; however, they should provide a more specific direction as we continue to minister in the twenty-first century. We must always remember to have love and compassion on those in their time of need. We must always remember that our Saviour came "not to be ministered unto, but to minister." Certainly it would be a shame for any servant of God to feel that he or she is above helping the needy. This would be a sign of carnality and something that is not pleasing to the Saviour. The pastor and pastoral staff deal daily with these particular types of needs; however, our deacons will help fulfill this role in and around service times to allow the pastoral staff to more effectively lead, direct, and guide the overall flock of the church. Special situations and questions may be directed to the pastor during the regular meetings or at other times should the need be of an urgent nature.

Altar Work

General Guidelines for Leading Someone to Christ

1. Always be patient and thorough when presenting the Gospel. Do not feel as though you must rush back into the church to announce the person's decision.

2. When dealing with a person who has learned English as a second language, be especially cautious to make sure they understand each term.

3. Thoroughly present the fact that all are sinners who fall short of God's glory.

4. Share several Scriptures related to the atonement of Jesus Christ for our sin and the necessity of complete reliance upon His finished work for salvation.

5. After the person prays to accept Jesus Christ as Saviour, thoroughly fill out the decision card.

6. Bring the new convert to two or three church and staff members who will then rejoice with him in his decision.

7. Be concerned for this person and encourage him to become involved in an adult Bible class in the coming days.

General Guidelines for Counseling Those Burdened with Sin

1. Ask the Holy Spirit to help you be very sensitive to the burden of the person's heart.

2. Avoid being judgmental of this person who is showing repentance at the altar.

3. Write down specific verses he can use that will help him find a way of escape should the temptation or trial come to him again.

4. Pray with him and ask God for victory in his life.

5. Maintain confidentiality about things discussed with him at the altar.

General Guidelines for Transfers and Membership

1. Transfers are to be handled by the deacons and their wives.

2. Ask to hear their testimony. (When were they saved? Baptized?)

3. Explain re-baptism if they have been baptized in a church that is not of like faith.

4. Verify that the "authority" of the previous church believes the same things (Bible, like faith, unity of doctrines). "If we accept your baptism, we will be accepting the authority of the other church."

5. The church they are coming from must be "of like faith and practice" to protect doctrinal purity (Philippians 1:27).

6. The pastor will have to give an account for the church. (Hebrews 13)

When Filling Out A Decision Card

See CD 1.2 for an example of a decision card.

1. Always remember to put the date the decision was made.

2. If the person making the decision is a child, try to get the age of the child.

3. Print the name legibly so it can be read by the secretaries in the office.

4. Always get the address from the person making the decision. If his mailing address is different from the street address, write it down as well.

5. If the person has a phone, get his number for our records.

6. It is very important to obtain birthday and anniversary information (if applicable), especially if they are baptized, so we may update our records with all the needed information.

7. Remember to find out the person's marital status.

8. Make sure you check the correct decision, whether it is salvation or another decision on the card.

Offering Counting Procedures

The offering counting procedures of Lancaster Baptist Church are in accordance with the Policies Manual of the church. These policies have helped us maintain the integrity of the financial dealings of the church and are in accordance of the counsel we have received from legal seminars at the Christian Law Association, as well as our certified public accountants.

The following policies should be adhered to by any church when counting and handling the offerings.

Purpose

To establish proper control and accountability in the handling of all cash for the ministry.

Policy

It is the policy of Lancaster Baptist Church that all currency, coinage, checks, money orders, and debit or credit card receipts shall be deposited in their entirety in the appropriate ministry account within 24 hours of receipt or collection. There shall be no withholding of cash from incoming cash receipts to cover current or past due ministry expenses, savings for future expenditures, payroll, bonuses, gifts, love offerings, travel expenses, expense reimbursements, cash advances, or any other unapproved cash need.

Procedure

OFFERINGS:

1. Separate individuals shall be assigned to the task of counting and depositing the offerings than those responsible for recording donor contributions. No fewer than two unrelated deacons must be present and active in any given task related to the handling of offerings.

2. All cash shall be properly inventoried and recorded on a Deposit Transmittal Form (see CD 13.2) by the individuals counting and depositing the offerings.

3. All checks and money orders shall be documented by adding machine tape and shall have a corresponding offering envelope for reconciliation purposes. If loose checks or money orders are contributed, then an envelope shall be prepared by the counters to document the contribution.

4. All checks shall be immediately stamped "For Deposit Only" by those individuals responsible for counting and depositing the offerings.

5. All offerings shall be secured behind at least two locked doors from the time of collection to the time of counting. The door to the offering counting room shall be separately

keyed and keys distributed only to individuals specified by the financial administrator and the primary deacon(s) responsible for offering collection and counting.

6. All offerings not secured in accordance with number 5 above shall be in the custody of at least two unrelated deacons until they have been safely deposited in a bank or placed in a secure night depository.

7. Offerings in the form of cash should never be received by a ministry employee unless it can be receipted within 24 hours by another individual. Pre-numbered triplicate receipts shall be used. One copy of the receipt shall be mailed to the contributor, one copy shall accompany the contribution to the appropriate bookkeeper, and one copy shall be retained in the receipt book.

8. Offerings received by mail shall be immediately receipted by the person opening the mail. Pre-numbered triplicate receipts shall be used. One copy of the receipt shall be mailed to the contributor, one copy shall accompany the contribution to the appropriate bookkeeper, and one copy shall be retained in the receipt book.

9. Offerings received by mail shall be recorded in the same manner as noted in items 2, 3, and 4 above and shall be deposited within 48 hours of receipt and shall remain locked in a secure cabinet until they are deposited.

10. Cash should never be removed from the offering for any purpose prior to its being counted. It is absolutely essential to maintain the integrity of the offerings as given. If an emergency cash need arises, it can be met by cashing a church check in the offering and then depositing that check in the regular manner. If a check is not available, then as a last resort in an emergency, cash may be retained and documented by use of a petty cash receipt. This is highly discouraged, again to maintain the integrity of the

offerings as given. Finally, checks should never be cashed for church members.

11. All deposit slips and transmittals shall be signed by the deacons performing the count and the deposit.

12. Any discrepancy between the actual deposit counted by the bank and the deposit and transmittal documents provided to the bank shall be immediately reviewed by the financial administrator and the primary deacon(s) in charge of the count and deposit for that particular deposit.

OTHER CASH RECEIPTS:

1. All disbursements of funds for this ministry shall be made by check. All supporting documentation such as receipts, purchase orders, and invoices shall remain on file.

2. Cash advances shall be made only by a check made payable to an individual. That individual is then responsible for cashing the check and settling up with the bookkeeper with the receipt and change.

3. Transfers of cash between savings and checking accounts shall require a purchase order in triplicate with the signature of the financial administrator. One copy of the purchase order shall go to the financial administrator, one copy shall be matched up with the bank statement, and one copy shall reside with the bookkeeper requesting the transfer.

4. Vending machine cash and coinage shall be collected once per week. Two trustworthy, unrelated ministry employees shall be assigned this task. All cash and coinage shall be separately counted and deposited within 72 hours and shall remain locked in a secure cabinet until deposited.

5. Pre-numbered triplicate receipts shall be issued for all cash payments received by any point of sale or payment

collection point in the ministry. One copy shall go to the person making the payment, one copy shall accompany the deposit documentation, and one copy shall stay in the receipt book. One copy of all voided receipts shall accompany deposit documentation, and one copy shall stay in the receipt book.

6. Separate deposit transmittals shall be prepared at the end of each operating day for each source of income (e.g., Bookstore, Tape Ministry, WCBC, LBS, West Coast Café, College Cafeteria, Information Center collections for retreats and other events, offering collections, etc.) unless otherwise instructed by the financial administrator or bookkeeper. Copies of all receipts shall accompany the deposit transmittal given to the appropriate bookkeeper. Funds for deposit shall either be hand-delivered to the appropriate ministry bookkeeper during regular business hours **or** must be placed in the ministry's drop safe.

7. All deposit slips and transmittals shall be signed by the person performing the count and the deposit.

8. All cash shall be deposited in its entirety. No funds shall be removed from the cash to reimburse expenses, reserve for future expenditures, pay consignment fees, cash checks, or for any other reason.

CHAPTER FOURTEEN

Nursery Ministry

*"For God is not the author of confusion, but of
peace, as in all churches of the saints."*
I Corinthians 14:33

If you are planning to reach families through the ministry of your church, you are going to have to start with the nursery. Take a walk through your nurseries, and as you do, ask yourself this simple question, "If I were an unsaved, young parent—nervous about my first visit to this stranger-filled church—would I want to leave my child in this nursery?" One of the first exposures that your church has to a young family is the nursery. The greeter, the lighting, the décor, the organization, the workers, the condition of the carpet, the smell—they all create a first impression that can either put a parent at ease and encourage an open heart, or put a parent on guard and harden the heart.

A well-equipped, well-staffed, and well-organized nursery will put parents at ease, soften their hearts, and create incredible open doors for ministry. Every young family needs a high comfort level with the church nursery, and without it, you will be hard pressed to find spiritual inroads to their hearts.

For this reason, the church nurseries must be well organized to provide quality ministry. The church nursery should provide the following:

1. **Uninterrupted Services**

   One of the primary goals of the nursery is to remove distraction from the church services and Sunday school classes. Ushers should be trained to lovingly encourage people to place their children in the nurseries, or to sit toward the rear of the auditorium so they can slip out. Nursery workers should be motivated by the fact that every task they handle in the nursery—changing, feeding, biting, rocking, etc.—is another task that a young parent does not have to deal with during a potentially life-changing sermon.

2. **Peace of Mind**

   The nursery environment, the staff manner, the equipment (or lack thereof) will all collectively either put a parent at ease or put a parent on edge. It is not selfish or unspiritual for parents to have a keen interest in the well being of their children in the nursery. It is every parent's God-given duty to carry such concerns, and it is the responsibility of the nursery team to understand and address those concerns with care. It may take time for a newcomer to feel a comfort level with the nurseries, but we should do everything within our power to provide well for the concerns of young parents and to care for each child in a way that pleases every parent.

3. **Safety and Cleanliness**

   Health and safety must be priorities to your nursery team, and these issues must be constantly addressed. Schedule regular times to clean the toys, replace carpet, paint walls, and repair damaged facilities that could present risk.

Determine to maintain a standard of excellence in this area.

4. **Early Learning Experiences**

The nursery can be more than simply childcare. Each age can be spiritually nurtured through songs, prayers, Scripture readings, and even some interactive games and activities (in some of the older nurseries). Help your nursery staff understand the typical learning abilities of each age, and provide resources and ideas for the transferring of spiritual truth to these toddler hearts.

5. **Ministry Opportunities**

There are members of your church family who truly love to care for and nurture infants and toddlers. It is even more exciting to do this for young families so that Mom and Dad can listen to the preaching and teaching of God's Word. The Nursery Ministry is a wonderful opportunity for Christian ladies to use their God-given gifts and abilities in a way that truly makes an impact for eternity. Make it your goal to help people find this place of service where God can use them.

6. **Encouragement**

Obviously, the above-mentioned items of service provided by the nursery workers are invaluable, not only to the parents, but also to the pastor of the church. We highly recommend that the pastor and Children's Ministries director take time, throughout the year, to encourage the nursery workers with notes of encouragement and, perhaps, gift certificates or even public appreciation for these wonderful volunteer workers. Most pastors would agree that they will probably stand in the back of the line behind the nursery workers at the Judgment Seat of Christ! Let us do our best to support these godly laborers who do so much to support the church services.

The following pages contain samples of the Lancaster Baptist Nursery Ministry Handbook, calendars, and other organizational tools.

The Nursery Ministry

Dear Friend,

I want to welcome you to the Nursery Ministry! It is a privilege to be able to serve the Lord here in any way or fashion. Through this area of service, I pray that you will grow spiritually as you meet the needs of others.

The purposes of the nursery is to minister to the children and parents of our church, to provide the best nursery care in a loving Christian environment, and to teach the children at an early age about their Saviour Jesus Christ.

As you serve in this ministry I would like you to keep in mind Colossians 3:23–24, "And whatsoever ye do, do it heartily, as to the Lord, and not unto men; Knowing that of the Lord ye shall receive the reward of the inheritance: for ye serve the Lord Christ." As you serve the Lord in the Nursery Ministry, be mindful that your service is unto the Lord and whatever we do for Him should be our best.

The thought of "commitment to excellence" comes to my mind when I read those verses. As servants of God, our attitude toward the Lord's work should be on a different level of excellence because of who we are serving—the Lord.

Finally, let me express how excited I am that the Lord has led you to serve in this ministry, and may the Lord bless you because of your faithfulness in this area of service.

Your friend,

Pastor

Qualifications of a Nursery Caregiver

The idea that "anyone" can care for small children is a myth. A nursery caregiver is a very special person, having some distinct qualities that are fit for a nursery caregiver.

Jesus said, *"Take heed that ye despise not one of these little ones; for I say unto you, That in heaven their angels do always behold the face of my Father which is in heaven. Even so it is not the will of your Father which is in heaven, that one of these little ones should perish"* (Matthew 18:10, 14).

Qualifications:

1. Must be a member of the church

2. Must be willing to abide by the nursery guidelines

3. Must be willing to abide by the leadership requirements of the church

4. The nursery caregiver must be committed and dedicated to her task. She must consider her work with young children a holy task for God. Her life should reflect her faith, her loyalty to the church, and her ever increasing understanding and application of biblical truth.

5. A nursery caregiver must genuinely love children. That love will be transmitted through her voice, facial expressions, touch—through her whole being. A child instinctively knows if the nursery worker loves him.

6. As any other servant for Christ, the nursery caregiver is to be dependable. This means she will be there when scheduled, on time, and stay until every job is completed.

7. The nursery caregiver needs to be a good team member. She will need to be able to get along well with others. Her suggestions, cooperation, and support are needed.

8. Certainly a nursery caregiver should be friendly and cheerful, a person who radiates Christian joy and the warmth of the fullness of the Holy Spirit in her life.

Nursery Director Job Description

The nursery director needs to be a very organized, positive person who will work hard to maintain the nurseries of the church. She will answer to the pastor in charge of the Children's Ministries.

Nursery Leader Job Description

The nursery leader's task is to make sure her nursery is properly staffed, cleaned, and organized for every service and to help recruit and train new caregivers.

Responsibilities:

1. To distribute nursery schedules and make reminder phone calls to the caregivers

2. To attend Christian Education Clinics and monthly leadership meetings

3. To open her nursery before each service

4. To organize the visitation of the children in her nursery (Every child should receive a visit, a card, and a phone call before graduating.)

5. To create themed bulletin boards for her nursery

6. To oversee safety in her nursery (broken toys, doors, windows, etc.)

7. To ensure all policies and guidelines are being followed in the nursery as described in the Nursery Handbook

8. To encourage the caregivers in their nursery with notes, phone calls, or small gifts of appreciation

9. To communicate with the nursery director

Nursery Caregiver Job Description

Task: To lovingly care for babies and toddlers and to teach them the love of Jesus.

Responsibilities:

1. To be in the nursery 30 minutes prior to service time

2. To attend Christian Education Clinics

3. To go soulwinning regularly and visit the children

4. To provide physical and emotional care for children

5. To clean up the nursery after each service

6. To oversee safety in her nursery (broken toys, doors, windows, etc.)

7. To follow policies and guidelines for diapering, feeding, and caring for children as described in the nursery procedures

8. To teach the children about Jesus, interact while playing, sing songs, color, etc.

What does being a nursery worker mean to you?

1. Contacting visitors' parents in their homes

2. Taking a gift to a brand new mother and father

3. Singing Christ-honoring songs to children

4. Writing birthday cards and encouraging notes

5. Providing clean, safe toys

6. Displaying a consistent Christian life to parents

7. Greeting families with a smile

8. Helping visiting parents find their way around

9. Providing fun and bright decorations

10. Praying for babies and their parents

11. Arriving at class 30 minutes early

Nursery Procedures

The nursery procedures that follow are to help the nursery caregiver to understand how the nurseries operate. *"And we know that all things work together for good to them that love God, to them who are the called according to his purpose"* (Romans 8:28).

Procedures:

1. Cheerfully greet each parent and child. Assure them that their child will be well taken care of during the service. A smile and good attitude always go a long way.

2. Make sure each child has been registered at the nursery registration counter before accepting them into the nursery. Parents are given the security card at the registration counter. This will be explained in more detail later in the handbook.

3. Have the parent sign the child's name on the sign-in sheet for the nursery their child will be in during the service (see CD 14.1). Make sure they fill out the "Special Instructions" if they have any (e.g., potty training, when to feed, what to feed, etc.). If given a pager, write number in pager section.

4. Pagers are mainly for the newborn and infant nurseries. They are used for emergencies and nursing mothers. Always offer a pager to a visitor; it may make them feel

better, and if we need them, it makes it easier to find them during the service. Remember to write the number of the pager on the sign-in sheet and always remember to get the pager back from the parents.

5. All babies that are nursing are to be nursed in the nursing room, not in the nurseries.

6. Make sure that all belongings (bottles, blankets, toys) that belong to a particular baby are marked. Make sure each bag has a church diaper bag tag. All of these belongings should go in the correct cubby hole. (The cubby hole number and the sign-in sheet number should correspond.)

7. We provide a snack for children ages nine months and older. Make sure when giving them their snack that you place it in a cup, hand it to them, or put it in their hands. Do not place food on the floor and do not allow them to eat food that has been on the floor. It is extremely messy and unsanitary.

8. Make sure that all diapers are changed and checked each service hour. Do not forget to take the potty-training children to the rest room! If you notice a child is dirty when ready to leave, make sure you change him before returning him to the parents.

9. Use sanitary gloves when changing each child. Use a new pair of gloves after each child. Always wash hands or use antibacterial lotion after each changing.

10. Babies should not share bottles, drinks, etc.

11. When church is almost over, make sure that each child is ready to go. Gather up all belongings, make sure noses are wiped, faces are clean, and shoes are on. During the winter, place their coats on before giving them to their parents. Make sure they have their cup!

12. Always ask for the security card before giving a child to anyone. If they do not have the card, they must go to the registration counter.

13. Thank parents for entrusting children to us.

Nursery Security System

Purpose:

The purpose of a nursery security system is to ensure the safety of the children who are in the nursery at church and to help ease the flow during registration.

Procedures:

1. Visitors with infants or toddlers will need to enroll their children at the receptionist window (see CD 14.2 for Childcare Registration Form). They need to register no matter what service it is that they are attending—Sunday morning, Sunday night, or Wednesday night. At registration, they will receive a security card and a security identification tag for their diaper bag (see CD 14.3 and CD 14.4). The security card is what they will show to the nursery workers to identify themselves and to be able to get their children from the nursery. The security card is to be kept with them at all times while at church.

2. After they are registered, they will be escorted to the appropriate nursery by one of the nursery greeters.

3. When the child is signed in at the nursery, the worker will make sure that the parents have their security card. It is important to remind them that they need the card to pick up their child. Also they need to remember that whoever has the card can get the child—guard it carefully. If they

want someone else to get their child, they would need to give that person the security card.

4. The nursery greeter will give all the child's information (name, address, etc.) to the nursery worker. Then the nursery worker will put the information on the back of the attendance form.

5. At check-out time, if they DO NOT have the security card with them, they will have to go to the registration counter to get another security card. They will be asked to show that security card to get their child back.

6. We must be diligent to consistently ask to see the security card.

Caring for the Nursery

Nursery caregivers should know how to care for the rooms God has given us.

Nursery Care:

1. Remember to keep your area tidy during the service time. Be careful not to let the children spill their juice, water, bottle, etc., on the carpet. Only give them a little bit of snack at a time.

2. If you lay a child on the floor, please lay a blanket down for them first.

3. Keep the counters inside and outside neat and tidy.

4. During the service, be sure to put trash in the trash can. Have the children pick up toys as they play.

5. After the service:

   a. Put all toys, blankets, and cups where they belong.
   b. Empty trash cans and install new liners.

   c. Vacuum the nursery and wipe down counters.

   d. Make sure that the closet and cubby holes are neat.

   e. Put the laundry in the laundry bag as well as any toys that need cleaning. If there is a broken toy, please throw it away.

   f. Throw away the sign-in sheet and put the clipboard and pens in the drawer. Make sure the lights are off.

Nursery Guidelines

The nursery guidelines contain information for the nursery caregivers to let them know what is expected of them while serving in the nursery at our church.

"For God is not the author of confusion, but of peace, as in all churches of the saints" (I Corinthians 14:33).

Guidelines:

1. Please be on time when serving in the nursery:

    Sunday Morning Service
    8:15, in position by 7:45
    9:30, in position by 9:00
    11:00, in position by 10:45

    Sunday Evening Service
    5:30, in position by 5:00

    Wednesday Evening Bible Study
    7:00, in position by 6:30

2. If you are unable to serve your scheduled time, please contact your nursery leader as soon as possible. Also, please let her know of your vacation dates ahead of time. The nursery schedules for the evening services and soulwinning days are completed by the 15th of the prior month. Please remember to put dates in writing.

3. If you are in the choir, please **do not** sing on the nights you are scheduled for nursery.

4. Always be mindful of the parents and children. Keep your conversation pleasing to the Lord. Never **complain** about the children or their parents to other workers. Do not say things like "shut up" or raise your voice in an angry manner. All children need love; show the love of Christ through your attitude.

5. Do not complain to parents about their child. Say nothing negative to a parent about his child. We want to encourage parents to come hear God's Word. The last thing a parent needs is an excuse to stay home from church. All complaints should be directed to the nursery leader. She, in turn, will talk to the nursery director.

6. We **do not** use any form of physical discipline in the nursery. Discipline in any physical way is absolutely forbidden. Do not swat or spank babies. Even if the child is your own, this should not be done in the nursery.

7. If a child needs to be disciplined (for throwing toys, hitting, etc.), set him in a playpen or high chair for a "time out." Do not leave him there the entire service; use discipline wisely. It is not intended for long periods of time. We want the children to love the nursery, not hate it. If you have a continual problem, let the nursery leader know about the situation, and she will take care of it.

8. Always remember the "line of sight" rule: you should always have the children in your line of sight. Do not leave them unattended for any reason.

9. The nursery caregiver needs to keep track of sending notes, calling, and visiting the children in her class. You need to attend an organized soulwinning time at church for this. Even though the children we care for are too young to be

saved, their parents are to know that we minister to them also.

10. If there is an accident in the nursery (a cut, a bump, falling down, biting, etc.), you must fill out an Incident Report Form (see CD 14.5). Put into detail what happened, who was present, and what was done. Make sure you inform the parents of what happened. Give details such as this, "Billy tripped over a toy and bumped his head, and we put ice on it."

11. If a child bites or hits, immediately separate him from the other children. Tell him biting is a "no-no" and will not be allowed. Take care of the child who was bitten or hit; wash any cuts with antibacterial soap. Use Band-Aids if needed, and apply ice if needed. Be sure to fill out the Incident Report Form and turn it in to your nursery leader. When the parents come to pick up their child, inform them that their child was bitten and what you did to take care of it (washed it, etc.). Let the parents of the child who did the biting know what happened. Never tell the parents who did what; no names are to be given. This is our policy, and if they have a problem, send them to the nursery director.

Miscellaneous Nursery Forms

To view a monthly nursery workers calendar, see CD 14.6. To view the nursery worker questionnaire, see CD 14.7.

Screening

For the protection of the young children, the workers, and the church as a whole, you may choose to have policies and procedures in place to do background checks and fingerprinting on all ministry workers involved in any Children's Ministries. This is mandatory in some states. See your local sheriff's office for details and laws.

CHAPTER FIFTEEN

Children's Sunday School & Ministries

"...Suffer the little children to come unto me,
and forbid them not: for of such is the kingdom of God."
Mark 10:14

When we began serving the Lord in Lancaster back in 1986, the children's Sunday school consisted of one class for nursery through the sixth grade. My wife, Terrie, taught the class and did a great job. Down through the years we have developed dozens of classes and several departments for our Children's Ministry.

A thriving children's program is essential for any church that seeks to effectively meet the needs of its community. When a child who becomes excited about the activities in his class at church conveys that excitement to his parents, it encourages them to be faithful in their attendance. Many parents have been won to the Lord through the faithful persistence of children! Likewise, if a child does not want to attend his Sunday school class and complains about going to church, or if his parents do not approve of his classroom environment, they will use it as an excuse not to attend. The church that does not focus on expanding its Children's Ministries is stifling its own growth.

Additionally, Children's Ministries are vital because we are literally training "the church of tomorrow." It has been said that if one could train a child until he was merely five years old, then that child would be his follower for the rest of his life. From that statement, Christians can see the necessity of properly training our children while they are young! Proverbs 22:6 says to "*train up a child in the way he should go: and when he is old, he will not depart from it.*" A gardener can easily manipulate a young sapling to grow a certain way, but once that sapling has become a deep-rooted tree, it is no longer workable. Teachers *must* teach the children in Sunday school classes to follow the Lord while their hearts are still tender, before they become hardened by the wickedness of this world. If Christians do not teach their children to live godly, separated lives at a young age, they cannot be expected to develop a holy lifestyle as young adults.

Christ placed a special emphasis on children throughout his ministry, setting aside special time for them and speaking of their significance to His Father. He even tells us to come to Him "*as a little child*" (Mark 10:15). Many lessons can be learned by observing the faith of young children!

As children arrive at class each week, they desire to be greeted with a warm smile and friendly conversation. Regardless of whether or not the child comes from a godly home, he needs the teacher to be his friend, to keep him accountable for saying his verses, and to remember his birthday and special events. The task of working with children extends beyond merely entertaining them while the parents are in church.

Some of the Children's Ministries of Lancaster Baptist Church include the Baptist Boys' Club on Saturday mornings (for boys in third through sixth grades), and the Joy Club on Saturday mornings (for girls in third through sixth grades). Additionally, the Cactus Kids' Club is a Wednesday evening Bible memory and game time for children.

The guidelines in these next pages detail an assortment of responsibilities and procedures. Included are duties for childcare workers, general childcare procedures, and precautions.

Children's Ministries

Dear Friend,

Welcome to the Children's Ministry! Jesus made it clear as He taught that children are very important to Him and to His Kingdom. I am glad you have chosen to join Him as He works in their lives on a weekly basis, through the various Children's Ministries of Lancaster Baptist Church.

The purposes of our Children's Ministry is to help children know Christ, grow in Christ, and show Christ to others. This mission is accomplished through a variety of ministry opportunities, and I am thrilled that you will be part of such an eternally significant work.

One of our goals is that ministry might be done "decently, and in order," so please endeavor to give your very best as you minister to children and their families. You can do this by attending training events; by giving attention to policies, procedures, and ministry descriptions; and by seeking God's power as you do His work.

If there is any way I can be a blessing to you as you serve the Lord by serving children, please do not hesitate to let me know. It is my joy to serve our Lord, our church family, and our community along with you!

Your friend,

Pastor

Children's Ministries Director

The Children's Ministries director (the children's education director) oversees the various Children's Ministries and departments. He is directly responsible to the senior pastor.

See CD 15.1 to view the leadership structure for the Children's Ministries.

The Department Director

Definition

The department director serves Christ and his church by *assisting* the Children's Ministries director, *equipping* and *encouraging* his teachers and workers, *praying* for his department, and *leading by example* in servanthood, separation, and soulwinning.

Description

A. He meets all the leadership requirements of the Sunday school.

B. He is a team player and leader.

C. He is dependable.

1. Punctual in his schedule
2. Faithful in his duties

D. He has a desire for excellence, as well as a drive to learn more and to institute it into the Sunday school program.

E. He has a heart and burden for the Sunday school and especially his department.

Duties

A. The department director answers to the children's education director:

1. Report problems, needs, or requests to children's education director.
2. Report material and equipment needs to children's education director.

B. The department director is to give a weekly report on Wednesday evenings, which will consist of the following:

1. Number of students in attendance
2. Number of students saved and baptized
3. Number of workers involved in soulwinning and/or visitation

C. The department director is responsible to contact all workers in his department:

1. To remind them about workers' meetings
2. To contact them when there are special conferences, workshops, revival meetings, or workers' meetings
3. To encourage them as the Lord lays them on his heart

D. The department director is to assist the workers in checking on classroom needs and discipline matters to report to the children's education director.

E. The department director will assist the children's education director by suggesting, but not contacting, prospective Sunday school workers.

F. The department director will ensure his department is maintaining attendance, visitation, and enrollment records.

G. The department director will collect all roll sheets and turn them in to the Sunday school secretary each week.

The Children's Teacher

Definition

A children's teacher has a love for the Lord and for children. His desire is to see children saved, growing in faith, and enjoying Sunday school. This person must have a hunger to teach God's truths effectively and creatively.

Description

    A. The teacher is dependable.

        1. Punctual in schedule
        2. Faithful in duties

    B. The teacher is faithful to the leadership requirements.

    C. The teacher provides mentorship and on-the-job training for his class helpers.

Duties

    A. Prepare for each Sunday's lesson and class time well in advance.

    B. Delegate responsibilities such as taking roll, leading songs, object lessons, crafts, and a portion of the absentee contacts to the class helpers.

    C. Pray regularly for each class member.

    D. Contact each class member regularly by phone, note, or visit.

    E. Notify department director of any classroom needs or discipline concerns.

    F. Notify department director of absence ten days in advance, if possible.

    G. Learn and grow in teaching children.

The Children's Helper

Definition

The class helper is vital! He sees the needs of his teacher and the children, and then takes the lead in meeting those needs. The helper has a love and a servant's heart toward the Lord and children.

Description

A. He is dependable.

B. He is faithful to the leadership requirements.

C. He has a desire to actively participate in the life of each child.

D. He shows initiative in being involved in the class time with creative ideas.

Duties

A. Take on a portion of the class responsibilities (e.g., roll, song-leading, object lesson, crafts, absentee contacts).

B. Pray for each member of the class regularly.

C. Contact each member of the class regularly by phone, visit, or note.

Sharing the Burden of the Class

It is a great responsibility to be a helper for a Sunday school teacher. A helper is there to support and help the teacher teach the students the Word of God. Without a good helper, a teacher is not very effective because he cannot concentrate on the most important part of being a teacher—teaching. If a teacher has good helpers, all he has to worry about is meeting the needs of the students through the teaching of God's Word. Here are a few practical tips to be of help in sharing the burden carried by a teacher:

I. Be Prepared

   A. Be a help in any way.

   B. Always have an object lesson ready.

   C. Have an extra game or color sheet available.

II. Be on Time

   A. Early is on time—on time is late.

   B. Be in class 30-40 minutes early.

   C. Being late puts a burden on the teacher.

   D. Lateness shows a lack of interest and dedication.

III. Be Watchful

   A. Always look for a way to be a blessing to the teacher.

   B. Look for things that could be distracting to the teacher or students and take care of them.

   C. Notice how the children are responding to the lesson and invitation. This will be a help in knowing who to pray for and who might need to be prayed with.

IV. Be Burdened for the Children

   A. Help visit part of the class.

   B. Pray for each of them by name every day.

   C. Help in baptism follow-up.

   D. Take a personal interest in a student who needs some attention.

V. Be An Encouragement to the Teacher

   A. Write the teacher a note telling him how much he is appreciated.

   B. Find out when his birthday is and have a surprise party in class.

   C. Ask to lead the songs or do a game.

   D. Always be happy and cheerful when around the teacher.

   E. Do whatever the teacher needs done.

Conclusion

To reach young people with the Word of God, dedicated teachers need dedicated helpers who will help carry the burden so the teacher can focus on what he has been called to do—teach.

General Ministry Guidelines

The following is a list of ministry guidelines that will help the church program operate more effectively.

1. Any worker who leads a person to Christ should always fill out a decision card and get it to the church office or department superintendent.

2. Any worker desiring to organize a class or group activity of any kind must call the church office and clear the date and time on the calendar.

3. Any worker desiring to have an announcement made in the services should call the announcement in to the church office.

4. Any Sunday school teacher who has a first-time visitor in class should fill out the triplicate visitor card and give one copy to the church office or department director.

5. Any worker needing additional teaching supplies should submit, in writing, the list of items to the children's education director for these items to be ordered.

6. Any worker having difficulty in ministry should set up an appointment with the children's education director to discuss the situation. Workers should not complain about ministry problems to other workers.

7. Any new member or inactive member who returns to church may need to wait as long as six months before working in a ministry. Anyone in this category who desires to serve

in the ministry should contact the children's education director.

8. The proper procedure for resigning a ministry is to contact the children's education director for an appointment.

9. All church workers should arrive at church early, and the Sunday school teachers should be 30 minutes early in order to prepare the room, etc.

10. When absent from class on a given Sunday:

    a. If you know in advance, please give the information in writing to the children's education director and the department director.
    b. If it is short notice, call your department director or the children's education director.
    c. NEVER, NEVER, NEVER assume that no one will miss you or they will get by without you if you do not show up! We are counting on you.

11. All workers must fill out the attendance and student contact section of the weekly roll sheet (e.g., PH=phone calls, V=visits, C=cards or letters, SW=soulwinning) (see CD 15.2).

12. Every worker, regardless of class, should persistently and consistently visit the students.

13. Procedures of safety:

    a. Always keep children in the "line of sight."
    b. Two adults must always escort children to the restroom. Stand just outside, and check on them regularly.
    c. If something is peculiar or out of place, please report it at once.
    d. Report any type of suspected or stated child abuse and/or sexual abuse.
    e. Men, never place a child on the lap. Use as little physical contact as possible.

    f.   Never use any form of physical discipline or spanking. ALWAYS use a controlled voice.

    g.   Never leave a classroom unattended.

    h.   Always take accurate attendance. The roll sheet is a legal document.

    i.   Always report immediately any accident or injury in the classroom. Document it on an Incident Report Form (see CD 14.5), and turn it in to the department director.

    j.   Never turn over a child to an adult unless it is the parent. Better safe than sorry.

14.   Workers must follow stated procedures when children are baptized (see Chapter 2).

15.   These policies relate to any Children's Ministry used during soulwinning activities and other activities requiring childcare:

    a.   There must always be at least two workers in a classroom.

    b.   In any class, the ratio of children to workers should never be greater than 14:1.

    c.   All accident or incident reports are to be turned in immediately to the church office.

    d.   No worker has authorization to change or give exception to these policies unless first cleared by the children's education director.

16.   Whenever teenagers are helping with childcare, an adult must be present to oversee and make sure responsible care is being given at all times.

Enlisting and Screening Workers

Parents entrust children's workers with a tremendous responsibility when they place their children under the worker's care. For this reason, it is important to ensure that all children's workers are qualified caregivers. Background checks and a personal interview should be performed for each person interested in working with children. If a candidate has committed any type of offense against a child previously, he should be discreetly directed to service in a different church ministry. The children's safety **must** have highest consideration when choosing workers.

When choosing workers, also keep in mind that many types of helpers are needed, even those who are not "gifted to teach." Children's workers must have patience, kindness, and a special love. If a worker does not feel comfortable standing in front of the class, then he can listen to verses, help during craft time, distribute the snack, or just sit with the children while the story is given.

Training Workers

Weekly Teachers' Meeting

A quick teachers' meeting after an evening service is an effective tool for communication between the children's education director and the teachers. The children's education director can inform the teachers of upcoming dates and events, curriculum can be distributed, and general announcements can be made during this time. The overall program of the Sunday school will go much more smoothly when the director and teachers are communicating consistently.

Quarterly Christian Education Clinics

C. E. Clinics are scheduled quarterly on a Saturday morning from 8:30–12:30. The clinic is a more in-depth teachers' meeting which includes a time of equipping and ministering to the Sunday school teachers and workers. The C. E. Clinic is a themed "mini-conference." There is a combined opening session which all teachers and workers attend. Uplifting, encouraging music and teaching will motivate the teachers and workers to have a heart to improve in their ministry. After the opening session, split sessions are planned which focus on the various levels of the Sunday school. There are sessions ranging from the security system of the nurseries to how to effectively communicate with teens. There will be sessions on crafts, flannel board, and games. Themes are unlimited! Just remember; improvement of all teachers is the goal.

Christian Education Room

To further assist the Sunday school teachers and workers, a C.E. room can be furnished with illustrated Bible stories and songs, bulletin board materials, coloring books and sheets, colored paper, easels, craft supplies, and much more.

Curriculum

Using a set curriculum throughout the year will greatly increase the efficiency of your Children's Ministry as a whole. Teachers will have a lesson plan to follow from week to week, the children will fall into a natural routine in the classroom, and class time will automatically be divided as the program dictates. It is extremely frustrating for both parents and pastors to find that the children have had a glorified baby-sitting time when they could have been taught about the Bible. There is certainly a time for games, and no class should have to sit still for the entire period—the key is balance. Having a set system of operation is vital for the success of the Children's Ministries.

Leading a Child to Christ

A teacher of young people has a God-given opportunity and responsibility to nurture and develop a child's knowledge and hunger for understanding salvation. Teachers and parents alike must be sensitive to the leading and guiding of the Holy Spirit when dealing with a child for salvation. Be careful not to lead a child into making a decision for Christ; make sure the Holy Spirit is guiding and convicting them to be saved.

Be clear about what the child needs to know and clear in your presentation. It needs to be simple yet complete. Here is a simple and clear explanation that a child can understand.

A. God loves you (John 3:16).

B. You have done wrong things (sinned) (Romans 3:23).

C. God says sin must be punished (Romans 6:23a).

D. God sent Jesus to take the punishment for you (Romans 6:23b).

E. Tell God you have sinned and want Jesus to be your Saviour (Romans 10:13).

Be familiar with the Scriptures.

God's Word is powerful. Do not use a lot of verses when dealing with a child. You do not want to confuse them or overwhelm them, but use verses that are easy to understand (John 3:16, Romans 3:23, and Romans 10:13).

Briefly explain terms:

A. Sin—doing wrong things/disobeying God's rules

B. Saved—to become part of God's family and go to heaven when they die

C. Forgive—to take away the punishment for doing wrong

D. Everlasting life—to live now and forever with Jesus

Be one-on-one.

When talking to a child, make sure he understands completely. When dealing with more than one child, it becomes difficult to make sure each of them understands completely.

Be careful not to force a decision.

Allow the child to make the free choice to be saved. Each child is eager to please and would be saved just because he was told to. **Make sure the child is responding because he *wants* to be saved.**

Be thorough on God's love and forgiveness.

Let the child know that there will still be times that he or she does wrong things, but that God still loves him and forgives sin.

Record Keeping in the Sunday School

Introduction

Is record keeping important? Some would say, "Let God keep the records." True, He has all the records, but if we asked of Mordecai (Esther 6:1–2) whether or not records were important, he would probably give a resounding "YES!" The king's records saved his life!

This section is presented to give a greater understanding of the importance of centralized record keeping in the Sunday school.

The Purpose for Centralized Records

A. Convenience—easy access and availability within minutes

B. Orderliness—organized so that a child can be contacted or traced

C. Protection—for legal purposes such as law suits

D. Visitation—to keep an accurate account of who was in each class on a specific Sunday (It also enables the teachers to visit absentees and visitors weekly.)

E. Evaluation—we will be able to watch growth patterns better, evaluate each teacher's performance, and keep up a weekly oversight of our students

The Procedures for Centralized Records

A. Distribution

1. The roll sheets are distributed to the teachers each Sunday morning before class begins (see CD 15.2).
2. Teachers/workers place an "X" beside the appropriate names of the students present that day.
   a. First-time visitors' names are printed on the attached visitor sheet (see CD 15.3). It is very important to obtain all information on the visitor sheets (e.g., first and last names, birth date, phone number, address, and bus number, if applicable).
   b. Teachers and workers are recorded on the front page, along with their visitation/soulwinning information for the week. If substitute workers are used, their names are written in on the teacher portion of the roll sheet.

B. Collection and Recording

1. Teachers or department directors collect the roll sheets at the end of the 11:00 hour each week and return them to the appropriate box at the receptionist desk. Rolls are to be turned in no later than Sunday afternoon. These are legal documents and are not to leave the church property!
2. The attendance is then recorded on a centralized database by a staff secretary. The software "Shelby Systems" is used for all Sunday school records.
3. Visitation lists will be printed weekly for department meetings and also upon request.

The Product of Centralized Records

A. The church has a master list of names, addresses, and specific facts on each person enrolled in the Sunday school.

B. This database can be used for mass mailings, phone calls, etc.

C. This database can be used for charting statistics for teacher/worker visitation and soulwinning records.

D. This database provides a case history for each enrollee in the Sunday school.

Practical Helps

How to Teach a Bible Lesson

1. Pray and prepare.
   The best way to do this is through your own daily Bible reading. Keep a list of ideas and story-time passages that you find through reading.

2. Read the story over several times.
   Familiarize yourself with the story so it can be told vividly.

3. Use imagination.
   Think about the story. Use imagination and make it exciting without "abusing" it. The only way to do this is to spend time thinking about it and living it out in your mind. Consider all the events and surrounding circumstances. Apply events to realistic situations.

4. Think of illustrations.
   Illustrations are keys to applying biblical principles in our lives. Children must have illustrations. (Stories that apply to childhood and humor always work well.)

5. Use object lessons when possible.

   Kids love tricks, objects, and teaching tools. Be creative and think of an object lesson for the story. Children will remember object lessons for the rest of their lives.

6. Use voice control and a variety of vocal tones.

   This is a key in keeping the attention of your young audience. Raising and lowering volume, changing tones, showing emotion, and acting out parts will keep all eyes fixed on the teacher, and will have a far greater influence. Avoid speaking in a monotone voice or yelling in frustration at all costs!

7. Use a wide variety of facial expressions.

   The face will communicate a point almost as much as your voice. Show emotions vividly on your face. You will keep them laughing as well as listening.

8. Use sudden attention getters.

   Clapping the hands, whispering, a sudden increase in volume, talking faster, snapping your fingers, sudden body movements, or key attention getting phrases (e.g., Guess what?, Hey!, Wow!, etc.) are absolutely essential with young audiences. Every few minutes, a child's attention will wander and must be regained! Keep them aware.

9. Be enthusiastic, dynamic, exciting, and vibrant.

   If the teacher is not exciting, the young audience will quickly find other amusing interests, whether it be toys, neighbors, or other fun things.

10. Demand their undivided attention.

    Correct talkers or those causing distraction on the spot. Do not be hateful, but do be firm and stern. Do not let a child continue distracting others. Deal with the problem; separate the child if needed, and then continue the lesson.

How to Use Visual Aids

What are visual aids?

A. Anything visual (able to be seen) which aids the teaching of a concept or idea

B. Some examples of visual aids:

1. Chalkboard, white board
2. Overhead projector
3. Film strip
4. Pictures
5. Flannel graph
6. Drama
7. Word strips, flashcards
8. Charts, graphs, maps
9. Objects
10. Bulletin boards, banners
11. Video
12. Puppets
13. Songs

Why use visual aids?

A. People remember 70 percent more of what they see than of what they only hear.

B. Teachers may capture attention more quickly through the "eye-gate."

C. As visuals are used and changed, they help keep the attention.

How important is the use of visual aids?

A. One cannot effectively teach children, and sometimes adults, without the use of visual aids.

B. No teacher is fully prepared to teach children without visual aids.

C. Our Lord, the Master Teacher, made constant use of visual aids (e.g., the lilies, the sower, the birds, and the water).

The Purpose of Visual Aids

A. To capture the attention of children

B. To teach an object lesson

C. To present the Bible lesson or application

D. To illustrate a truth

E. To teach the memory verse

F. To present salvation and invitation

G. To make announcements

Pointers for Storytelling

The Story

1. Choose the theme. Look for the memory verse; it is the theme or it should be. If choosing the verse, ask the Lord's guidance in picking one that the story can illustrate.

2. Repeat the theme. Refer to the meaning of the verse several times during the story.

3. Close with the theme. Use the verse as part of the application and/or invitation.

4. Drive home one central truth.

Some Dos and Don'ts

1. Don't read it to the audience.

2. Don't memorize verbatim.

3. Do be thoroughly familiar with the story, including the details.

4. Don't just tell it—live it!

5. Do remember that the span of attention varies. Be sensitive to your children and gear the story to their receptiveness.

Introduction

1. Teachers will win or lose their audience in the first three minutes, depending on how they begin. Capture their interest immediately.

2. Arouse their curiosity.

3. Be careful when asking questions that the child does not take up all your time.

4. Never talk down to the children in arrogance.

Delivery

1. Be enthusiastic.

2. Be sincere and wholehearted in telling it. Be yourself—do not mimic other storytellers.

3. Vary the tone of voice to fit moods, characters, etc. (practice sounding excited, sad, burdened, proud, glad, mean, etc.).

4. Pace it—speed up or slow down for variety in action.

5. Pause to emphasize a point or command attention.

6. Dramatize—they love it. Whisper or get louder for effect to emphasize.

7. Interpret—let every character build and become real. Paint a word picture and relate to the listeners. Use imagination.

8. Involve individuals in the story. ("What would you have done, Jim?") (Have kids represent characters.)

Application

1. Make it as real as the story—weave the application throughout the story.

2. Apply it to the listeners personally.

3. Keep it simple.

4. After the application, STOP!

5. When telling a continued story, leave the ending on a high point, so the kids will look forward to the next class!

The Storyteller

1. Preparation

   a. Read the Scriptural account first.
   b. Pray.
   c. Rely upon the Holy Spirit.

2. Grooming

   a. Be neat and modest.
   b. Avoid extremes in dress.
   c. Watch posture. (Do not slouch.)
   d. Watch breath. (Make sure it is pleasant.)
   e. Be poised. Poise is a combination of confidence and humility. Confidence is essential for a good presentation. Humility is remembering who gave you the raw material with which to work, so the good presentation is possible.

3. Gestures

   a. Do not overdo gestures; use natural gestures.
   b. Do not become addicted to one gesture.

c. Do not become known for eccentric gestures.

4. Voice

a. Avoid shrill, nasal tones.
b. A good voice depends on a relaxed throat, proper breathing, and focused tone.

5. Commission

a. To show God's plan of salvation (Matthew 28:19–20)
b. To show forth His praises (I Peter 2:9)
c. To be a faithful steward of His grace (I Peter 4:10)
d. To be a minister of reconciliation (II Corinthians 5:18)
e. To trust God to *"create the fruit of the lips"* and to remember that my message is *"peace to him that is far off, and to him that is near"* (Isaiah 57:19)
f. To show thankfulness to be *"allowed of God to be put in trust with the gospel"* (I Thessalonians 2:4)

Control in the Classroom

1. Never lose control, yell, get angry, or show a temper in any way. By losing control of yourself, you will lose more control of the kids. They will try you, and if they can frustrate you, they will! If you cannot control yourself, do not expect to control 75–100 kids.

2. Never get physical in any way when dealing with discipline problems.

3. Get the kids to respond. Noise is fine as long as the teacher is controlling it. The first step to control is to begin to bring all uncontrolled noise and chaos into the arena of "ordered noise." Do this by using "1–2–3 Zip" or other games. Also use, "If you are glad to be here today/tonight say, 'AMEN!' "

4. Sing a few songs. This is conditioning the kids to respond to your commands. While singing, be looking for trouble makers and keep an eye on them. Start with fast, loud songs and taper down to slower, milder songs. This will begin to settle them down.

5. Use praise. Praise someone for doing good, and he will do it again. If the kids know that the teacher is proud of their behavior, they will keep trying to make him proud. Say things like, "Aren't these kids being good?" "They must be the BEST boys and girls in the world." Compliment them.

6. Tell them what is expected. Tell them the rules (e.g., sitting up, listening, no talking, etc.) and look them in the eyes as you do. Also begin pointing out talkers and trouble makers at this time. Warn them of the punishment for misbehaving.

7. Separate troublemakers quickly. While you are still getting started, remove troublemakers and talkers. Be firm, quick, and stern. Do not put up with constant disruption, or control will be lost.

8. Move around and use eye contact. Look them in the eye and move around the class so everyone knows the teacher is aware of what they are doing and how they are behaving.

9. Occasionally stop and praise them for being good. Praise will do wonders!

10. If troublemakers persist, take them out of the room. Do not tolerate misbehavior.

Handling Class Disruptions

Here are some common words said by Sunday school teachers: "Why can't little children sit still?"—"What these kids need is discipline!"—"Why is a child's behavior sometimes puzzling and frustrating?"—"Why do children act like this?"

No two children are alike. The different experiences each child has had in the first six years of life are innumerable. Knowing these things, teachers continue to be surprised when children do not act the way they expect them to.

By the same token, no two teachers are alike. Yet, when surrounded by a whole room full of children, they are all similar. All they want is for children to behave, which means teachers want them to act the way they think they should. Discipline is the guidance a teacher gives so children learn to control their impulsive behavior.

Realizing that all teachers have the same problem—how to get them to behave properly, to be in control and not be disruptive—and knowing there are no perfect children, one can only try different techniques of guiding each child's behavior. Through this section, materials and tools will be given to help guide each student's behavior.

Requirements of Good Behavior

A. Set limits to help children feel a sense of security and order.

B. An ounce of prevention is worth a pound of cure.

C. Rules need to be reasonable and simple enough for kids to remember.

D. Develop an atmosphere of love and acceptance.

    1. Every child who enters the class needs to feel that someone cares about him.

    2. Love needs to be demonstrated in a way children can understand.

        a. Talk with them at their eye level.

        b. Listen attentively to what they have to say.

E. Children need classroom orderliness.

1. Children respond in a positive manner to a neatly arranged room with fresh and interesting things to do.
2. The temperature of the room will determine how they act and respond to a teacher. It needs to be comfortable.

F. Provide an interesting schedule of activities.

1. If the teacher is asking them to sit and be quiet for a whole class period, he is asking them to be miniature adults. Children often misbehave because they are bored.
2. Children need action.
   a. Singing—action songs that direct their behavior
   b. Games—allow for interaction and involvement
   c. Surprises—keep them on their toes, wondering what could come next
   d. Physical activity—allows them to release their pent-up energy

Respond to the Behavior Challenge

When dealing with a behavior challenge, we can respond two ways—ignore it or respond to it. Most try to ignore it, and then it becomes more difficult to handle.

A. Deal with the problem individually. Avoid embarrassing the child in front of the class.

B. Avoid long explanations.

C. Have the child tell what he or she did wrong. Do not ask why he acted that way—this only invites him to justify the offense. Only deal with the current situation—do not bring up past offenses.

D. Be sure the child understands why the behavior is not acceptable in the classroom.

E. What to do when a child:

1. Hits, kicks, or scratches—Separate him and explain to him that those things hurt and he may not hurt other people.
2. Bites—Explain that teeth are for chewing food and that biting hurts. Do not encourage the child to bite back to show how it feels.
3. Throws a tantrum—Separate him from the rest of the class. Allow time to calm down and then address the problem.

Redirect the Child to a Positive Behavior

A. Focus on good behavior. Ask what better thing he could have done instead or what he can do now and in the future.

B. Simply state what the child is to be doing. It is also appropriate to tell the child what will happen if he continues to disturb and to follow through. Effectiveness depends on ability to follow through on a promise. Avoid repeated threats. A threat is a form of dare that increases tension while an explanation of consequences defines the limits of what he or she can or cannot do.

C. When a child consistently misbehaves during activities, remove the child from the scene of difficulty. Always keep your conversation cheerful even though you are redirecting his misbehavior.

D. Misbehavior is sometimes a bid for attention. If given proper attention in the first place, they will not have to misbehave to get it.

E. As a child makes changes in his behavior, give honest and sincere encouragement to reward good behavior.

Reward Good Behavior

When children know they will receive attention for positive behavior, their display of disruptive behavior often diminishes.

Conclusion

Your positive, loving approach to the individual needs of the students is one of the most helpful approaches in making the classroom a place of good behavior. Guiding a child in class not only helps the teacher, but it also helps that child take the first step toward ultimately obeying the Lord with his life.

Causes of Misbehavior

Misbehavior due to learning tasks

A. Three important causes related to tasks or activities of a lesson:

1. *Fatigue*—The students become tired and seek rest or change of activity.
2. *Boredom*—The teacher fails to hold the children's attention and they seek other things to do.
3. *Frustration*—The activity is too difficult, resulting either in excess nervous energy that takes either the form of hostility or aggression or in withdrawal, apathy, crying, etc.

B. Ways to improve learning tasks:

1. Variety
2. Time—shorter periods, know the group's attention span.

3. Simplicity—DO NOT have projects, activities, or crafts with multiple rules or steps.

Misbehavior due to the teacher

A. Four important causes of misbehavior which relate to the teacher:

1. *Lack of clarity*—students do not understand what is expected and sit idly or do inappropriate things.
2. *Poor voice characteristics*—weak/soft, whining, too loud, monotone, filler words, out of control.
3. *Inconsistency*—lax one day, strict the next, does not treat all students fairly. Students become resentful.
4. *Poor classroom climate*—temperature, limited space, lack of activity

B. Suggestions to correct this behavior:

1. Tape the class—listen to tone of voice, for words too difficult for the age group.
2. Work on voice inflection, grammar, etc.
3. Be consistent, controlled, and filled with the Spirit.
4. Brighten the classroom with bulletin boards and proper lighting, and make sure the temperature is comfortable.

Misbehavior due to the student

A. Four causes which reside in the student:

1. *Ignorance*—they just do not know what is acceptable or unacceptable behavior from a class leader.
2. *Mimicry*—students imitate each other.
3. *Habit*—students often misbehave because of habits developed in other classrooms or other places.

    4. *Displacement*—aggression, defiance, and withdrawal result from pressures outside of Sunday school—abuse, broken homes, unloved children.

B. Remedies to correct these areas:

    1. Train and inform—children cannot do what they do not know.

    2. Example—find someone with good behavior and elevate him.

    3. Separate and isolate the child who is misbehaving. Put him near a worker.

    4. Visit the home—it may not change anything but at least the teacher can understand the family.

Misbehavior due to other causes

A. Two other causes which bring about misbehavior:

    1. *Special events*—holidays, trips, relatives visiting

    2. *The unexpected*—weather changes, accidents, natural disasters, startling news

B. Possible cures:

    1. Be flexible, give assurance to the class.

    2. Redirect their activity.

    3. Explain disturbance.

    4. Holiday—use their excitement and bring it around to the spiritual.

Growing a Sunday School Class

I. Understand the purpose of your Sunday school class.

A. To reach people

B. To teach people

C. To win people

D. To care for people

II. Understand your priorities as the Sunday school leader.

   A. Lead the class.

   B. Feed the class.

      1. Consider the students' learning levels.

         a. Knowledge

         b. Comprehension

         c. Application

         d. Analysis

         e. Synthesis

         f. Evaluation

      2. Consider your central truth.

      3. Consider your teaching aims.

         a. To fill the mind

         b. To stir the emotions

         c. To challenge the will

   C. Care for the class.

III. Understand how to pray for your Sunday school class.

   A. Pray for a teachable spirit.

   B. Pray for the ministry of the Holy Spirit.

   C. Pray for guidance in lesson preparation.

   D. Pray for your students.

Age Divisions

Churches of different sizes will have different needs regarding their children's classes. A church may start off with combined grades and as the ministry grows, divide these classes as necessary. A good goal is to have all the classes divided by grade and gender. For instance, the Sunday school ministry could eventually work toward having a 5th grade boys' class and a 5th grade girls' class. (To view the LBC children's class schedule, see CD 12.3—Information Guide.)

Dividing a Growing Class

When does a class get too large? Setting a ratio of students to workers is subjective. Different teachers have different levels of control. Some teachers can handle 40 students with a worker or two. Other teachers have a difficult time handling 40 with 5 workers. Observe the class and know the teachers. When the class grows too large for the teacher's abilities, split it.

Thought: If the discipline trouble is due to a weak teacher, discuss this with the teacher.

Other Children's Ministries

Cactus Kids' Club

Most churches find that conducting a Wednesday night program separate from their Sunday school helps draw more children. Lancaster Baptist Church conducts "The Cactus Kids' Club." It meets every Wednesday night, and each member receives a Cactus Kids' shirt. Every grade level has a book of different verses to memorize, varying in length and difficulty. The children receive a copy of the verse book to study throughout the week with their parents, who can initial the verses once they are learned. When an entire section of the book is learned, the child receives a "star" patch that can be sewn onto his shirt. This encourages the child to continue learning verses in order to earn more stars, and an award is given at the end of the year for anyone who has completed his entire book. Classroom time consists of saying and learning verses, Bible story time, craft and snack time, and game time.

Kiddie Church

Kiddie Church is held for children ages 3–5 during regular church services on Sunday night and Wednesday night. The classes are divided by age and when the classes become too large, the boys and girls can be placed in separate classes.

During Kiddie Church there should be plenty of singing, teaching, crafts, snacks, and games. It is important to guard against workers just "watching" the children. Children this age need to be taught the stories and principles of God's Word. This should not just be a play time.

The Joy Club & Baptist Boys' Club

The Joy Club and Baptist Boys' Club are other variations of children's programs. The Joy Club is a girls-only group that can meet weekly or monthly, depending on the church's schedule. The girls learn to sew, do needlepoint, to iron, etc., as well as learn verses each week. They have special activities such as going to the zoo or to the park, and the girls go out soulwinning with the teachers occasionally and learn how to share the Gospel with others. The Baptist Boys' Club focuses more on outdoor activities for the boys and teaches them how to be leaders from an early age. These programs encourage relationship building and character development. They pinpoint specific traits, such as teamwork, ingenuity, and creativity, more easily than in a typical classroom setting because of the nature of the activities.

Children's Adventure Fridays

Throughout the summer months, the Children's Ministries plan a monthly Adventure Friday. This all-day activity is an exciting field trip that involves the workers of the Children's Ministries and volunteer parents. The activities can be held in a variety of places such as amusement parks, museums, and aquariums. Whatever the activity, the Adventure Friday should be advertised for several weeks prior to the day. Announcements could be placed in the bulletin and reminders could be made at the end of services. Have registration tables set up in the lobby for parents to sign up and pay for the activities.

It is a good idea to design a brightly colored shirt that the parents must purchase. If all the children are wearing the same bright shirt, it is easier for the workers to supervise their group. The shirts could be sold starting at the first Adventure Friday. The children could wear the shirt for all the following Adventure Fridays. It is helpful to the parents if they only have to purchase one shirt for the whole summer.

Vacation Bible School

Held annually during the summer, this one-week special emphasis on the children of your community is a very effective tool in giving children the Gospel and reaching their parents and families for the Lord. Listed below is the planning guide for holding this event:

1. Set the date. Monday–Friday; 6:00–8:00 P.M. has been effective.

2. Establish a theme.

3. Acquire a curriculum.

4. Divide the classes by age group. Larger grades can be separated by boys and girls.

5. Enlist volunteers through the adult Bible classes. Teachers and workers are needed.

6. Set a schedule. Have a timeline for each night.

Children's Choir

Children's Choir meets on Sunday afternoons during the adult choir practice. This is a great opportunity to begin developing the musical talents of the young people in the church. The Children's Choir can sing regularly and give special performances such as Easter, patriotic, and Christmas musicals. Parents enjoy seeing their children participate in the ministry, and it is a good opportunity to invite extended family members to hear the Gospel.

A one-time yearly fee is charged per child to cover the costs of the music and outfit. The children wear coordinating outfits. The girls receive a dress and the boys wear dress pants, shirt, and tie that coordinate with the girls.

Pastor's Summer Pals

When a child gets out of school for the summer, he has one thing on his mind—PLAY! Bible reading, prayer, helping Mom out—all of this vanishes from his thoughts. Pastor's Summer Pals is a great way to encourage the children to stay faithful in church attendance, Bible reading, prayer, and other good behavior.

Pastor's Summer Pals is a contest run through the children's Sunday school classes. Here's how it works:

1. The first Sunday of summer break, each child is given a scorecard to check off what he accomplished during the week (see CD 15.4).

2. The contest rules are explained both in the children's Sunday school classes and in the evening services to the parents. The prize(s) are announced. The prizes can vary from every child who turns in a card every week receiving an ice cream sundae party to the child with the most points at the end of summer break receiving a nice prize. Be creative with the prizes; they do not need to be expensive to be effective.

3. Sunday school teachers collect the scorecards weekly and turn them in to the director's office. The director will keep the tally and announce the winners at the end of summer break.

Pastor's Summer Pals is a fun way to encourage faithfulness even during the summer months.

Boys' Basketball League

The Boys' Basketball League is an "extra-curricular" ministry in the church. It is an intramural program designed to teach elementary boys the rules of basketball and give them an opportunity to play team sports in a Christian setting. The league director and the coaches are volunteers from within the church. Since the competition can get fierce, they should be godly men who are able to keep their anger and emotions in control.

Steps to starting an intramural basketball league:

1. Appoint a league director—He needs to have a good knowledge of the game and how to set up a tournament. He will set the game schedule and keep the statistics.

2. Recruit volunteer coaches—They will need to be able to attend practice times for their team during the week.

3. Provide times after services for parents to sign up their boys. There can be tables at the exits and sign-up sheets available.

4. A one-time charge can pay for team shirts to be designed. The shirts do not need to be fancy. Have different colors for each team, and the team name on the shirt. Numbers and player names are a nice option.

5. Decide on how many teams will be needed. Each team needs to have 5–8 players. If the group is large, grade divisions can be made such as 3rd–4th grades and 5th–6th grades.

6. Set a game schedule.

7. Keep statistics.

8. The last day of games can be a championship tournament with trophies and/or ribbons for winning teams and individual players with outstanding performances.

This should be a time of not only teaching rules but also encouraging a spiritual response to peers and to the coaches and referees. It is a good idea to have the coaches prepare a devotion to teach their team after each game. This keeps a spiritual emphasis throughout the season.

Annual Children's Offering

During the months prior to the collection of the annual Victory Night Offering (see Chapter 22), the children's education director leads a special emphasis to teach the children the importance of worship through giving. It is announced to the children that they will participate in the Victory Offering, and a goal is set. Each child receives a cardstock church bank that can be used to save up his change. The special offering is collected each Sunday in Sunday school and a running total is announced weekly in their classes. At the end of the allotted time, a giant-sized check is made out to the Victory Night Offering. The children's education director brings the children up to the platform on a Sunday or Wednesday night before the Victory Offering and presents the check to the pastor and the people. This is a very effective way of helping the children be involved in their church.

Conclusion

Obviously, time and space limit the discussion of every available children's program. Above all else, choose programs that will enhance the quality of a particular ministry. In a smaller church setting, separating the boys and girls into different classes may not be feasible. Time, workers, and attendance all factor into the programs each church will be able to establish. But whatever program is chosen, it should be focused around the teaching of God's Word, and what the children are being taught should be applicable to their lives both now and in the future.

CHAPTER SIXTEEN

Student Ministries

"As arrows are in the hand of a mighty man;
so are children of the ***youth****."*
Psalm 127:4

I will never forget the first youth activity at Lancaster Baptist Church! We had three teenagers in attendance and Terrie and I were excited to be a blessing to them.

One of the games we played was one that required the teens to take off their shoes and socks, catch a styrofoam cup with their toes, and then jump across the parking lot about forty yards to win the race. There were several problems with this game, the least of which was the wind blowing the cups all over the parking lot and the fact that the parking lot was extremely porous and rough on the feet of the teenagers. After losing several cups to the wind and spending time administering first aid to the toes of the teenagers, I began to realize this "youth ministry stuff" was not as easy as it seemed.

Over the years, God has truly blessed the development of the Youth Ministry here at Lancaster Baptist Church. Today, hundreds of teenagers meet each week and dozens of teenagers annually are following the path of the Lord into full-time service.

Much of the material in this chapter has been developed by the director of our Student Ministries, Brother Cary Schmidt. Cary has been a fantastic influence in the lives of hundreds of young people. I believe he is the best youth pastor in America today. One of the reasons I state this is because of his influence on our four children. He has helped each of them to have a love for God and the things of God. The biblical lessons he has taught them and the tremendous memories he has given them are gifts for which Terrie and I will be eternally grateful.

I would strongly encourage each reader of *Order in the Church* to purchase a copy of Brother Schmidt's book, *Discover Your Destiny*. It will give you a sample of the biblical philosophy of ministry he has employed in directing our teens to discover the will of God for their lives.

A character study of youths in the Bible reveals that the teen years are typically either when decisions are made to live faithfully for God, or corruption is born for a life of sin. Ecclesiastes 12:1 says, *"Remember now thy Creator in the days of thy youth, while the evil days come not, nor the years draw nigh, when thou shalt say, I have no pleasure in them."* God wants young people to develop a heart for Him from their youth, and the Youth Ministry of the church is one of the keys to helping this process happen.

In II Corinthians 6:4, Paul said, *"But in all things approving ourselves as the ministers of God..."* The youth pastor and those working with youth in your local church must take this verse seriously. We are commanded to consider ourselves as "ministers of God" and to "approve" ourselves in His sight. So often, Youth Ministry is less than effective because of the impure motives and the immaturity of those in leadership.

Many people enter Youth Ministry because they want to have fun, they want to be accepted by a younger crowd, they want to recapture some youthful memories, or they want to tell others of their youthful mistakes. While Youth Ministry ought to be enjoyable and memorable, these motives will not produce an effective ministry.

At the core, like all personal work in ministry, effective Youth Ministry involves hard work, personal sacrifice, detailed organization, Spirit-filled Bible teaching and preaching, leadership ability, spiritual maturity, pastoral "watch-care," discernment, and an understanding of the pastor's heart for the whole church. Often times there is a "great gulf fixed" between "why" people enter Youth Ministry, and "what" effective Youth Ministry really calls for.

The result of this "gulf" is that our youth ministries are often nothing more than glorified "childcare." Rather than true heart and life transformation, young people are coming together to goof off, waste time, and "do church"—all under the sanction of the Youth Ministry. Often Youth Ministry is shallow, surface, and "juvenile." The problem with "juvenile" Youth Ministry is that the Christian life is not "juvenile"—it is not something that teens "grow out of" or "grow beyond." Fun activities are not the criteria for a successful Youth Ministry.

In addition to this, there is a movement in our world to bring modern pop-culture into the youth church experience, and to bring God down to the level of an MTV party enthusiast. This trap places the emphasis of Youth Ministry on the culture rather than on the cross and redefines God as a "hip pocket good luck charm" rather than a sovereign, holy Lord. The excuse that many churches are buying into is that we have to "connect" with our modern day youth culture.

While there is value in understanding the needs and challenges of today's youth culture, there is no biblical basis for the nonsense that is happening in the name of God in many youth groups. In our attempts to lower God to the level of a pop-culture rock concert, we fail to raise the spiritual maturity and biblical discernment of Christian teens. In this process, church becomes an entertainment venue much like a nightclub or a late night talk show, and the Christian life becomes a warm feeling rather than a dynamic, supernatural process of life transformation. Lowering God to a place where culture approves of Him can only result in a culture that does not change. The Youth Ministry should function to salvage kids from an ungodly culture, not help them remain in it.

It is time for youth ministries to return to the biblical call of helping youths "remember their Creator." It is time that we raise the standard of God's majesty and holiness and that we call young people away from culture and into a dynamic life of surrender to their Creator. Youth ministry ought to focus on helping teens meet God, know God, surrender to God, and experience God at work in their lives on a daily basis. Our desire ought to be to raise the spiritual maturity of young people rather than to lower the definition of God. Our focus should be the teaching and preaching of the perfect Word of God, and our efforts should be to prepare young lives to live faithfully for God "all the days of their life."

In addition, the Youth Ministry ought to be a "microcosm" of the church as a whole and should be structured to support the entire vision and function of the church. Teens should not be an "identity" unto themselves, doing their own thing, running their own program, and expecting the church to support them. The Student Ministry should support the church by carrying out the church vision in the lives of young people. The spirit of the teens should positively influence the church as a whole, and the schedule and structure of the group should involve the young people in the core values and ministries of the church. Why? Simply put, young people will quickly outgrow "youth group," but they should never outgrow the church! And the total desire and focus of those leading the Youth Ministry should be to prepare young people for "the rest of their lives." Bonding teens to a youth group will not necessarily prepare them to be faithful to God for life; yet building them to and through the church will lay the foundation for a life of faithfulness.

Finally, Youth Ministry should partner with parents. Too often, the Youth Ministry conflicts with families, and the youth pastor views parents as a threat. This view is completely contrary to Scripture, counter-productive to God's purposes, and anti-family in its outcome. In Scripture, God never established the "youth pastor" as a teenager's primary authority. He never gave a mandate to "bringing children up in the nurture and admonition of the Lord" to a youth pastor. He did give clear instructions in Malachi that we are to turn the hearts of children and parents toward each other. More than a teenager needs a youth group or a youth pastor, he needs godly parents. Where parents are out of the picture or have failed to provide godly leadership, the church should "stand in the gap," but we should do everything we can to build the whole family.

Huge problems result in the lives of kids when the Youth Ministry comes between parent and child. Whether this happens through an event schedule that never allows for family time, through a counseling session in which the youth pastor promises "not to tell parents," or simply through the lack of a servant's heart from the youth pastor—the results are always destructive. The foundational authority in every teenager's life is the parent. When this authority is minimized or usurped by a well-intentioned Youth Ministry, the results are always harmful to the teen.

The Youth Ministry should exist to partner with parents in bringing up young lives for God—it should support the families of the church and help to build their relationships. The youth pastor should give himself to encourage, equip, and assist parents, and he should consistently encourage teens to love, obey, honor, and submit to their parents. No program, teaching series, or retreat can have the significant spiritual impact that a strong parent/teen relationship can have. A Youth Ministry that focuses on building the entire family will have far greater fruit that will last for generations.

Youth Ministry Must Have a Purpose

At some point, early in the life of your Youth Ministry, you must define your purpose and vision. Someone once said, "If you do not know where you are going, you will probably end up somewhere else." Your purposes should be biblical and foundational, and should create the entire framework for this part of your church. Weak purposes of Youth Ministry would be: "to keep teens busy," "to get teens around good influences," or "to provide good clean fun." While there is nothing wrong with these things, there are far greater and deeper scriptural reasons for having a youth group.

Consider the following purposes as a part of your vision:

1. To reach lost teens

2. To inspire love and commitment to Christ

3. To grow strong Christians

4. To prepare young people for adulthood and God's will

5. To strengthen family relationships

6. To protect from Satan's attacks

7. To develop godly character

The pastor of the church should be the originator of this vision and the youth pastor should then determine to own and fulfill that vision. As a youth pastor, ask yourself this question, "Do I know the heart and passion of our pastor for our Youth Ministry?" If not, then your first assignment would be to sit down with the pastor and have him articulate his vision to you. Take notes, restate the purpose to him, and refine it into a concise definition that will clarify your mission. From this articulated vision, you should make a list of priorities for your Youth Ministry and consider fitting those priorities into a statement that your team can own and implement.

Youth Ministry Must Have a Plan

From the purpose should flow a plan. If you are not planning, then you are not leading. You may be reacting or responding, but you are not leading. Later in this book, there is a chapter about planning the church calendar and creating a staff planner. We suggest that you approach each ministry of your church with an annual planner. This planner will help you target specific steps and projects to fulfill your purpose in Youth Ministry. Purpose or vision without a detailed plan is really nothing more than good intentions.

This annual plan should address every major activity, class, or event in Youth Ministry and should give a one-year overview that clearly points back to the overall purpose. It will take a few days to create, and the pastor should review it before the year begins, but it will also clarify the direction and motivate the entire Youth Ministry team to press forward into spiritual progress. Putting a well-defined plan into action is a lot of fun.

Youth Ministry Must Have a Balance

Perhaps one of the biggest struggles in any ministry is how to "cover all the bases." This will be a constant balancing act to which you must be sensitive all the time. In ministry, there is a tendency to lose the big picture and to focus on one area at the expense of another. There are countless ways that ministry can become "imbalanced." Here are a few thoughts on developing a balanced Youth Ministry.

Regularly review your purpose and plan

Stay in touch with the direction God has given you and consistently look at this big picture to evaluate your progress.

Understand major priorities of Youth Ministry

At Lancaster Baptist Church we have defined our major priorities in Youth Ministry as follows:

1. Outreach—reaching new Christians and training soulwinners

2. Discipleship—building strong, committed Christians

3. Fellowship—building relationships, friendships, activities

4. Family Ministry—encouraging and equipping parents

5. Youth Leadership Team—enlisting and equipping adult leaders

6. Annual Planning—creating an annual plan for the entire Youth Ministry

7. Office Support for Youth Ministry—clerical work to support the ministry

8. Personal Ministry—one-on-one personal work

Every event, every sermon, every meeting, and every program of the Student Ministry falls under one of the above priorities. In youth meetings these priorities are addressed constantly.

Stand guard against typical imbalances in Youth Ministry

The following balances are areas we try to address regularly.

1. Blending public school kids with Christian school kids

2. Working with troubled teens versus working with soft teens

3. Addressing the different needs of junior high teens and senior high teens

4. Encouraging teens and encouraging parents

5. Hosting fun activities with a spiritual purpose

6. Bonding the kids to the church and the pastor versus the youth group and the youth pastor

7. Ministering to kids with strong families as well as those from broken homes

8. Nurturing new Christians while also building mature Christians

9. Making God's Word understandable without making it "juvenile"

10. Building a close-knit group that is not "cliquish"

11. Maintaining high standards without ostracizing those who do not hold to the same standards.

Youth Ministry Summarized

The Student Ministry at Lancaster Baptist Church is defined by four groups of young people—each with different needs, different activities, different classes, and different workers.

These four groups are defined as follows:

1. **Junior High**—7th–8th grade boys and girls led by the junior high youth director and a team of volunteer youth workers. This group focuses on early faith building and helping young people transition from childhood into teen years, preparing for the spiritual battles ahead.

2. **Middle Senior High**—9th–10th grades led by the senior high youth director as well as several volunteer couples. This group focuses on issues of spiritual maturity and spiritual battles that are at their greatest intensity during these years.

3. **Upper Senior High**—11th–12th grades led by the Student Ministries pastor with volunteer workers. This group focuses on preparing teens for adulthood and for critical decisions that must be made at the end of high school.

4. **College and Career**—includes all students within the first five years out of high school. This group provides an identity for those young people who stay local for college, career, or both, and focuses on helping them survive the "testing of their faith" that is so prevalent during these years. It is a bridge into adulthood that keeps these young

lives connected to their "group" rather than disconnected right after high school. This group is led by the Student Ministry pastor and is intentionally staffed with lay leaders/teachers (role models) who work in the secular work place.

A summary of the LBC Student Ministry for 7ᵗʰ-12ᵗʰ grades

DISCIPLESHIP

1. Winter Retreat

2. Youth Conference

3. Summer Teen Camp

4. Bible Class—Sunday morning class

5. One-on-One Discipleship—lunch, soulwinning, etc.

6. Pastor/Teen Relationship—regular gifts, occasional activities

7. STRIVE Offering—stewardship emphasis

8. ALIVE—summer small group discipleship program

9. Visitation Saturation—one-on-one visitation program through the rosters

OUTREACH

1. Teen Soulwinning—weekly doorknocking

2. Open House Sunday—major student soulwinning effort

3. Kings of the Court Tournament—major student soulwinning effort

4. Summer Missions Trip

5. Public School Bible Clubs

6. Visitor and Prospect Follow-up—youth leaders and teens visiting

FELLOWSHIP

1. Monthly Activities—one larger and one smaller (e.g., fast food on Sunday night)

2. After Church Fellowships—usually by grade at the leader's home

3. Miscellaneous Group Gatherings

FAMILY MINISTRY

1. Quarterly Teen Parent Meetings

2. Counseling Appointments

3. Regular Letters to Parents

4. Family Fellowships at Leader's Home

YOUTH LEADERSHIP TEAM

1. Annual Enlistment of New Workers

2. Quarterly Training Clinics

3. Weekly Teachers' Meeting

4. Weekly Youth Ministry Communiqué Newsletter

5. Weekly Statistics Sheet of Visitors and Attendance

6. Curriculum and Tools Needed

7. Leadership Fellowships

8. One-on-One Leader Training

9. Weekly Visitation and Follow-up

10. Class Development

11. Personal Touch with Teens—calls, visits, notes, e-mails

ANNUAL PLANNING FOR ENTIRE YOUTH MINISTRY

1. Prayer, Vision, and Strategy for the new year

2. Goals for the New Year

3. List of All Foreseeable Projects and Events for One Year

4. Description and Details of All Events and Projects

5. Details and Tasks Placed on the Calendar

OFFICE SUPPORT FOR YOUTH MINISTRY

1. Weekly Teen Bulletins

2. Weekly Workers' Statistics Sheet

3. Weekly Communiqué (Newsletter)

4. Weekly Absentee Letters

5. Weekly Visitor Letters

6. Weekly Personal Notes and Letters

7. Assembling Follow-up Visits

8. Tracking Salvations and Baptisms

Public School Bible Clubs

"Columbine." The very name invokes tragic memories for each of us. Columbine was one in a series of high school shootings that riveted America at the turn of the century. Millions of teenagers attend America's public schools and are crying for some form of love and direction in this needy hour.

While our church had reached hundreds of public school teenagers through the Bus Ministry and other forms of evangelism, it was not until Columbine that God smote my heart with the necessity of having effective Bible clubs on the public school campuses. The testimony of Cassie Bernal from Columbine and her willingness to testify unflinchingly for Christ in the face of death were used greatly in my own heart.

I am thankful for several public school teachers who attend our church and willingly sponsor our youth workers on the public school campuses for the purpose of extending God's love and care to these needy students.

Today's teens are faced with a level of peer pressure that we in the generation preceding them cannot comprehend. Every day, situations arise that challenge their resolve to "live purely in an impure world." Teenagers who have not received proper biblical instruction are at a much greater risk of falling prey to Satan's wiles than those who have been *"taught in the word..."* (Galatians 6:6). Notice the urgency in the psalmist's writings as he pledges to share God's faithfulness with his children:

> *I will open my mouth in a parable: I will utter dark sayings of old: Which we have heard and known, and our fathers have told us. We will not hide them from their children, shewing to the generation to come the praises of the Lord, and his strength, and his wonderful works that he hath done. For he established a testimony in Jacob, and appointed a law in Israel, which he commanded our fathers, that they should make them known to their children: That the generation to come might know them, even the children which should be born; who should arise and declare them to their children: That they might set their hope in God, and not forget the works of God, but keep his commandments: And might not be as their fathers...* Psalm 78:2–8

Unfortunately, not all children are blessed with godly parents who will teach them about God's love and faithfulness. Many children are left on their own to determine what is right and wrong, with little help from friends at school. Neither can every Christian parent afford to send his child to private school, where he is at least partially sheltered from temptations such as smoking, alcohol, and drug use. We must meet them where they are, and beginning a Bible club at your local public school is a great way to establish a connection between your church and the youth in your community.

There are no set standards for establishing a Bible club. Some are conducted 30 minutes or an hour before school starts; others meet after school on a weekly or bi-weekly basis. Before you begin, check with your local public school on the guidelines for starting a student club. Most schools have certain criteria for a club name and constitution (see the regulations found at the end of this chapter). If there is someone in your church who works at the school, he may be a good contact and information source for you.

Once you know how to begin your club, gather a small group of students from that particular school to begin praying and spreading the news about the club. Make sure you have a starting date and time for them to pass along to their friends! If your youth group has home schoolers or teens from a private school that starts at a later time than the public school, encourage them to become involved, too. They will enjoy the contact with other students, and they can provide a solid core group at the first meeting, which will encourage more students to attend.

Meetings should begin with singing and a short prayer to get everyone involved from the start. It is best to choose songs that will appeal to teens and have words that are easy to learn. After singing, share a short devotional that will apply to each teenager in the room. It is essential to share lessons that are both challenging and easy to understand, as the ultimate goal of a Bible club is to bring in new souls for Christ while helping the Christians to grow spiritually. Time at the end may be used for prayer requests and prayer in partners or as a group, followed by light refreshments, such as doughnuts and juice. Try to leave a good impression at the school by dismissing on time and cleaning the room when finished.

There are many ways to vary your schedule as your Bible club develops, such as having a teen give the devotion, having someone from your youth group open in prayer, and by playing quick "ice-breaker" games at the beginning of your time. Attendance may vary from week to week, but realize that the increase is in the Lord's hands. If you are faithful in your labor, He **will** provide the harvest. *"And let us not be weary in well doing: for in due season we shall reap, if we faint not"* (Galatians 6:9).

For the Youth Pastor:

STARTING A CLUB

1. Obtain permission from the school administration to hold Bible club meetings there.

2. Obtain guidelines and rules from the public school administration.

3. Locate one student who attends the public school who is willing to "lead" the club. He is also referred to as the student advisor.

4. Assist the "leader" with the club start-up rules. These follow in the next section.

5. Locate a faculty member from the public school who is willing to act as a sponsor. He will be the intermediary between the student "leader" of the Bible club and the administration of the public school. Be sure to introduce the student "leader" and the faculty "sponsor."

6. Set a time for the Bible club to meet. It can be before or after school; it can be weekly, bi-weekly, or monthly. Try to make it convenient for the students so they can attend.

7. Develop an "order of service,"—a plan for the meeting.

HELPFUL HINT:

Contact the Christian Law Association for a packet of information on the "Equal Access Act." This packet will supply you with the various laws regarding access to the public schools.

For the Student:

STARTING A CLUB

Students wishing to start a club need to do six things:

1. Get a start-up group together and decide what the purpose of your club will be.

2. Find a faculty sponsor (unless the youth pastor has already done this).

3. Recruit members.

4. Elect officers.

5. Draft a constitution and submit it with your officer slate and membership list to the school board for recognition.

6. Once recognized by the school board, set up an account with the bookkeeper at the student store.

Now you are in business.

Guidelines for Drafting a Club Constitution

PREAMBLE

The preamble consists of a brief statement of the aims and purposes of the organization.

ARTICLE I—NAME

States the name of the organization and, if the preamble is omitted, it contains a short statement of the purpose of the organization.

ARTICLE II—MEMBERSHIP

Defines the general requirements necessary for membership.

ARTICLE III—OFFICERS

Contains a list of the officers of the organization and the length of their term of office.

ARTICLE IV—TERMS OF ELECTION

Includes how officers are elected, who elects them, the length of their terms, and what the qualifications of the officers shall be.

ARTICLE V—MEETINGS

States the time for regular meetings and provides a method by which special meetings may be called.

ARTICLE VI—AMENDMENTS

Contains a statement of the method of amending the constitution and the vote required for such amendments.

ARTICLE VII—SCHEDULE

States date on which constitution becomes effective.

Once the Club is Started:

1. The club has to be student "led." You are acting as a guest speaker.

2. You, as the guest speaker, cannot promote or propagate your church's name, activities, functions, or meetings. The student advisor can promote any church activity, function, or meeting that he would like.

3. Any flyers must have A.S.B. (Associated Student Body) approval on them to be handed out on school campus. Posters, articles in the school newspaper, banners, or displays can be used as long as they are made available to other clubs.

4. Always check in with the school secretary before going to your room.

5. As the guest speaker you cannot contact students outside of the set club meeting time, unless they are a part of your youth group.

6. Attend as many games and competitions as you can that your club members participate in. Use this time to meet their parents and meet other students.

7. Do not "preach" at them. Teach easy-to-grasp simple truths.

8. Always present salvation to them.

The following pages give instructional materials for youth staff, program ideas, and general operating guidelines for the Student Ministries of Lancaster Baptist Church.

The Student Ministry

Dear Friend,

I want to welcome you to the Student Ministry! It is a privilege to be able to serve the Lord here in any way or fashion. Through this area of service, I pray that you will grow spiritually as you meet the needs of others.

As you serve in this ministry, I would like you to keep in mind Colossians 3:23–24, "And whatsoever ye do, do it heartily, as to the Lord, and not unto men; Knowing that of the Lord ye shall receive the reward of the inheritance: for ye serve the Lord Christ." As you serve the Lord in the Student Ministry, be mindful that your service is unto the Lord and whatever we do for Him should be our best.

The thought of "commitment to excellence" comes to my mind when I read those verses. As servants of God, our attitude toward the Lord's work should be on a different level of excellence because of who we are serving—the Lord.

Finally, let me express how excited I am that the Lord has led you to serve in this ministry, and may the Lord bless you because of your faithfulness in this area of service.

Your friend,

Pastor

Principles for Youth Ministry

1. **Give praise, not flattery.**
   Flattery deals with outward changeable characteristics and appearance. Praise focuses on spiritual character qualities. Every teen has some, though they may be few.

2. **Never make fun of a young person in a harmful way.**
   Teenagers are very sensitive when it comes to being teased or ridiculed. Teasing and joking must be done discreetly and with discernment. Please be very careful not to belittle or hurt them in any way.

3. **When teaching, do so practically and relevantly.**
   You are preparing teens to face real life and death issues. Our teaching must be very practical. When preparing a challenge or lesson, constantly ask yourself, "So what?" If need be, place yourself in their shoes. Remember when you were a teenager. Use personal illustrations of when you were a teenager, but somehow bring the biblical truth down to a level that applies to their lives.

4. **Always give biblical reasons for what you believe.**
   The teenager often struggles with reasons. That is why when a boy turns 12 or 13, he begins asking Mom and Dad, "Why?" whenever they request something. Teens begin searching for answers and wanting real-life reasons for why they do what they do. This may mean that, as a youth worker, you will have to dedicate yourself to Bible study and searching the Scriptures, but never leave a teenager hanging as he seeks you out for answers and reasons. Always try to be prepared to share God's Word and to show him that God's Word is credible and reliable. In the long run, the teens will see that God's Word is what they must build their lives upon.

5. **Choose activities that reinforce character.**

If you are ever put in charge of games or activities please never use games in which someone will be humiliated or ridiculed. Be sensitive to those who are uncoordinated, nonathletic, or slow learners. One simple example is when dividing up teams, it may be better to count off (one, two, one, two) than to have team captains choose a team.

Realize that every activity is held for a purpose. That purpose is to build spiritual character. Though each activity should be fun and lighthearted, there is a real purpose behind it. Keep this foremost in your mind.

6. **Be a real person with the teens.**

Teenagers can immediately spot a phony and if they feel you are trying to put on a hypocritical air to impress them, or if they sense that you are not being genuine with them, they will close up to you. Nothing can build respect and break down barriers quicker than just being yourself with the teenagers.

7. **Follow through on commitments.**

When making a promise, be sure to keep it. A teenager has the longest memory in the world when it comes to broken promises and unkept commitments. You cannot afford to hurt the spiritual progress of a teenager by not fulfilling a commitment.

8. **Be patient.**

Youth workers must realize that teenagers are unstable, inconsistent, emotional, immature, and sporadic. Be prepared for these teenage normalities and commit to working consistently with them, developing them to be stronger spiritually.

Always be careful not to snap or lash out at teenagers at the wrong time. They may get on your nerves or do something really stupid, but always be patient.

9. **Create ways for new teens to fit in and meet friends.**

This may involve a game, social event, lunch, or something very simple. The most successful way to involve new teenagers in a youth group is to involve them in games and activities that require them to get to know new friends.

10. **Live above reproach.**

In other words, be blameless. For the most part, teenagers live in a world of phonies and hypocrites. Teens are constantly living a lie and posing to be somebody they are not. As teens see in your lifestyle that you are a real person, and as they see your godly walk, it will have an enormous impact.

Always guard your speech, conduct, and actions. Everything you say and do has an effect for good or bad.

Starting a Youth Group

Introduction:

Suppose you are starting a church, or have been called to a church as youth pastor. Perhaps there are no teenagers, or very few. Where do you start in guiding a program that will be honoring to God and will draw teens and their parents to church? Starting a youth group or helping a small one grow can be an exciting challenge. Here are some proven steps toward developing a strong youth program:

I. Soulwinning

   A. Personal soulwinning

      1. Look for teen prospects and then go after them.

      2. Go where teenagers are (e.g., malls, high schools, parks, ball games, etc.).

   B. Teaching soulwinning to those who are saved

      1. Teach them how to go door-to-door.

      2. Teach the plan of salvation to use and assign verses to memorize.

3. Demonstrate.

4. Practice techniques in the class.

C. Take teenagers with you to go soulwinning.

1. Go to their contacts or friends.

2. Teens need a good example as well as step-by-step instructions on what to say and how to act.

D. Teach them to follow up on the converts. Let them make contact with the converts at least once a week. This is the only way the group will grow from the soulwinning effort.

II. Public School Bible Clubs

A. Work in and through the local church youth group.

B. Gather teens together from a particular high school or junior high. Have them meet in your home or at one of the teen's homes. Teens from the youth group may only come if they bring someone with them who is lost.

C. Sing some choruses, have a testimony, give an evangelistic message and a short Bible study.

D. Have some light refreshments and a game after the meeting.

E. Encourage the saved teens to M&M and D&C ("Mix and Mingle" and "Divide and Conquer").

III. Evangelistic Meetings

A. Several different activities or meetings can be used with evangelism as the goal.

1. A week of meetings just for teenagers

2. Special youth rallies

3. Special activities

B. Regular attending teens must get involved in this to bring in lost teenagers.

C. Good music, testimonies, and sound Bible preaching are necessary.

D. Have a way to register the visitors. Give them a gift with a card to fill out or have a sign-in table.

E. Have competent personal workers.

F. Register all decisions.

G. Follow up on them as soon as possible.

IV. Activities

A. Young people are drawn to:
   1. Fun
   2. Food
   3. Other teens

B. Be organized.

C. Have plenty of help and supervision.

D. Always have a time to preach the Gospel.

V. Music

A. Always have good music in the meetings and services. If it's important to adults—it's important to teens.

B. Start some groups or even a choir.
   1. This is a good way to involve teens in service.
   2. It is a good testimony to unsaved teenagers.

VI. Sports

A. Develop a regular intramural program that will not only excite your regulars but draw in visitors.

B. Everyone should be allowed to play, whether saved or unsaved, regular attender or not.

C. Have a separate program for guys and girls or use sports where they can both play, such as volleyball or softball.

D. Always present the Gospel.

VII. Some General Considerations

A. Keep senior high separate from junior high.
1. There is a temptation to combine them to have larger numbers.
2. The senior highers will drop out because they feel junior highers are too immature to be around.

B. Always make the program appeal to young men.
1. If the program appeals to girls it will make Christianity look like it is just for ladies and children (often a preconceived notion already).
2. The girls will be where the guys are.

C. Friendliness is a key.
1. Every visitor must feel special.
2. A good youth leader will attend high school functions of their teens.
3. Have a high visibility at teen activities, fast food places, etc. This will show that you care and are interested in them.

Conclusion:

If teenagers are reached, their parents will automatically be impacted. They rejoice in positive changes in their teens. Don't squelch their sometimes fanatical zeal. They may want to have all-night prayer meetings, go on extended fasts, rent an airplane and bomb the city with Gospel tracts, etc. Channel these ideas and energies into productive outlets. A balanced, stable, and productive youth group can be built.

Qualities of a Successful Youth Leader

Introduction:

Success is knowing God's will and faithfully doing it. It is God's will that a youth leader or pastor is filled with the Holy Spirit, has an intimate relationship with Jesus Christ, prays, is holy in behavior, has a fervency to reach people with the Gospel, rules well his own household, preaches the Word, and obeys God's commandments. With these basic requirements, a successful youth worker will possess the following characteristics:

1. He has a burning desire to reach as many people as possible with the Gospel of Jesus Christ. He seizes every opportunity afforded him to preach, pass out tracts, witness, disciple new converts, and support missionaries and other Christian workers. He is on the "Gospel Trail" and believes it is always too soon to quit.

2. He has an unconditional friendliness. He is a "people person" without prejudice. He has an open friendliness in approach, voice, stance, and gestures. He goes out of his way to be friendly. This attitude creates opportunities for him.

3. He has a servant's attitude. He has a heart of love for people and will do almost anything for anyone at any time—sometimes to the point of people taking advantage of him—but he lets God balance those things out. He would rather give money than lend it, and he always has a bed or a meal for someone who needs it.

4. He is a goal setter. He writes down his daily, weekly, monthly, and yearly goals. He numbers them in order of importance and then prays, asking God what He wants him to do, knowing that God will not load him down to the point of exhaustion or hurting his relationship with Him or his family. He is flexible under the leadership of

the Holy Spirit so that God can work out His own plan and goals in his life.

5. He always has a positive attitude of faith. His approach is to praise the Lord and let Him run the show. Even when things go wrong, he gives thanks in every situation, knowing that God is in control and is working all things together for His good.

6. He has an enthusiastic attitude. Anything he does, he does wholeheartedly. Enthusiasm is based on good planning and on flexibility when the best-laid plans go awry. Enthusiasm can be genuine only when one knows what he is doing and how he is going to get it done. Uncertainty is the death of enthusiasm. Teens get enthusiastic when their leaders are excited about the activity, project, or event. These youth leaders want to do everything for the glory of God, and they give 100 percent to even the mundane things in life.

7. He recognizes and is willing to work with and through the local church in which God has placed him, seeking guidance and counsel from his pastor. He understands that God provides for, protects, and gives His promises to His institution—the church. Through his life and teaching, he helps young people submit to the leadership and counsel of the pastor that God has given them.

Conclusion:

These seven qualities are developed through an intimate relationship with Jesus Christ and a willingness to obey His will. If these qualities are cultivated continuously, you cannot help but be successful in youth work.

Being a Part of the Youth Worker Team

Introduction:

The simple fact is, this is a team! This is a team that God has assembled to operate and build the Youth Ministry. Please keep in mind that no matter what the role or position is on this team, it is an extremely important one. Not one of us could do what is required alone; each person is needed. God has brought us together to complete a task that would be impossible for any one of us to do single-handedly.

The success of the youth group, growth of the teenagers, and the salvation of many unsaved teens will depend on the spirit and cooperation that will take place as everyone works together as a team. With the idea of teamwork in mind, notice some important keys to developing a successful team and working with a team spirit.

> *But I trust in the Lord Jesus to send Timotheus shortly unto you, that I also may be of good comfort, when I know your state. For I have no man likeminded, who will naturally care for your state. For all seek their own, not the things which are Jesus Christ's. But ye know the proof of him, that, as a son with the father, he hath served with me in the gospel.* Philippians 2:19–22

> *And he gave some, apostles; and some, prophets; and some, evangelists; and some, pastors and teachers; For the perfecting of the saints, for the work of the ministry, for the edifying of the body of Christ.* Ephesians 4:11–12

Maintain a proper perspective.

It is always easy to get involved in the work of the ministry for the wrong motives. It would be easy to work with the youth for selfish motives. Examine your heart and remember that we are here to be servants. Of course, we are leaders in regard to the operation of the youth group, but the role of leadership simply means that we have the opportunity to serve people in a greater way. Let us each keep a servant's heart. Let our motivation be that of pleasing Christ and bringing glory to His name and not our own.

No one is above or below another person. There is not a political ladder of position or success. To impact and influence the lives of teenagers for the cause of Christ, everyone must serve and work together. Each team member has different gifts and abilities, and God has chosen to place us together so we can have a more effective ministry. If there is pulling against each other and fighting for selfish initiatives, our effectiveness in the ministry will be lost. We must bind together, remembering that we are here to be servants and to care for the needs of others.

Maintain a close walk with the Lord.

Remember that in general, teenagers will never experience a greater level of spiritual commitment than what they see in the staff. When a worker is introduced to the youth group, it communicates a message to the teenagers that says, "If you want to know how to live the Christian life, live like him or her." Be careful to maintain a spiritual direction in your own personal life. The need is for "FAT" youth workers (*faithful, available,* and *teachable*). Keep in mind that God is not looking for perfection in your life, but for the direction of your life.

Accept and commit to responsibility.

To be a successful team, each member has to accept the areas in which he is involved and perform them to the best of his ability. Everyone plays an important role in making the youth group work and grow, both spiritually and numerically.

Be faithful to regular youth worker meeting times.

Though these meetings are not frequent, they are extremely important. Part of the key to developing a workable team is practice. Every time there is a youth worker's fellowship or Saturday morning meeting, consider it as practice and training for the Youth Ministry. At each of these meetings, a direction is given regarding new training and insight that will create new ways to help the teens. These meetings bind the team together as a strong unit and make each member more capable of carrying out his duties.

Benefits of a Youth Worker Staff

1. It provides training for the youth workers in areas of hands-on ministry experience.

2. It creates a network of people accomplishing a ministry that one or two could never accomplish.

3. It creates a personal sense of accountability on the part of the youth pastor, as the youth workers will be watching every move he makes.

4. It enables the youth pastor to share responsibilities which allows them to be carried out more effectively.

5. It extends the pastor's influence as he reproduces himself in the youth pastor and then in the lives of the youth worker staff.

6. The youth group benefits from the gifts and talents of several people who have committed themselves to the same goals.

7. It provides the young people with a variety of individuals to whom they can go for counsel or encouragement.

8. It helps you maintain a personal nature in the group even when there is numerical growth.

9. It exposes the young people to different personalities, acknowledging the fact that not every teenager will click with just anyone.

10. It creates a forum from which creative ideas, plans, and decisions can flow.

Biblical Principles for Rebellion in Teens

Text: Ezekiel 18:4–30

1. **A rebellious teen is making a choice.**
   Realize that it is not the fault of the father, society, a tragedy, or a rough life. It is a personal choice on the part of the individual.

2. **A rebellious teen can choose right.**
   Realize that he can learn from his father either way. He can either learn from what the father did wrong and thus choose right, or he can learn from what his father did right. Either way—it is the same choice. A teen from a good family must make the same choice that a teen from a bad family must make.

3. **A rebellious teen must be warned of consequences.**
   In dealing with him, make it very clear that he is in a state of rebellion. This means telling him what he is doing wrong and why, and it is possible to do this in a spirit of love. As long as he is in this youth group, he must constantly understand that he has a problem. This may make him feel uncomfortable.

4. **A rebellious teen must have someone praying and burdened for him.**
   God's sorrow and brokenness over the rebellion of Israel is obvious in this passage. The youth leader must also carry a brokenness in his heart for this teen, sorrowing for what he will face because of his rebellion, and the

blessed life that he will miss. He must understand this burden and brokenness for his life. Never let him think his waywardness brings pleasure to those around him.

5. **A rebellious teen always has a way out.**
   God offers, to all who will ask, forgiveness, restoration, a new heart, a new spirit. Oftentimes the teen knows this but refuses to accept God's answer. A person who refuses help simply cannot be helped. Love him, pray for him, warn him, and express a burden for him. At any time, no matter what the condition or lifestyle, the teen can come back to God and obtain forgiveness and restoration.

How To Reach a Rebellious Youth

1. Begin with the father (Malachi 4:6).
   a. Acknowledge family iniquities (Nehemiah 9:2).
   b. Iniquities are passed on; particular willfulness is passed on (Exodus 20).
   c. Evaluate priorities around responsibilities.
   d. Teach fathers how to give daily praise. (Do not say, "how handsome…how beautiful…" Remember that Proverbs 26:28 teaches us that *"a flattering mouth worketh ruin,"* and Proverbs 29:5 states that a man *"spreadeth a net for his feet."*)
   e. Look for ways to bring praise daily to our children.
   f. Know the danger of being a perfectionist because children never feel they can please you.
   g. Ask forgiveness when wrong.

2. Separate youth from wrong friends and ALL rock music.
   a. There is the fear of losing teens from family, home, church, etc.
   b. Two things men gather—fruit (lasting reward) and firewood (instant heat and light) (John 15).

3. Surround youth with godly people.

4. Have a personal conference with each young person.
    a. Communicate genuine acceptance.
    b. Ask them, "Do you want God's best?"
    c. Bring secret sins to light. As long as they do not reveal hidden sins, Satan will continue to have dominion and authority in their lives. When brought to light, Satan is reproved. When they are willing to tell their parents, it enables them to free themselves.

Maintaining a Heart for Parents

"And he shall turn the heart of the fathers to the children, and the heart of the children to their fathers, lest I come and smite the earth with a curse." Malachi 4:6

In youth work, it is important to remember that first of all, God has given the primary authority over children to their parents. He did not place the youth pastor or the youth worker in this position. Second, the church exists to support and help families. In youth work, the primary responsibility is to come alongside the parents and be a source of support and help that they would not find elsewhere. In the Youth Ministry, the role of the parents cannot diminish in our minds. Our ministry to the parents is perhaps as great as our ministry to the teens themselves.

The Youth Ministry exists to support parents.

Never allow criticism of parents or parental authority within the group. Under no circumstances should criticism of any parent fall from the lips of a single youth worker. Wholeheartedly support parental authority in the lives of the teenagers.

The Youth Ministry exists to help parents.

This simply means if a parent expresses a certain desire or wish for the life of his teen, it is the youth worker's job to help see that it takes place. If a parent asks us to keep an eye on his teenager or to keep him away from a certain crowd, it is our duty to help and support his wishes. This may mean, at times, going against the grain of the group or even being thought of badly by the teenagers. Allowing yourself to become a wedge between the parents and the teens will do more damage to the home and the church than will ever be known.

The Youth Ministry exists to love and encourage parents.

Many times parents will be discouraged and frustrated at the direction or problems their teenager is facing. It is the youth worker's job to be a constant source of encouragement and edification. Do not pass a parent without stopping and speaking, shaking hands, or expressing some thoughtfulness. Parents have entrusted you to influence their teenagers, and it is imperative to have their support and confidence. It is important that you communicate with them as to what problems are developing and how their teens are doing.

Because of this important parent/youth worker relationship, never promise a teenager that you will not tell his parents about something. If a teenager expresses something that needs to be dealt with, you are duty bound as a youth worker to share that problem with the youth pastor and then take it to the parents. If a teenager ever asks you to promise not to tell his parents, simply say, "I'm sorry, I can't do that, but I will do my best to help with the problem."

The Youth Ministry exists to build the relationship between the teenagers and the parents.

It is interesting today, how many parents fall into the state of neglect when it comes to the relationship with their teenagers. This happens because of the many demanding priorities of life, whether they be career or otherwise. It is also interesting how teenagers seem to never want to spend time with their families. They seem to always want to be in their room or away with their friends. Yet, in the heart, every parent desperately needs a close relationship with his or her teenager, and every teenager desperately needs a close relationship with his or her parents.

It is the youth worker's responsibility first to remind the parents of their need for a close relationship with their teens, then to instill in the teens a love and appreciation for their parents. Constantly strive to build a relationship between parents and teens.

A teenager who grows up without a close relationship with his parents will face many struggles and heartaches that could be avoided. When in the presence of teens, always build up the parents, and always encourage a close relationship with the teens when speaking to parents.

The Youth Ministry exists to maintain close communication with the parents.

It is important to work together as a team in communicating with the parents of your teens. In a given week, many of you will bump into the parents of the teenagers. Use this time to communicate the direction of the group and of their teenagers. Use this time to be a help and encouragement and find out if there is anything that can be done for them.

When dealing with a specific teen, you may see needs and problems of which the parents are unaware. There may also be godly character traits developing of which the parents are unaware. It is important to take time to communicate these areas to the parents. Stay in close contact and build a relationship with the parents of the teenagers.

Before befriending the teens, help them grow spiritually. The youth workers are a part of the army in the fight for their lives. It is your job to communicate with the parents and the pastor to ensure a right direction for their lives. Please do not ever let a personal relationship with the teenagers keep you from being what they need spiritually in directing and helping them follow a proper direction.

In this area of communication it is also important to communicate the details of the actual youth program. It is important that the parents know the time, cost, location, and details of each activity. If everyone works as a team in communicating with the parents, there will be fewer times of offense and criticism. This will also build a confidence with the parents that will eventually allow the young people greater freedom to participate in the youth program.

How Can We Have A Greater Ministry To Parents?

As a worker, attend each parent-teen meeting.

These meetings are held once a month on a Sunday night after the service. This is an important time to interact and communicate with the parents.

Occasionally take some time to send a personal letter.

There is no way the youth pastor can contact the parents of all the teenagers the way they need to be contacted. For this reason, everyone must again bind together as a team and work at writing letters and making phone calls to show support and convey encouragement.

We must make it a point to invite the parents to participate in any and all activities or programs.

Does this mean that every parent will attend every meeting? Probably not. But it communicates an openness and accountability to the parents.

At church, be aware of teen parents around you.

Please take time to shake hands, greet them, and let them know that you are on their side.

Occasionally invite a teenager's family over for dinner.

Be sensitive. Sometimes the Holy Spirit may lay a family on your heart. Reach out, do something special for them. This may be all it takes.

Conclusion:

An effective ministry to the parents will result in an effective ministry with the teens. As you are united in a solid spiritual direction with the parents, there is a much better chance of reaching the teenagers. Work and strive to maintain a heart for parents. Love, encourage, and support them in any way possible. After all, you are here to help their families.

Teen Workers' Conduct Policies

1. Extreme caution and discretion should be used at all times in conducting yourselves with the teenagers.

2. A teen worker should never touch a teen of the opposite sex. It is imperative to avoid all appearance of evil and any cause for accusation.

3. A teen worker should never be alone in a house/room/ secluded area/car with a teenager of the opposite sex.

4. Inappropriate gestures, comments, or suggestive behavior should never occur and will be cause for dismissal from youth work.

5. Men do not counsel girls, and ladies do not counsel boys. If a teen of the opposite sex comes to you for counsel,

please make the youth pastor aware of it. Ladies, deal with girls' problems, and men deal with boys' problems.

6. When making a visit, if the parents are not home, make the visit brief and stay outside. Do not go in the house when parents are not home.

7. Be interested in the parents when you are visiting. Do not seem as though you are only interested in the teen. This may seem suspicious to some people.

8. In the joking, playing, and activities, always maintain a distance and a propriety with the teens of the opposite sex.

9. Make it a personal policy to reach out primarily to those of the same sex. This is why there are both men and ladies working with youth. Never have it appear that you are closer to a certain girl or boy.

10. Conduct that does not follow these policies will be cause for removal from the Youth Ministry.

The Personal Touch

"So being affectionately desirous of you, we were willing to have imparted unto you, not the gospel of God only, but also our own souls, because ye were dear unto us." I Thessalonians 2:8

Introduction:

In too many churches in society today, people, especially teenagers, have become mere statistics. Many churches have grown cold and calloused toward ministering to people. An effective Youth Ministry and effective youth work must always be person to person. The youth worker is primarily here to personally interact with the teens. Whatever the responsibility given, whether it be driving a bus or running an activity, it should always fall second to personal interaction and love for the teens.

As the youth group grows, there is a challenge to love and meet the needs of more kids. For this reason, one or two people cannot accomplish the task. It is imperative that every teenager at every event receives a personal touch. A personal touch can be defined every time a youth worker singles out a young person as an individual, apart from the mass. It is best for the Youth Ministry that every teenager is given the personal touch at least once every week. Mass mailings, flyers, visitor letters, absentee letters, and photocopied handouts do not communicate a personal touch, and nothing is as important to a teenager as being personally loved and encouraged.

In today's society, teenagers are starving for personal attention. Moms and dads have forsaken personal involvement for television, careers, hobbies and toys, and many of the teenagers in the group are longing for someone to reach out personally and invest in their lives.

How is a personal touch communicated? Here are some suggestions for how to effectively touch the lives of the teenagers, personally.

Greet the teens at every meeting.

It is vital that no teenager feels ignored or rejected. The only way to do this is work as a team to greet and welcome every teenager. A high five, handshake, pat on the back, slap on the shoulder, and a smile can do more than you could ever imagine.

Always look the teenagers in the eyes when you are talking to them and when you are communicating with them. This gives a sense of undivided attention, and it lets the teenagers know that they are really cared about.

Send an occasional note.

Every week, look at the list of teens and write five or six notes of encouragement to those the Lord lays on your heart. A note only takes a couple of minutes to write but will have a huge impact. Make these notes personal and encouraging and always make them feel loved.

Remember birthdays.

As a youth department, begin acknowledging birthdays on more occasions than just Sunday mornings. It is important to check the birthday list and send cards and notes. To a teenager, a birthday is the single most important event of the year, and when someone remembers a birthday, it means more than you will ever know.

Have a teenager in your home.

It may be a group of teens or a single teen whom the Lord lays on your heart, but to take a teen out to lunch or have them over for dinner indicates an investment of personal time and shows real love and concern.

Make phone calls every week.

Each week, pull anywhere from 5 to 20 names from your list, take a few minutes, and call the teenagers to tell them they were being thought of and that they are loved.

How to Teach Teenagers God's Truth

1. **Consider what is at stake.**
    What happens in their lives in the future if they do not get what you are trying to give them? If a burden for what the teens need will grow, so will a desire to really get through to them!

2. **Creatively approach the truth.**

    How can one creatively capture their attention and communicate the reality of this truth in an understandable way? Be appropriate but be willing to appear foolish in order to get the truth you teach across.

3. **Connect personally with the listeners.**

    How can a youth leader personally connect?

    a. Study them—attempt in every way possible, to understand their lives.
    b. Eyes—look at them.
    c. Body position—observe physical location as well as movements and habits.
    d. Facial expression—add life to the message.
    e. Heart—connect from the heart: be honest, transparent, open, and sincere.

4. **Create space for feedback.**

    a. From teens in the form of questions and responses
    b. From others who can honestly tell you your strengths and weaknesses in teaching
    c. From the Holy Spirit who will guide you into teaching material
    d. From yourself—not too critical, not too proud, sincerely honest—willing to grow
    e. Get the teens involved in the lesson somehow—rather than just sitting there hearing a lecture. Get them to think and discover the truth with you.

5. **Contain personal and practical illustrations in every lesson.**

    Sincere, humble, real situations can illustrate how you learned God's truth. Be transparent without glamorizing sin and wrong. Be real.

6. **Compel a personal response.**

   a. When preparing a lesson ask yourself two simple questions:

     1. What do I want them to know?

     2. What do I want them to do about it?

   b. Be clear; be specific; put action to what you teach. Give them specific ways to put into practice the truth you have taught.

7. Commit to personal touch outside class.

Be real, genuinely interested, fun, and a friend outside of the class. As relationships outside of class are built, the right to be heard inside of class is earned.

8. Commend yourself and your listeners to God.

Do not ever let the Devil convince you that what you are saying is not making a difference. God's Word will always work in their hearts. Whether you see the results you want to see or not, just keep teaching and let God do the rest.

9. Continually grow personally.

Your best teaching will be from that which God has recently taught you. If you have not learned anything recently, then your teaching will be dry and boring. Read, study, grow, and take the journey yourself.

10. Compliment spiritual growth.

Everyone is motivated by positive affirmation—so are teens when it comes to spiritual growth. How?

   a. Written notes

   b. Loving words

   c. Public praise

   d. Small encouraging gifts

   e. Personal time together

When you see a teen really "getting it," call attention to it in some way. Recognize and praise it. Look for the good and praise it.

Defining A Good Youth Worker

1. **Personally touch the lives of the teens.**
    Purpose: To lead teens to Christ; help them be baptized; and disciple them to grow in their faith.

    a. Visit class rosters.
    b. Call teens by phone.
    c. Write encouraging notes.
    d. Notice them at church.
    e. Be present and friendly at activities.
    f. Be consistent and compassionate.

2. **Be a help and presence in your Sunday class.**
    Purpose: To greet and fellowship with the teens; to help maintain focused attention upon the lesson; to assist with the flow of class time; to help in dealing with any disruptions.

    a. Be organized and prepared for your responsibility.
    b. Greet teens and talk to as many as possible.
    c. Assist the teacher when needed.
    d. Do not talk during the teaching.
    e. Greet teens after class.

3. **Encourage and serve teen parents.**
    Purpose: To be in touch with the whole family and in communication with parents regarding their teens; to encourage and minister to specific needs; and to bridge the gap between the teens and the parents.

    a. Praise the teens to the parents.
    b. Praise the parents to the teens.
    c. Share good news and decisions with the parents that the teens make.
    d. Write parents encouraging notes regularly.
    e. Attend teen parent meetings.
    f. View your ministry as to the whole family.

4. **Assist in youth functions.**

Purpose: To help serve the teens and conduct the activity in a controlled way; to supervise the group; to disciple and fellowship with the teens.

a. If possible, be present.
b. Participate in planning teams and details for youth functions.
c. Be excited about each activity, even if you cannot go.
d. Encourage and enlist teens to go to activities.
e. Be an authority, not just a buddy.

5. **Exhibit a strong Christian example.**

Purpose: To live and conduct your lives as living examples of fully committed Christians in every area of life.

a. Constantly guard your conduct with and without the teens.
b. Balance personal and family life to stay strong.
c. Remember you are constantly being watched.
d. Be above reproach in every way.
e. Behave properly with the opposite sex.
f. Do not act like a teenager; act like a mentor.

Youth Activity Preparation Guide

Introduction:

No part of a youth program can be more productive or disastrous than the activities and retreats of the church youth group. The responsibility of the youth pastor is to organize and coordinate every activity in such a way that they bring glory and honor to the Lord. The following procedures will help accomplish the goals of purposeful teen activities.

I. Planning

A. Plan a yearly calendar.

B. Plan each activity one month in advance (4–5 months for camps and retreats).

C. Clear all proposed activities and counseling with the pastor.

D. Plan for at least one counselor or worker per ten teens.

E. Always stay one step ahead of workers and ten steps ahead of the teens.

F. Develop separate junior high and senior high activities.

G. Visit the site of activity and analyze for safety and activity feasibility.

H. Publicize every activity.

   1. Every teen should receive a flyer and phone call to promote the activity.

   2. Teachers should visit class regulars, and helpers are required to make calls and attend activities.

I. If activity requires equipment, secure it ahead of time.

J. If activity requires a bus, request a bus from the bus director. (Only Class B or higher certified drivers may drive a bus.)

K. If activity has a fee, collect all funds before departure.

L. Never sign a contract without reviewing the contract with the pastor.

M. Never schedule a speaker without the pastor's approval first.

N. Always have an equal number of male and female counselors.

O. Always beware of first aid precautions and have a plan for emergencies.

P. Use Medical Release Forms for all retreats (see CD 16.1).

Q. Always arrive home 10 minutes before your announced time.

II. Perceptiveness

    A. Be perceptive of individual teen attitudes.

        1. Rebellious

        2. Quiet

        NOTE: Look for teens with responsive attitudes to develop as leaders.

    B. Be perceptive of teens who are trying to avoid "the group." Do everything with "groups" and insist that everyone participate.

    C. Remember the "line of sight" policy. Every teen must be kept within the line of sight. If they are ever out of sight and are injured or abducted, the church is responsible.

    D. Be perceptive of what others think about the youth group's testimony. Work hard to maintain a good testimony from within and without.

    E. Be perceptive of the youth workers.

        1. Expect them to be faithful.

        2. Encourage them when they are faithful.

        3. Watch them, and help them "avoid the appearance of evil."

III. Preaching

    A. Every youth activity should have a purpose. Do not have activities for youth workers to relive their youths.

    B. The best way to help is by having a "Bible time" at the end of the activity.

    C. Preaching is not screaming.

    D. Preaching is the impartation of a Bible truth that can help a young person develop spiritually.

    E. Plan the theme of the preaching in conjunction with specific goals for the youth group. Always preach salvation, as many visitors attend each activity.

Conclusion:

These activities must be planned thoroughly. Any questions may be directed to the pastor.

Material Taught to New 7th Graders

Surviving and Thriving in the Youth Group

Welcome to the Lancaster Baptist Youth Group! You will never know how thrilled I am that you are a new part of our great group. I will never forget when I was promoted into 7th grade—it was one of the most exciting and scary times of my life. In so many ways, I wanted to join the youth group, but in so many other ways I was really nervous about doing it.

I was the smallest guy around; I was not very strong; and I knew that I would get teased a little. Then, I was not sure how to act, or how to dress, or what kinds of things to talk about. Looking back—I can see some things that I wish I had not done, and I can see some things that I am glad I did. Either way, somehow I did survive and I am sure that you will too.

To be honest—I want you to do more than just survive; I want you to thrive! I mean I want you to grow, learn, mature, and have more fun than you have ever had. In six years, you will either be dedicated to God and on your way into life with your brain and heart packed and prepared to serve God, or you will be rebellious against God's will with a brain and heart packed full of sin and wrong. The next six years will be filled with decision-making times and needed spiritual growth that you must have to survive and to thrive. Where do you want to be in six years? Do you want to be right with God? Do you want to be doing His will? Do you want to have learned and grown and had a lot of fun? If so, then you will need to understand and do some things ahead of time.

1. Get Serious for God!—*"Remember now thy Creator in the days of thy youth, while the evil days come not, nor the years draw nigh, when thou shalt say, I have no pleasure in them;"* (Ecclesiastes 12:1).

All right, you have had 12 years of goofing off—now it is time to get serious at least about one thing. It is time to be serious about your spiritual life. Seventh grade is the breaking point—either you get serious now, or you probably never will. Now is the time to start listening intently to Pastor's preaching, to Bible study times, and to your class teacher. Now is the time to begin having your daily devotions. Now is the time to decide to get to know God. Now is the time to decide what you believe and why you believe it—and not just because your parents believe it. Talk to Him, prove Him, and learn about Him. Now is the time for you to make God your number-one priority. Do not allow yourself to slide through the youth group with no concern for spiritual things. First of all, you will feel out of place because the majority of the youth group teens are serious about God. Second, you will miss the real joy of being a teen and you will go into life completely unprepared. Get serious!

2. Get Fanatically Involved!—*"Whatsoever thy hand findeth to do, do it with thy might; for there is no work, nor device, nor knowledge, nor wisdom, in the grave, whither thou goest"* (Ecclesiastes 9:10). Hey! You have only got one shot at being in the youth group! Be as involved as you possibly can. Get all you can, while you can! Do everything that is available and be excited about it. If it is a picnic, a game, a retreat, or a ditch-digging party—remember, it is for you. Do not miss out on the fun. Everything our group does is planned and scrutinized so that you will grow spiritually and so that you will have a lot of fun—so why stay home? Be a faithful, active part of your youth group. Your excitement and involvement is what will keep our youth group great!

Be a youth group fanatic! Be at everything and be excited about it! I promise that you will have a lot more fun that way, and you will grow and learn more too. In six years as you walk across that platform to get your high school diploma, you will be able to look back at your youth group years and be glad that you were involved.

3. Get a Permanently Good Attitude!—*"He that hath no rule over his own spirit is like a city that is broken down, and without walls"*

(Proverbs 25:28). *"A merry heart doeth good like a medicine: but a broken spirit drieth the bones"* (Proverbs 17:22). *"He that is slow to anger is better than the mighty; and he that ruleth his spirit than he that taketh a city"* (Proverbs 16:32). *"Create in me a clean heart, O God; and renew a right spirit within me"* (Psalm 51:10). Your spirit is your attitude. Your attitude is the way you look at life and then the way you respond to it. The next few years will bring a lot of changes. The changes are not all that bad if you look at them the right way and respond to them the right way. Many times a very nice and respectable sixth grader becomes a troubled and rebellious eighth grader. Why? Because somewhere along about seventh grade he took a different approach to life. An approach that left God, Mom, Dad, and Pastor in the dust. An approach that says, "I am going to do things my way no matter what anybody says." Suddenly he becomes rebellious and troubled.

With this type of person, every youth activity is stupid, all of the Bible teaching is boring, Mom and Dad, and Pastor are despised, and all the "good teens" are jerks. Guess who this person makes friends with?—the trouble makers. Do you know what their life is like?—problems! Problems at school, fights with friends, in trouble with teachers and parents, failing grades, rock music, bad jokes, grounded at home—everybody seems to always be on their case; nobody can trust them; they seem to get blamed for almost everything. In short, their life is miserable—they do not love God, they do not have any good friends, and they are missing the real fun of being right and doing right like everybody else in the youth group.

Do you know where this person ends up? Remember Cain? Remember Lot? This teenager will end up running from God like Jonah. Before too many years, he will either turn and get his heart right or he will run away and be destroyed by sin. Again I ask you, where do you want to be in six years? Keep a good attitude! No matter what changes come, no matter how tough the problem, no matter how hard it is—keep a good attitude! Keep a good attitude toward parents, toward teachers, toward youth workers, toward Pastor and most of all, toward God.

4. Get Prepared for a Little Teasing—*"Great peace have they which love thy law: and nothing shall offend them"* (Psalm 119:165). We all hate to get it, but we all love to deliver it. Well, now is your turn to get a little. Suddenly you are going from being the top dog of the elementary group to being the littlest pup of the youth group. A little teasing is part of the territory. Be ready for it, and laugh at it when you get it. The seventh grader that gets upset and mad will be marked. One of the best ways to make a friend is to show that you can handle a little fun.

Don't worry about any initiations or radical forms of seventh grade torture. Our teens are not into that, but they are into joking around. Whatever you do—don't take it personally if you get teased. Just laugh at it. Next year you will be the one doing the teasing.

5. Get a Sensitivity Toward Your Parents—*"Honour thy father and mother; (which is the first commandment with promise;)"* (Ephesians 6:2). It happens too often. A person turns 12 and then he goes crazy for friends and fun and being "grown-up," and he flat leaves his parents in the dust. Do not do that! Remember, for 12 long years they have taken care of you, fed you, burped you, changed your stinking diapers, clothed you, and loved you—they deserve a little more than a pat on the head and a, "Thanks Mom, now can I have the car keys?" The easy mistake to make is to get so wrapped up in you, your friends, and your "new" status as a teenager that you completely forget your parents. Remember, they need time with you, they like being with you, and you need to be with them. Seeing you grow up is hard enough on them, don't kick 'em while they are down. Your parents need your love and attention! They want nothing more than to see you have a great time in the youth group, but I can guarantee they will be making you stay home and wash dishes if you forget to love, respect, honor, and obey them.

In six years you will be standing, getting a diploma, crying about how much you love your parents—shortly after that, you will be leaving and going to college where there will be no parents. Then you will wish you had loved them more. Love them NOW!

6. Get Barricaded Against Peer Pressure—*"Blessed is the man that walketh not in the counsel of the ungodly, nor standeth in the way of sinners, nor sitteth in the seat of the scornful. But his delight is in the law of the LORD; and in his law doth he meditate day and night. And he shall be like a tree planted by the rivers of water, that bringeth forth his fruit in his season; his leaf also shall not wither; and whatsoever he doeth shall prosper"* (Psalm 1:1–3). Peer pressure is one of the biggest battles you will face over the next few years. Thank goodness that in our group there is a good peer pressure. Peer pressure is doing something because someone else is. We all want to be accepted—we all want people to like us—we all want friends. Over the next years, you will have many opportunities to make a choice. The choice will be to do what others are doing so that they will like you, or to do what is right at the risk of losing your friends. It is a tough choice, and unless you are prepared for it—you will make the wrong choice. You see—that kind of peer pressure is a lie. It is based on the lie that good friends will only like you if you do what they are doing, and on the lie that if you don't do it—you won't have any friends!

First of all, it helps if you choose friends that will help you do right. Warning: stay away from those that you can tell have bad attitudes. They will not help you; they will hurt you. Second, a true friend would never ask you or pressure you to do wrong. Third, when you do take a stand for right at the risk of losing your friends, God always honors that by giving you better friends!

When you feel pressure to be something, do something, or say something that you know is not right—stand up and do right. When someone is bad-talking authority, talking wrong, or pressuring you in some wrong way—you do right and let God take care of the friends. And over the next six years, don't ever let yourself get stuck in the mode of doing things just because others are; this includes both good and bad things. You do what you do because God wants you to.

7. Get Buckled in for the Six Most Exciting Years of Your Life! — *"Let no man despise thy youth; but be thou an example of the believers, in word, in conversation, in charity, in spirit, in faith, in purity"* (I Timothy 4:12). The next six years can be awesome if you want them to be. They could be a nightmare if you make the wrong choices and go the wrong direction. You've only got one chance to be a teenager—make it the best it can be. Any time you need anything—let me know. Get ready for more fun than you have ever had!

PART THREE

Going Beyond:
Outreach Ministries

CHAPTER SEVENTEEN

Bus Ministry

"Whosoever therefore shall humble himself as this little child, the same is greatest in the kingdom of heaven. And whoso shall receive one such little child in my name receiveth me."
Matthew 18:4–5

It is interesting to observe, in many Baptist churches in America, that we have elevated certain ministries and forms of outreach to the point they have become a "badge of honor," or in some cases, even a litmus test for fellowship. It is my conviction that we should never support missionaries or develop a Bus Ministry simply to gain the acceptance of a group of peers or because we want to appear to be successful in the ministry. These outreach endeavors must be done as we respond to the leading of God's Holy Spirit and because of a true burden for souls.

The Lancaster Baptist Church Bus Ministry began about four or five months after our arrival in Lancaster because of the burden of a godly new member in the church. Our drive-in crowd attendance had neared the one hundred mark and one of our new members, Brother Eldon Lofgren, approached me and asked if we could use an old van to begin picking up boys and girls. On the first day of the Bus Ministry we brought in two riders to Sunday school. Since then, thousands of young people and adults have accepted Christ through this ministry, and hundreds arrive at our church every week.

Those who have had experience in the Bus Ministry know there is no ministry as rewarding as working on a bus route. While many churches have trimmed or deleted the Bus Ministry from their budget, we believe the Bus Ministry to be as viable and needed as ever before.

Mark 1 gives us insight into just one day in the life of Jesus. Our Saviour's example reminds us that real ministry involves real work. Christ's day begins when He is told that his cousin, John the Baptist, was imprisoned. He walks into Galilee, preaching to all who will listen, and sees Simon and Andrew out fishing. He tells them to follow Him, and they immediately abandon their fishing careers to do so. Walking a little further, He meets James and John, who also leave their jobs as fishermen to follow Him.

As they enter into Capernaum, Jesus immediately begins preaching in the temple and casts a demon out of a man. After they leave the synagogue, they enter Simon's house and find his mother-in-law sick with a fever. After Christ heals her, people from all around gather at the door, bringing the sick and demon-possessed to be healed, and He heals them. Finally, they are all ready to rest, but rather than sleeping in a little from the busyness of the previous day, Christ is found the next morning *"rising up a great while before day...and [he] departed into a solitary place, and there prayed."* Our Saviour certainly knew what it meant to work!

As we seek to imitate Christ in our work, let us remember how He treated the children who came to Him. After a full day of preaching and healing, when His disciples wanted to send the children away so their Master could rest, He said, *"Suffer the little children to come unto me, and forbid them not:"* (Mark 10:14).

When we are at our weakest from fatigue, sickness, or personal problems, we still have the privilege of ministering to the children on our buses. Many of them come from broken homes and abusive families; riding the bus is the highlight of their entire week. They know that when they come to church, they will be loved, protected, and cared for, and we must not let them down. We need to take every opportunity we can to talk individually with the children. We can help them find their places in their Bibles or share ours so they can follow along during the message. Small acts of kindness like these will not soon be forgotten.

We never know which of the troublesome teenagers will grow up to be a preacher because we took the time to mentor him. The same child who kicks everyone that sits by him may very well become a missionary one day, and God chose you to lead him to Christ on a bus ride.

The next time you become discouraged about a child's behavior, try looking at him through the Lord's eyes. In God's eyes, that child is a precious soul for which He cared enough to die. In God's eyes, that child is as important as you are. God sees the seeds of potential that lie in each little heart surrendered to Him, and it is our duty to help those seeds blossom and take root in God's Word. To be an effective bus worker, you do not have to have a great singing voice, an outgoing personality, or incredible speaking skills. You must simply be yielded to God's service and allow Him to love the children on your bus route *through* you. The guidelines will help bus workers and captains alike to establish proper systems and safeguards on their bus routes. Many of the guidelines and principles contained in the following handbook reflect legal advice gleaned over the years to protect churches from being negligent. We highly recommend that churches operating bus ministries attend an annual legal seminar sponsored by the Christian Law Association (727-399-8300).

The Bus Ministry

Dear Friend,

I want to welcome you to the Bus Ministry! It is a privilege to be able to serve the Lord here in any way or fashion. Through this area of service, I pray that you will grow spiritually as you meet the needs of others.

As you serve in this ministry, I would like you to keep in mind Colossians 3:23–24, "And whatsoever ye do, do it heartily, as to the Lord, and not unto men; Knowing that of the Lord ye shall receive the reward of the inheritance: for ye serve the Lord Christ." As you serve the Lord in the Bus Ministry, be mindful that your service is unto the Lord and whatever we do for Him should be our best.

The thought of "commitment to excellence" comes to my mind when I read those verses. As servants of God, our attitude toward the Lord's work should be on a different level of excellence because of who we are serving—the Lord.

Finally, let me express how excited I am that the Lord has led you to serve in this ministry, and may the Lord bless you because of your faithfulness in this area of service.

Your friend,

Pastor

Purpose

The ultimate goal of all ministries is to impact the lost with the Gospel of Christ. Because you represent the Lord in this ministry, it is important that you set up some standards for those who participate. Everyone is a leader in some way. Each bus worker should be the right kind of example before the people who ride the bus each week.

Also, you must remember that your community always has their eyes focused on you. Because of this, remember to uphold these standards as you endeavor to serve the Lord.

It has been said, "People would rather see a sermon than hear a sermon." Truly you need to understand that you will teach by example, whether good or bad.

You must realize that as a servant of the Lord, teacher, and preacher of the Word of God, you have the awesome responsibility of shaping lives for eternity. The church leadership requirements are to be adhered to by all teachers and workers.

Job Description for Bus Captains:

1. Meet all the leadership requirements of the Bus Ministry.

2. Attend workers' meetings, clinics, etc.

3. Keep accurate and updated records (attendance, salvations, baptisms, enrollment, discipline problems, accidents/injuries).

4. Pray for riders and their families, your driver, and your workers on a regular basis.

5. Submit names of potential bus workers to the bus director.

6. Follow up on all absentees every week.

7. Visit your riders on a weekly basis.

8. Maintain proper order on the bus.

9. Make sure the driver has conducted a safety check of the bus before you begin picking up your riders.

10. Make sure your bus is clean before and after your route.

11. Make sure you have the full name, complete address, and telephone number of all riders before they enter the bus (permission slips).

12. Keep the riders in the line of sight of bus workers at all times.

13. Always strive to improve your program on the bus (variety, exciting games and prizes, relevant Bible lessons, etc.)

14. The aisle of your bus must be kept clear.

15. Remind workers of the "no-touch" policy. (No child sitting on a male worker's lap. Only female workers are allowed to give comfort or attention. Never use any form of physical discipline.)

16. Make sure the procedures for "pick up" and "drop off" at church and home are carefully observed. (Outlined later in this chapter.)

17. Notify the bus director of any problems on your bus (discipline, parents, workers, mechanical, etc.).

18. Express appreciation to your workers for their help and support.

19. Make sure all teachers have correct information on each student.

20. Observe age limits for bus riders. Do not allow any riders under age 5 without an adult guardian.

21. Take part in any special outreach programs such as Open House or Country Harvest Days.

22. Support the pastor in any changes in the Bus Ministry.

Job Description for Bus Workers:

1. Meet all the leadership requirements of the Bus Ministry.
2. Attend workers' meetings, clinics, etc.
3. Pray for riders and their families, your driver, bus captain, and other bus workers on a regular basis.
4. Be on time for bus visitation and for the actual bus route.
5. Help keep control of the riders.
6. Help visit your riders.
7. Teach the riders to appreciate their bus captain.
8. Be careful to observe all "pick up" and "drop off" procedures on the bus.
9. Be familiar with and observe the "no-touch" policies.
10. Help keep accurate records of new riders (full name, complete address, phone number, etc.).
11. Notify the bus captain of any problems on the bus (discipline, parents, mechanical, etc.).
12. Notify the bus captain of any changes in your schedule (illness, vacation, resignation, etc.).
13. Always help clean the bus before and after your route.
14. Take part in any special outreach programs such as Open House and Country Harvest Days.
15. Support the pastor in any changes in the Bus Ministry.

Job Description for Bus Drivers:

1. Meet all leadership requirements of the Bus Ministry.

2. Attend workers' meetings, clinics, etc.

3. Pray for riders and their families, your captain, and other bus workers on a regular basis.

4. Be early for the actual bus route and complete a pre-trip inspection on your bus before the bus route.

5. Be sure the bus and its equipment are in safe and good working condition before leaving the church.

6. Be aware of and observe all traffic laws.

7. Be careful to observe all "pick up" and "drop off" procedures on the bus.

8. Be familiar with and observe the "no-touch" policies.

9. Notify the bus captain of any behavior issues on the bus.

10. Notify the bus director of any mechanical troubles with any equipment and/or vehicles.

11. Ensure that the bus is clean and fueled after the bus route.

12. Follow and support the bus captain with any decisions made on the route.

13. Notify the bus director of any changes in your schedule (illness, vacation, resignation, etc.).

14. Support the pastor in any changes in the Bus Ministry.

Procedures for Visitation

1. Never talk to children on the streets without permission from their parents first. (Basic greetings like "Hello" or "Hi, Kids!" are permitted.)

2. Bus workers should never go into any child's house when parents are not home. (Wear I.D. tags if available.)

3. Always introduce yourself and your church immediately.

4. Always be kind, even if the people are not interested in sending their child on the bus.

5. Remember you are representing the church and, most importantly, Jesus Christ.

6. Follow up on all absentees every week.

7. Make each visit quick but friendly.

8. Remember, the parents are always right.

9. If you have a problem child on your bus, deal with the problem immediately.

   a. First, warn the child you will not pick him up next week.

   b. Second, if the child continues, suspend him for two weeks.

   c. Third, if the child comes back after his suspension and still is a problem, visit the parents that week and tell them: "We think that it would be best if _____ would be brought to church by some other means. For some reason, _____ does not like the program we have on the bus. Maybe the answer for your child is for you to bring them to church."

   d. Please keep accurate information when warnings are given to families (e.g., date, offense, nature of warning, etc.).

10. Always try to get address information on your new riders when you visit them during the week.

11. While visiting, you must have a partner with you at all times.

12. While visiting when parents are not home, do not carry on a conversation with the child. Tell him you will come back or call him on the phone later.

13. Get parents to sign the permission slip that authorizes their child to ride the bus to church (see CD 17.1).

14. Be consistent in your visitation time on your route.

15. Go straight to your bus route. (Do not let small errands take half of your day.)

16. Keep every visit brief.

17. Tell of your love for the children.

18. Be "folksy" with families.

    a. Make them feel important (use their names).
    b. Find something to discuss that interests them.

19. Get to the point of your visit.

    a. Look for an opportunity to share the Gospel.
    b. Invite them to church.

20. Pray with them before you leave.

21. Look for new riders while visiting your regulars.

Procedures for Pick Up

1. The bus comes to a complete stop.

2. The bus driver disengages the gears.

3. Then, ONLY the bus driver opens the door.

4. The runner goes to the house and picks up the children who will be riding for that day. (Runners must be 9th grade or above.)

5. Use your time wisely as you walk back to the bus.

    a. Talk to the children.
    b. Make them feel important.
    c. Tell them you prayed for them this week.
    d. Tell them how much you love them.

e. Praise them (tie, dress, bringing Bible, coming to church, etc.).

6. Have a bus worker mark each rider's hand with your bus route number.

7. Check the rider's name off on your roster as he gets on the bus.

8. Seat the rider on the bus.

9. Bus driver then proceeds to the next stop.

10. No new children under the age of five are allowed on the bus. The only exception is if a child comes with a parent.

11. Every bus must have a female adult worker.

12. Never pick up a child who is screaming before they get on the bus.

13. No child is to be brought to church unless you have his full name, complete address, and telephone number. Do not put the child on the bus if you do not have this important information.

Procedures on the Bus

1. The bus captain should always be in control of his bus riders and program.

2. Every rider must be seated.

3. Never exceed the capacity of the bus.

4. Arms and heads must stay inside the windows.

5. You must conduct some kind of bus program on the bus.

   a. This will help to eliminate discipline problems with your riders.
   b. The time on the bus is a great opportunity to influence children for the Lord.

   c. It is a time for training the children.

   d. It builds an atmosphere of fun.

   e. It helps the children enjoy the ride to church.

6. Remember, having a fun and exciting bus program will eliminate most of the discipline problems on your bus.

7. The aisle must be clear.

8. Always calm down your program as you get closer to church. Your Sunday school teachers will greatly appreciate you for this.

9. It would be wise to have the smaller children sit toward the front of the bus and the older ones toward the back.

10. Workers must remember—there is to be no yelling on the bus.

11. The "no-touch" rule must be adhered to at all times on the bus by all male workers.

12. No child should be sitting on the lap of a male bus worker.

13. If a child needs some comfort or attention, only a female bus worker is allowed to give the child this comfort or attention.

Procedures for Drop Off at Church

1. If you need to back a bus into its stall to unload, have two spotters help the driver back up. This will help eliminate any accidents.

2. No children are allowed off the bus:

   a. Until the bus comes to a complete stop, the gears are disengaged and the emergency brake is applied.

   b. Until the Sunday school teachers are in their places.

3. There will be a designated unloading area for the buses. Only one bus at a time should unload its riders. This will be done in the order of arrival unless the bus director or Sunday school superintendent indicates otherwise.

4. Five-year olds should be walked to their class by a worker.

5. The remaining bus riders may then be unloaded by bus workers according to age.

6. The bus workers are required to help their riders get to their classes.

7. Every bus child must be in the **line of sight** of an adult worker.

8. Male bus workers are allowed to offer a hand to assist people off the bus if they require assistance.

Procedures for Pick Up at Church

1. A worker from each bus should go to the five-year olds class and pick them up.

2. For all other grades, the classroom teachers and workers will escort the children to the appropriate buses.

3. No child will be released from a class without an adult worker assisting the child to the bus.

4. As the children are getting on your bus, you must have a worker checking names so you know that you have all of your riders.

5. Once a child gets on a bus, that child should not get off the bus for any reason.

6. A final check should be made before the bus leaves to drop off the riders.

Procedures for Drop Off at Home

1. The bus comes to a complete stop.

2. The driver disengages the gears.

3. The hazard lights are turned on.

4. The emergency brake is applied.

5. The bus worker gets off the bus first.

6. The riders get off the bus second.

7. If you have to cross the street, walk in front of the bus with the children.

8. The worker should walk the child to the door of the house to make sure the child gets in safely.

9. For NO reason are the riders allowed to get off the bus by themselves without an adult supervisor.

10. Do not leave a child in an unattended home.

11. Please make sure the bus has been swept out and the windows put up when your route is finished.

Other Important Procedures

1. A bus worker will be standing at the unloading zone. His responsibilities are as follows:
   a. Write down arrival time.
   b. Write down your attendance.
   c. Video the unloading of your riders.

2. Each bus must have at least one female worker.

3. All church bus/van drivers must have the appropriate driver's license to operate any of the church's vehicles.

4. Make sure that the parents are aware if the children are going to a separate or different location for Sunday school.

5. All workers must be approved by the bus director before they are allowed to do anything on your bus.

6. Do not talk to anyone concerning working on your bus. If you think someone would be a good bus worker, submit his name to the bus director.

7. If someone approaches you concerning working on your bus, please inform him that he must see the bus director.

8. Be protective of your bus route! Do not put your whole bus route in jeopardy for one problem child.

9. If you are ever threatened by a parent, please refer them to the bus director or to the pastor.

10. While you are visiting your bus route, never enter a home when the parents are not in view.

11. While visiting, you must have a partner with you, preferably someone of the same gender.

12. Whenever the driver has to back up, always have at least one spotter.

Procedures for Follow-Up on Children

I. The Mandate of Follow-Up (Matthew 28:19–20)

A. Christ's commission to us in Matthew 28 gives a three-fold responsibility. This commission was Christ's direct command to us, not an option.

    1. *"Go teach"*—This means to go make disciples. In other words, evangelize and lead them to Christ.

2. *"Baptizing them"*—The second step is to be baptized, publicly identifying with Christ's death, burial, and resurrection.

3. *"Teaching them"*—The third step is to train and teach them God's Word so they may grow.

B. Acts 2:41–42 gives us the biblical order of the Christian life.

1. Received Jesus as Saviour
2. Were baptized
3. Added to the church

   a. To be grounded in doctrine

   b. To have Christian fellowship

   c. To participate in the local church for growth and service

II. The Method of Follow-Up

A. The four-fold purpose of follow-up

1. Renew contact—It is important that you visit to help them renew the decisions in their minds by seeing you again.

2. Re-enforce their decisions—You want to review the decisions they made and make sure they understood them.

3. Reassure their faith—Many times, between the time they accept Christ and the time of your next contact, the Devil has already planted doubts. You need to give them Scripture to assure them of their salvation.

4. Re-establish steps of growth—You want to cover assurance of salvation, baptism, Bible reading and study, prayer, witnessing, and church attendance. The basics and progressive steps of the Christian life are essential for growth.

B. How to do a baptism follow-up call on children

   1. Setting up the call

      a. It may be possible to contact the parents and arrange a time when you can visit.

      b. How you speak to the parents is very important. When you call, introduce yourself by giving your name, church, and your relationship with their child. Example: "Hello, Mr. Davis, my name is Bill Smith, and I am Johnny's Sunday school teacher at _____. The reason I am calling is that I have some exciting news about Johnny and wanted to stop by and share with you a wonderful decision he made in class recently."

   2. When you arrive at the home, whether or not you set up an appointment, follow these guidelines.

      a. Introduce yourself at the door.

      b. Ask about the child and the family; be folksy for a few minutes.

      c. Get to the point of the visit.

         (1.) State the reason you came. Example: "As you know, I said I had something to share with you regarding a decision your child made recently."

         (2.) Explain how you taught or the student heard a lesson from the Bible, then it was explained how he could be sure he was on his way to Heaven. Explain that their child accepted Jesus Christ's death, burial, and resurrection as the payment for sin.

   3. Using Acts 2:41–42 (people are less likely to argue against Scripture), explain the pattern God

gave us in the verses—salvation, baptism, church membership.

4. Then explain baptism using the baptism brochure, emphasizing that it is a public identification with Christ and a step of obedience to His command. Explain that it does not wash away sins or help one get to Heaven.

5. Reassure the parents no one is baptized unless he understands what baptism is.

6. As you explain this to the parents and child, be sure the child also understands.

   a. Use hand motions to show going under and coming back up.

   b. Use a wedding ring as an object lesson to explain the purpose of baptism. (It is a symbol of marriage, but just because you put one on does not mean you are married.)

7. Explain the procedure on the day of their baptism.

   a. Come down front to Pastor at the invitation.

   b. You or a personal worker will accompany the child to the changing rooms.

   c. Special gowns and towels are provided for them.

   d. Parents are encouraged to come and watch.

   e. Mention that baptisms are video taped on the service videos and can be purchased. They can also take photographs.

8. Be sure the child understands and the parents agree. Have them sign the permission slip and turn it in with the decision card for filing (see CD 2.1 for Baptism Permission Slip).

9. Be sure to thank the parents for their time.

C. Negative responses

1. If parents are negative, do not give up, but try again in a month or two. In the meantime, encourage the child to grow in his Christian faith.
2. If the child does not understand, then continue to work with him.
3. Teach about baptism once a month during your program.

Procedures for Baptism Visits

1. The participants for baptism are those who are saved.

2. The purpose of baptism

   a. Step of obedience
   b. Step of faith

3. The pattern for baptism is found in Acts 2:41—immediately after salvation.

4. The plan for a baptism call

   a. Catch the importance of the new believer taking that first step of baptism!
   b. Express your appreciation to the parent for allowing the child to come to church.
   c. Share with them how their child is growing and participating in class.
   d. Share with them the truths that their child has been learning.
   e. Explain the important decision that their child made to accept Jesus Christ as his personal Saviour.
   f. Share with them what baptism is and how their child can make that next step for Christ special.
   g. Try to get them to commit to it.
   h. Invite them to come to the service where they can share this special time in the life of their child.

i. Ease all of their fears by explaining what will take place when their child is baptized.

j. Express your love for the family and how much you are looking forward to seeing their child follow the Lord in baptism. Close in prayer.

Visitation and Record Keeping

1. Consistency

    a. Unsaved parents appreciate consistent concern for their children.

    b. Lead the children as you are led by the Holy Spirit.

2. Faithfulness

    a. You have to be everything you are trying to get your children to be.

    b. Continually pray over all names on the roll.

    "As every man hath received the gift, even so minister the same one to another, as good stewards of the manifold grace of God." I Peter 4:10

3. Manners

    a. Much work can be wasted by poor manners.

    "Behold, I send you forth as sheep in the midst of wolves: be ye therefore wise as serpents, and harmless as doves." Matthew 10:16

    b. Avoid the "interview" syndrome. Listen for details about the family that may help later in witnessing.

    c. Do not assume families are "traditional."

4. Importance of Good Record Keeping

    a. They save time and money.

    b. They prevent embarrassing situations.

    c. Make sure necessary data is current and available.

    d. Use system to track absentees.

Procedures for Discipline

Always act in love, do not proceed in anger, and do not yell at any time.

1. If the child has a discipline problem, give him a verbal WARNING.

2. If the problem persists, give them a second WARNING and discuss the problem with his parents.

3. If the problem still persists, restrict him from riding the bus for two weeks.

4. If the problem arises, kindly ask his parents to bring him to church, and let him know he can no longer ride the bus.

5. You must document each disciplinary act you take. Make sure you turn this in to your Bus Ministry director.

6. There are no exceptions to these procedures, unless permitted by the bus director.

Keys to Unlock Salvation to Children

1. Dealing with a Child:
   Matthew 19:13–15
   Matthew 18:3

2. Six Keys to Dealing with a Child

   a. Scriptural (use Bible)—do not use terms like: "ask Jesus into your heart"
   b. Involvement (one-on-one)—ask questions when dealing with a child
   c. Mindful—be aware of reaction, understanding, age, attention
   d. Patience—do not rush through plan of salvation
   e. Lead gently—do not force or scare, threaten or bribe

     f. Explanation of terms (use simple words)—explain again. Use literal terms.

  3. The A-B-C's of Salvation

     a. Acknowledge they are a sinner/agree (Romans 3:23 or 6:23)

     b. Believe—Jesus died for their sins and rose from the grave

     c. Call on the Lord (Romans 10:13)

Forms

A folder with all necessary forms is kept on each bus. It can include Bus Rider Permission Slips (see CD 17.1), Captain's Report Forms (see CD 17.2), Bus Decision Cards (see CD 17.3), and Incident Report Forms (see CD 14.5).

CHAPTER EIGHTEEN

Open House Sunday

"And the lord said unto the servant,
Go out into the highways and hedges, and
compel them to come in, that my house may be filled."
Luke 14:23

It is my firm belief that every church should do its best to impact its entire area with the Gospel of Christ. Because of this belief, we conduct an annual special day at Lancaster Baptist Church called "Open House Sunday."

One of the primary goals of Open House Sunday is to saturate our entire valley with the Gospel of Jesus Christ and an invitation to attend Lancaster Baptist Church. In the early years, we would attempt to saturate entire neighborhoods. In recent years, we have saturated the entire population of three or four cities around us. The principle of saturation evangelism is vital for a church that wants to truly make an impact on its area for Christ.

Open House Sunday is the single biggest evangelistic outreach day of the year for Lancaster Baptist Church. This one Sunday is the culmination of months of prayerful planning and preparation.

The focus of the day is to bring as many first-time visitors to church as possible and to present the Gospel as clearly as possible. A secondary goal is to involve the entire church family as a team in bringing guests and conducting the day.

Though every year Open House Sunday varies slightly, the general approach includes one month of advertising on TV, newspaper, radio, billboards, community posters, etc. Two weeks prior to the Open House, special doorknocking brochures are put into use and a two-week saturation campaign is begun with the church family. During this two-week span, soulwinning is held every morning and every night with the goal being to knock on every door in our valley within two weeks (approximately 80,000 doors).

The final Saturday prior to the Open House wraps up the soulwinning campaign with a breakfast, a rally, and one final community blitz. It is usually our goal to get the entire church family to be a part of soulwinning on that morning. It is one of the most exciting times of the year to sense the anticipation at this particular soulwinning rally. Later that evening, the entire church family gathers again for a special time of prayer and testimonies.

On Open House Sunday, every ministry attempts to increase its outreach and attendance. Buses are added to the Bus Ministry; special services are held for teens, children, Spanish, etc. Most of our willing church members are assigned to help in ministry on that day which makes room for visitors in the church service. Over the weeks prior, city officials, law enforcement officers, and elected officials are all invited and committed to come to church on that day.

The morning service is meticulously planned from start to finish and includes familiar hymns, songs about salvation, special presentations to guests, and a crystal clear salvation message and invitation. Counselors are ready, and God always gives a great response to the labor of His people. There is nothing quite like seeing lost people come to Christ by the dozens in this kind of special service.

After the service, the visitors are usually invited to lunch on the campus where they can meet folks in our church family and learn more about the Lord. Every year, people accept Christ even during this luncheon. Across the property and even sometimes in rented locations, special services are held, the Gospel is preached, and decisions are made for Christ. By the day's end, the entire church family gathers for the evening service where reports are given, testimonies are shared, and the results of the day are enjoyed.

It is at this point that the Open House follow-up effort begins—an effort to personally visit and follow up on every visitor. This follow-up usually lasts for several months and careful tracking is done weekly to account for the awesome stewardship that God blesses us with on Open House Sunday. Not one life can fall through the cracks, and it is often in the weeks after Open House that the greatest fruit is seen in additional salvations, baptisms, new members, and growing new Christians.

The Open House Sunday is a church-wide effort to "go the extra mile" in fulfilling the Great Commission—from start to finish, and God has blessed it miraculously over the years.

Here are some practical thoughts on hosting an Open House Sunday.

1. **Begin with a Pastoral Planning Meeting.**
    Open House Sunday usually begins four to six months in advance with a creative planning meeting of the pastoral staff. This meeting is often off property away from phones and interruptions, and is completely dedicated to prayer and idea gathering for this special day. Over the years, the Lord has given direction and clarity through this all-day meeting, and He has also stirred our hearts in prayer and discussion. The ideas generated in a meeting like this can vary from advertising themes, to special guests to invite, to special services or locations. From this meeting, the

pastoral staff begins to put the leg work into the ideas that were settled on.

2. **Create an Organizational Book.**

This book contains every area of responsibility for the day with a list of those who should be asked or enlisted to help with each area. The goal of this book is to create an exhaustive list of responsibilities from decorations, to music, to food preparations, and then to meticulously assign every member of your church family to an area of service. Each responsibility will have a leader who will then contact every member on his list to personally ask for his help. While not everyone is always interested in helping, within a month or so from the Open House Sunday, a majority of the church family has been enlisted to an area of service.

3. **Develop an Advertising Theme and Strategy.**

Your community needs a theme that they will see from every different direction. Some of the themes we have used over the years are: "Experience the Difference," "Be Our Guest," "Celebrate Freedom" (more of a patriotic theme during war time, etc.), "A Million Smiles and Counting," "Be Refreshed." Once the theme is chosen, a generous advertising budget and strategy is developed. This theme is placed in TV spots, radio spots, on billboards, on posters, and on doorknocking tracts. One of the most effective advertising methods is a simple business card that our church family can carry in their pockets and hand out as they go about their day.

The goal of the early advertising is to prepare the way for the doorknocking campaign. By the time the door knockers arrive, most of the community has already heard about the day, which makes people much more responsive at the door.

The key to this advertising campaign is to have attractive materials so that people actually read them. Catch their attention and have a high standard of excellence with these materials.

Finally, be sure to take advantage of free advertising. Send out public service announcements. Ask your local paper to do a story about the day. Get on a local radio or TV talk show. Use any idea the Lord gives you to get the word out.

4. **Assign Every Responsibility to a Leader.**
    These leaders could be staff or lay leaders, but every area must have an owner, and every area must be in progress shortly after your planning meeting. This will give plenty of time for preparation and execution of every area of responsibility.

5. **Conduct Follow-Up Meetings.**
    At least once a month, and more frequently as the day draws nearer, the leaders need to meet together to track progress, to pray, and to communicate on vital details.

6. **Host a Church-Wide Organizational Meeting.**
    During this meeting, the pastor hands out the organization book, goes through the vision and plan for the day, and shares with the church family what God can do on this one day. Afterwards (and for several weeks prior to the Open House), the pastor preaches on soulwinning and passionately challenges the church family to be involved in reaching the community. Nothing stirs the heart and motivates the church family like the right message from God's man.

7. **Organize and Execute an Exhaustive Doorknocking Campaign.**
    Map out your city, create individual maps of doorknocking areas, order more tracts than you believe you can use,

and then lead the church family in knocking on as many doors as possible. Over the years, we have never set an attendance goal for this special day, but we have set "work goals." Rather than say how many you hope to have in church, set goals for how many doors you hope to knock on, how many soulwinners you hope to enlist, and how many church members you hope to involve. Give your best effort and leave the results up to God.

8. **Invite Special Guests and City Leaders.**

Six to eight weeks in advance, the pastor should personally invite key leaders to be a part of the Open House Sunday. When appropriate, you might even invite your city Mayor to give a word of greeting or you might present these guests with a gift Bible.

9. **Host a Saturday Morning Soulwinning Rally.**

This rally is the culmination of the doorknocking campaign. The morning begins with breakfast and fellowship. The rally begins with music, instructions for door knockers, and then a challenge from the pastor. During the rally, the pastoral staff works to partner experienced soulwinners with new soulwinners. At dismissal, every doorknocking team receives a map and a bundle of tracts for the morning.

10. **Host an All-Church Prayer Meeting.**

One of the sweetest times prior to Open House Sunday is this prayer meeting. At the beginning, testimonies are shared of salvations in the community, people who have committed to come, and prayer requests for the day. Afterward, the church family breaks up into groups of two or three to spend a season in prayer asking the Lord to bless Open House Sunday.

11. **Provide Lunch for Every Visitor.**

    This will require some investment, but over the years this luncheon has proven to be a great tool for reaching the lost, meeting visitors, and paving the way for future follow-up. If the budget is not available, consider asking your church family to host their guests to lunch after the service.

12. **Prayerfully Execute a Quality Day.**

    From the parking lot, to the nursery, to the service, to the luncheon—make this day excellent in every way. Make your Gospel message clear, the invitation simple, the music strong, and the fellowship sweet. Ask the Lord to work in every heart and do your best to truly "roll out the red carpet" to your community on this day.

13. **Meticulously Track Follow-Up.**

    Whether you have 10 visitors or 500, God has entrusted you with a stewardship. Many of your visitors will be saved during a follow-up visit, and all of the long term fruit of this day will be a result of your careful follow-up. The week after the Open House is somewhat of a recovery week, but it is also critical as every visitor is accounted for and assigned to a soulwinner. These visits are tracked in staff meetings, on dry erase boards, on Excel spreadsheets, and on individual prospect lists—and no visitor is "dropped" from the list until a definite determination has been made on his spiritual progress. Every person saved on Open House Sunday receives a baptism follow-up call. Every visitor receives a visit, and many of them are later saved in their homes. The follow-up from Open House Sunday is as critical as the day itself—do not miss this vital part of the day.

The rest of this chapter includes a manual on how to conduct an Open House Sunday.

Open House Sunday

Conducting an Open House

Deuteronomy 31:12
Luke 14:16–23
Acts 2:40–42

The Purpose of an Open House

- To obey Christ's command
- To win people to Jesus Christ
- To bring visiting families to the church
- To let the community know about the church

The Planning of an Open House

A. Develop a theme that will catch the community's attention. Examples:

1. "You have Never Been So Loved"
2. "Be Our Guest"
3. "A Million Smiles and Counting"
4. "You've Got a Friend in Me"
5. "You'll Love It Too"
6. "Celebrate Freedom"
7. "Be Refreshed"

B. Determine the tasks that must be accomplished.

1. Print materials
2. Mail promotional pieces
3. Choose teams and team leaders
    a. Sunday School
    b. Teen Services
    c. Music Ministry

    d. Spanish Ministry

    e. Saturday Bus Ministry

    f. Sunday Bus Ministry

    g. Military Outreach

    h. Neighboring Communities Outreach

    i. Welcome Teams (parking lot, hospitality, ushers)

    j. Assimilation (gifts, visitor packets, bulletin, information center, bookstore, guest's center, receptionists)

    k. Campus Activities

    l. Campus Enhancement

    m. Support Ministries (prayer team, childcare workers, baptistry, security, counselors)

    n. Food Services

4. Assign members to various teams

5. Conduct meetings

6. Order equipment

7. Rally church members

8. Schedule soulwinning

9. Order/prepare food

10. Prepare campus

C. Design a timeline for the completion of those tasks.

D. Delegate the tasks to staff and volunteers.

The People of an Open House

A. Include every member possible in outreach.
(Have a soulwinning theme like, "Be 1 of 800!")

B. Involve every member possible in ministry.
Open House Sunday ministry examples: Bus Routes, Bus Rallies, Nursery, Children's Classes, Teen Service, Photography, Set-up, Mechanics, Games, Landscaping, Maintenance/Janitorial, Hospitality, Clowns, Traffic

Flow, Ushers, Gift Preparation, Prayer Team, Security, Food Preparation/Serving, Clean-up

C. Create a Team Booklet to give church members who are involved on the various teams. This will keep members organized. (The cover can include the Open House theme.)

The Promotions of an Open House

A. A catered meal for all first-time guests and those who bring them

B. Recognition of community servants (firefighters, law enforcement officers, paramedics)

C. Special guests from the community or public

D. Games/Activities for children

The Publicity of an Open House

A. Personal invitations at every door in the community

B. Bus workers going to every neighborhood to canvass

C. Buttons and business cards for every member of the church (buttons that say, "Ask Me About May 5th," and cards with information about the Open House to give to a person who asks about May 5th)

D. Mail sent and visits made to every police and fire station nearby

E. Varied forms of advertising around every corner

   1. Postcards
   2. Billboards
   3. Radio
   4. Television
   5. Direct mail
   6. Newspaper

7. Posters in businesses and public places
8. Bus-stop benches
9. Signs on public buses
10. Banners
11. Community bulletin boards

The Program of an Open House

A. Drive-in Worship Service (see CD 18.1 to view a sample Open House Cue Card).

1. Bulletin and materials are provided that showcase today's and future events.
2. Choir, special groups, and soloists sing their best and most evangelistic songs.
3. Familiar congregational hymns are chosen.
4. First-time guests are welcomed; they remain seated as members and regular attenders stand. The guests are given an information packet and card during the handshaking.
5. Special guests are recognized and honored.
6. A community leader welcomes all attendees. (This is planned ahead.)
7. Guests are asked to place the filled-out information card in the offering plate as it passes.
8. Evangelistic message is given, often using a striking visual aid.
9. As invitation is given; those who just received Christ and those who would like to are invited to come forward for counsel. They receive a free Bible.
10. Announcements are given, and the service is dismissed.

B. Drive-in Childcare and Classes

1. Visitors' guides are provided and special signage is posted.

2. Hospitality team shows guests where classes are located.
3. Costumed greeters welcome families.
4. Each classroom has a greeter, a registrar, and multiple class leaders.
5. Refreshments and activities are provided for students as they are welcomed.
6. A simple, visual, and evangelistic lesson is presented.
7. Students make take-home crafts.
8. An invitation is given in 1st-6th grade classes.
9. Children are counseled carefully and decision cards are completed.
10. Those children who receive Christ as their Saviour are presented with a discipleship booklet, a baptism brochure, and a letter to parents.

C. Bus Ministry Program

1. Routes run twice.
2. Greeter team welcomes buses.
3. Registration team welcomes students.
4. Parents are invited to participate.
5. Large rallies are held.
6. Giveaways are donated and purchased.
7. Time is allotted for games and refreshments.
8. Game equipment is rented and promoted.
9. Food is donated and prepared.
10. Counselors are trained and ready.
11. Follow-up calls are created and tracked.

The Products of an Open House

A. New Christians—follow up for baptism and discipleship

B. New visitors—follow up for salvation and baptism

C. New prospects—follow up for attendance and salvation

CHAPTER NINETEEN

Country Harvest Days

"For God so loved the world, that he gave his only begotten Son, that whosoever believeth in him should not perish, but have everlasting life."
John 3:16

The harvest season—September, October, and early November—is a wonderful time to conduct a focused emphasis on outreach, soulwinning, and world missions. Over the years at LBC, we have conducted our T.E.A.M. soulwinning kick-off in September, with the training running throughout the fall season. In conjunction with this, we host "Country Harvest Days" during the month of October—which gives every soulwinner the opportunity to use what he is learning!

The foremost goal of Country Harvest Days is to reach the lost with the Gospel of Christ. A special doorknocking plan is organized, and special themes are developed for each Sunday in October. In addition to this, special brochures and advertising tools are created to promote the month to the community. The themes involve promotional ideas that welcome visitors, encourage outreach, and provide fellowship opportunities where first-time visitors can meet the church family and possibly be led to Christ.

Country Harvest Days are usually planned during the summer months, and each special Sunday is assigned to a pastoral staff member. This key leader is then responsible to develop the theme for the day, propose a plan and budget, and enlist lay leaders and teams to help conduct the various details.

The church family has grown to love the outreach, the fellowship, and the fun related to Country Harvest Days. Throughout the month a family would experience a variety of fun after the morning services, such as a church-wide picnic, a chili cook-off, a pie and cake baking contest, an international tasting buffet, a pumpkin patch, an old west stunt show, games and treats for the kids, and more. These events following the services are more than "promotional tools"—they are times when visitors are made to feel at home with new faces and where the Christian life takes on a personality for a newcomer. Every year, people are saved at these "post service" events due to the personal follow-up that happens after the morning message.

Finally, one of the highlights of Country Harvest Days is the World-Wide Missions and Stewardship Conference. During this conference, missionaries from all over the world join us for three days of preaching and testimonies. (See Chapter 21 for more information.)

The following pages include a practical overview of how Lancaster Baptist Church plans and implements each of the special Sundays of Country Harvest Days.

Missions Sunday

Missions Sunday is a special Sunday with an international flavor and is the start of the annual Missions Conference. This allows many missionaries to attend the services. Missionaries speak in all adult Bible classes, and make short visits to all the teen and children's Sunday school classes. Another fun idea is to encourage people to dress in modest international costumes. This adds to the visual flavor of the day. There can be contests such as coloring contests for the children, essay contests for the pre-teens and teens, and costume contests for all ages. The International Tasting Buffet is also a big hit!

Purpose

- To offer a special day that will draw people to the services to hear the message of the Gospel.

- To expose and excite our church family, especially getting new members involved and interested in the opportunity to see missions in action and to understand the history, biblical basis, and how the local church is involved.

- To create an atmosphere where a Christian's heart will be touched and motivated to give, to pray for our missionaries, and to see young people surrender to go to the foreign field if God calls them.

Promotion

TO ADULTS:

1. Select five to six young men to dress like former missionaries and promote Missions Sunday to the adult Bible classes the Sunday before. (No dates are given below but can be filled in according to when the event is held.)

   a. Select young men to dress like missionaries.
   b. Select the missionaries.

    c. Write script and have memorized.

    d. Line up costumes for rental.

    e. Pick-up costumes.

    f. Make a schedule so every adult Bible class is attended by one of the men.

    g. Design/write the biographies for each missionary and place them on card stock.

    h. Proofread and send to print.

    i. Pick up cards.

2. Have a possible skit ready for the Sunday before Missions Sunday.

    a. Choose skit participants.

    b. Write up lines and theme.

    c. Practice at least two times.

    d. Perform for leader for approval.

TO CHILDREN:

1. Coloring Contest (Three year olds–4th graders)

    a. Choose missions theme coloring sheet.

    b. Order paper and fill out a purchase order (P.O.) for it.

    c. Make copies.

    d. Distribute in children's classes.

    e. Collect coloring sheets on Missions Sunday.

    f. Announce winners in Sunday school.

2. Essay Contest (5th grade–high school)

    a. Choose missions theme for essay.

    b. Make up essay sheet and P.O. paper.

    c. Make copies.

    d. Distribute in Sunday school.

    e. Collect essays.

    f. Announce winners in classes.

3. Children's International Costume Contest
    a. Write up guidelines.
    b. Make copies.
    c. Distribute in Sunday school classes.
    d. Line up judges.
    e. Judge in classes.
    f. Announce winners in classes.

International Decorations

1. Gather materials needed.

2. Ask people to help.

3. Put in P.O. for materials.

4. Build and assemble.

International Greeters

1. Contact potential greeters.

2. Set a meeting time for greeters.

3. Line up costumes for greeters.

4. Commit and confirm greeters.

International Buffets

PRELIMINARIES

1. Type sign-up sheets.

2 Distribute sign-up sheets to adult Bible classes.

3. Designate a division of adult classes for breakfast and lunch buffet.

4. Line up table in lobby for sign-ups.

5. Line up couples to man tables.

6. Promote at all services starting three weeks prior:

    a. Main bulletin announcements

    b. Adult class bulletins (instructions on where to deliver food, etc.)

SET-UP CREW FOR SATURDAY

1. Contact men to help with canopies.

2. Line up canopies and get cost.

3. P.O. for canopy rental and donuts.

4. Set time for men to meet for set-up on Saturday morning.

5. Provide donuts and coffee for set-up crew.

SET-UP CREW FOR SUNDAY

1. Contact ladies to set up and serve.

2. Put in P.O. for paper supplies, table coverings, and plasticware.

3. Arrange tables, chairs, and electrical for food warmers.

CLEAN-UP CREW FOR SUNDAY

1. Contact people to help.

2. Confirm and give time schedule to those helping with buffet breakfast and lunch.

Dinner on the Grounds Sunday

This Sunday takes on a "country" flare with a picnic on the grounds after the morning services. Decorations are made easily during the autumn by using hay bales, scarecrows, antique farm equipment, and tools. "Dinner on the Grounds" could also be titled "Country Neighbor Day," but whichever title is used, the important emphasis of the day is for everyone to invite his neighbors to church. Members can be encouraged to pack a picnic large enough for their families and a neighbor family that they bring. Promote this day through announcements in all services a couple of weeks prior, in the main church bulletin, and all adult Bible class bulletins. Sign-ups for all activities and contests help encourage people to participate and should be distributed to all adult Bible classes on each of the two Sundays before.

Sign-ups

1. Choose a member of each adult Bible class to supervise the distribution of all sign-up sheets.

2. Have sign-up tables in the main lobby for two Sundays prior with sign-ups for each contest.

3. Announce in adult Bible class teachers' meeting.

4. Have pulpit announcements regarding sign-ups.

Set up/Tear down

1. Complete P.O. for all tents needed for the day (well in advance).

2. Pick up tents and transport them to church.

3. Set up Pastor's tent.

4. Set up tents for food.

5. Set up tents for shade. (Encourage members to bring their own tents. Adult Bible classes could also set up their own tent areas.)

6. Tear down and return tents after event.

7. Set up a picture spot.

    a. Face in such a way that the background is open sky.
    b. Sun should not be behind the people in the picture.
    c. Decor—hay, wood rail fencing, farm implements

8. Tear down picture spot after event.

Clean up/Trash Cans

1. Check trash cans periodically during the picnic and empty as needed.

2. Have crew ready at the end of the picnic as people are leaving and discarding all trash items at once.

3. Pick up trash from picnic area after all people have gone.

4. Check baking contest area after all people have gone.

5. Check contest areas after all people have gone.

Activities

1. Reserve games.

   a. Air Bounce Houses
   b. Inflatable Rock Climber
   c. Air Bounce Caterpillar
   d. Inflatable obstacle course

2. Meet representative from air bounce company and show where to set up.

3. Line up workers to supervise the activities during the picnic.

4. Submit a schedule of workers to leadership.

Food/Drinks for Sale

1. This encourages those who do not wish to pack food to still attend the picnic for fellowship.

2. Can be hosted by the senior class to raise funds for senior trip.

3. Assign a senior class teacher/sponsor to be in charge.

4. Advertise in bulletins.

5. Have tent set up for the sale of food.

6. Post signs advertising prices.

Sound

1. Set up P.A. system with microphone and CD player.

2. Select and play music suitable for a picnic.

3. Take down P.A. system after event.

Contests

1. Create a time schedule of events and announce this over the P.A. system periodically at the picnic.

2. Assign people to oversee the various contests and keep accurate records of the winners to announce in the Sunday night service. (Ribbons/certificates can be awarded.)

   a. Nail Driving—set up wooden work horses with wood attached that can be nailed into. Have plenty of hammers and nails.

   b. Horse Shoes (Singles/Partners)—set up enough pits to have games move quickly.

   c. Tug-of-war—Make teams using five men from each adult Bible class. The classes have fun cheering for their team. Have a long rope with bandana tied in the middle. Mark team starting lines and winning lines clearly.

   d. Arm Wrestling by weight class

      (1.) Under 150 lbs.

      (2.) 150–200 lbs.

      (3.) Above 201 lbs. (could add Superweight class—250 lbs. +)

e. Baking

    (1.) Advertise sign-ups in bulletins listing the categories.

    (2.) Determine the location and announce in adult Bible classes.

    (3.) Post signage for directions and for judges. (You can use new members to judge this tasty event!)

    (4.) Select a panel of judges ahead of time.

Awards

1. Select a group to prepare the awards as events close and winners are declared.

2. Get certificates from local restaurants donated (or the church can purchase them).

3. Deliver winners' list and awards to Pastor or person who will present the awards in the Sunday night service.

Photography

1. Know where the "picture spot" is located.

2. Set up equipment.

3. Complete a P.O. for film and developing.

4. Take names and phone numbers of those having their picture taken.

5. Develop the pictures and assist leader in getting the pictures to the individuals.

6. Have a table set up in foyer for several services following the event to distribute pictures to church families.

7. Have this table announced in the services.

Harvest Sunday

Harvest Sunday has a strong emphasis to "Bring a friend!" Citing this emphasis, the day could also be called "Friend Day." No matter which title is chosen, all the activities on this day are designed to encourage folks to bring a friend with them to church!

"Friend" Prayer Sheet Sign-up

Encourage all the adults to think of friends who need to hear the gospel. Through the adult Bible classes, sign-up sheets could be passed around for the two weeks prior to "Harvest/Friend Day." At the mid-week prayer service prior to "Harvest/Friend Day," the names listed on the sign-ups can be distributed for the entire church family to use during prayer time. Remind the church family to pray for those individuals that hearts would be touched and people would be saved as a result of this important Sunday.

Decorations

The Country Harvest Days decorations that are already in place are used for this Sunday. If more are desired, a team should be established ahead of time.

Pumpkin Patch

All children 6th grade and under can "pick" a pumpkin from the patch! The children love this event and it should be promoted through the children's Sunday school classes and through the Bus Ministry and advertised through pulpit and bulletin announcements.

SET-UP

1. Designate an area of cleared lawn that would be large enough for all the children to meander through to pick just the right pumpkin!

2. This area should be decorated with the "Harvest" theme and can be a nice picture spot for parents.

3. Visiting families will enjoy this event with their children. To keep this event organized and pleasant, a different "patch" can be placed in another location for the Bus Ministry.

4. Enlist a team of volunteers to locate a place to purchase the amount of pumpkins needed. This team may need to transport the pumpkins to the designated area.

5. This team should place the pumpkins to resemble a "patch," leaving enough room for people to walk through.

6. Create signage to direct families and children to the "patch."

MONITORING

1. Have a team of volunteers who will arrive early and leave after the last child has "picked" his pumpkin.

2. They would stand in strategic places to be able to view all the children. This will keep running to a minimum, and they could pleasantly assist any children who decide to argue for their pumpkin!

CLEAN-UP

1. This crew would arrive at a designated time to clean up and discard all unclaimed and broken pumpkins.

2. The pumpkins can be left through the evening service and made available to church members. Then the crew would clean up after the evening service.

Ideas

1. Pumpkin pie slices served with whipped cream

2. A gift for all visiting "friends"

3. Hay maze

4. Bobbing for apples

Round-Up Sunday

The purpose of Round-Up Sunday is to "round up" all of our family, friends, neighbors, and co-workers and get them to church to hear the message of salvation. The western theme is fun and exciting making this day a great opportunity to reach the lost.

Activities

ADULT

1. Chili Cook-Off (Steakhouse certificates for 1st place winners of 3 categories)
2. Wild West Stunt Show (outdoor skit)
3. Adult Bible class group "western" photos
4. Family hayrides

CHILDREN

1. Pony rides (3 years–4th grade)
2. Licorice lassos (3 years–6th grade)
3. Cowboy Gospel singers (3 years–6th grade)
4. Family hayrides

Advertising

1. Mail postcards to all Sunday school enrollment approximately 7–10 days prior to event.
2. Cowboys from stunt show visit adult/teen/children's Sunday school classes the Sunday before, do short skit, and pass out flyers to children/teen classes.
3. Cowboy/cowgirl greeters at church
4. Western sign at church entrance
5. Bulletin insert on Sunday prior to and day of event

6. Saturday phone blitz day before event (can be done by children's and teen's teachers/helpers and by adult Bible class care group leaders)

Preparation

1. Recruit phone callers to call everyone on the church roll.

2. Prepare classroom skits/cowboy greeters.

3. Prepare for stunt show.

4. Recruit chili hosts/servers.

5. Recruit pony ride helpers.

6. Recruit chili judges.

7. P.O. and order paper products, tablecloths, etc. for chili cook-off.

8. Reserve tents.

9. Prepare drink station for judges and for guests.

10. Arrange for sound at chili cook-off and stunt show.

11. Arrange for power supply for chili cook-off (lots of crock pots!).

12. Prepare and distribute chili cook-off sign-ups through the adult Bible classes.

13. Mail postcards to Sunday school enrollment.

14. Set goals for adult/teen/children's classes (can give certificates as awards to teachers who reach goal).

15. Arrange for hayrides.

16. Arrange for class photos.

17. P.O. and purchase gift certificates for prizes.

18. Rent ponies.

19. P.O. and purchase licorice lassos.

20. Arrange for any wagons needed (whether for decorations or hay ride).

21. Host special guest cowboy Gospel singers.

22. Arrange Saturday set-up crew.

23. Arrange bales of hay around campus.

24. Arrange Sunday clean-up crew.

25. Obtain many water cooler jugs and cups for chili cook-off beverage stations.

PART FOUR

Great Expectations:
Church Calendar & Events

CHAPTER TWENTY

Developing Your Annual Church Calendar

"Walk in wisdom toward them
that are without, redeeming the time."
Colossians 4:5

A study of Scripture reveals that God is interested in how we use our time, how we steward our resources, and how we order His work in the local church. It has often been said, "To fail to plan is to plan to fail!" Perhaps you have heard the phrase, "He who aims at nothing hits it every time!" How often in the highest calling of life—the ministry of the Lord Jesus Christ—we aim at nothing! And indeed, we hit it every time! Too many churches default into a new year, a new season, or a new month with little or no plan of attack—no strategy, no thought, no prayer, and no road map.

God's Word is very clear that He has placed leaders within the church to *"set in order the things that are wanting"* (Titus 1:5). He has commanded us that *"...all things be done decently and in order"* (I Corinthians 14:40). God tells us about Himself that He *"is not the author of confusion"* (I Corinthians 14:33). It is apparent that God wants His work done with order, with planning, and with premeditation, and it is incumbent upon every pastor to assume this responsibility. "Not being an organized person" is not an acceptable excuse for allowing God's church to falter or stagnate for lack of planning.

Planning, the wise use of time and resources, is not a "cure-all" in ministry, but it is a vital and necessary habit if we desire to truly be effective and fruitful in the service of the Lord. Making wise use of your time, planning the months ahead for your church family, and organizing the ministry that God has given to you will, in effect, remove many of the common "road-blocks" to spiritual and numerical growth in the life of your church. It has been said, "What gets planned—gets done and what gets budgeted—gets done." Many times we miss out on God's greatest blessings or spiritual victories simply because we "got in the way!" We set up personal or organizational barriers that hinder the free flowing power of God's Holy Spirit.

When we fail to take time in planning and organizing a ministry or event, we are sure to discover unanticipated problems, confusion, frustration, and limitations. Yet, planning a ministry or event well in advance has exactly the opposite effect. A well-planned event is like a well-oiled machine or a free-flowing river—no barriers, no blockage, no hindrances. And the fruit of such planning can be seen as God's people enjoy serving Him, as Christians experience personal growth, and as new souls come to the Saviour.

As leaders, we cannot manufacture growth—numerical or spiritual. Growth is the product of God's hand at work. Growth is the outflowing of the Holy Spirit at work in an individual life or in a church. In addition to this, the church is a living, breathing organism! It is natural and healthy for a church to grow. It is God's plan for His church to grow. A healthy church **will** grow. Proper spiritual planning and organization contribute to the health of a church and literally help to "make way" for God-given growth.

Consider a bridge under construction. If you were building a bridge, you would first have to build the support structure. You would have to dig well below the surface to establish a strong pillar of support. Once this is established, you could span the distance from the land to your first support. You could not build much farther beyond your first support simply because your bridge would collapse. So, you would launch out beyond your span and dig down again to establish another pillar of support. Only then could you extend your bridge to your next pillar.

In this illustration, the church is the bridge. The planning, organization, and careful structuring that you as God's man put in place with God's help become the support. What kind of support do you have in place? Are you trying to extend beyond the support structure that you have currently established? This will not work. Go to God; spend time alone with Him, and seek His guidance in placing the right support structure deep in the foundation of Christ. From this position, God will begin to extend the bridge farther than you ever dreamed He would!

As this chapter deals with personal time management, annual planning, and annual theme development—each of these topics contributes to the support structure that you are building under the spiritual life of your church. These pages will guide you through the process of strategically planning one full year in the life of your church with the guiding help of the Holy Spirit of God.

This planning process will help you create an "annual plan" for ministry. Once you have developed this plan, you will need to clearly and carefully communicate it with staff, deacons, and finally the church family. This is literally the act of "laying the tracks" so the church can move forward for another year, and over the years this process has become a part of the life-blood of Lancaster Baptist Church. It is something that begins with the pastor, involves the key leaders, involves many ministry teams, and then ultimately is presented to the entire church family on "Vision Night"—the one night each year when the vision for the new year is shared with God's people. It is a very invigorating and energizing process as the church family catches the vision and spirit of what God might desire to do in the coming 12 months. It is literally one of the most exciting services of the year for our church family.

Please note that you must not approach this "planning process" with a secular mindset. This process is innately spiritual and must flow primarily from time alone with God and with trusted leaders in prayerfully seeking God's heart and mind. If this process does not start in silent seeking before Almighty God, then it has failed before it begins! Do not think that you can read the latest corporate strategy book and simply "activate" the newest leadership idea or organizational theory in your church. Not only will this "not work" in the spiritual realm, it will probably cost you dearly as you follow corporate whim rather than the voice of God. Please recognize that everything in this chapter is written under the context of this truth. All planning, organization, strategy, and structuring must come from God's guidance through His Word and in prayer. God will not bless a plan that circumvents His chief plan! God will not move in the midst of a secular mindset.

Finally, recognize that there are many aspects of ministry that simply cannot be and should not be planned. Any attempt to become completely "planned" is simply an attempt to take away God's sovereignty. The best-laid spiritual plan is, at best, a human attempt to sense and anticipate the leading of God. Sometimes, God chooses not to reveal His leading. Sometimes God completely circumvents what we anticipated as His plan to accomplish something we never imagined! This is God's way of working! He works in ways that we cannot see or understand, and He plainly tells us that His ways are not our ways (Isaiah 55:8).

Though we should make every effort to be organized and well-planned, we must also rest in the sovereignty of God from day to day and moment to moment. When God completely rewrites the script at the last minute, we must recognize that He is God, and He is probably about to do something far greater that we ever imagined.

You cannot plan trials, hospital visitation, setbacks, problems, and heartaches. You cannot anticipate disasters or personal suffering. You cannot schedule crisis counseling or urgent needs. Yet, a well-ordered ministry life (in other areas) will certainly make more room for God's intervention with the urgent or immediate. As you plan and order your ministry, you will find that urgent needs, God-ordained opportunities, and even unforeseen setbacks can be more effectively ministered to and handled.

Key Thoughts About Time

1. **Time is a Gift from God.**

   We are called to be faithful stewards of everything that God has entrusted to us. Time is our most valuable resource and must be recognized as a precious gift from God. With this perspective, every moment will be viewed with care and caution, and you will be less likely to squander or waste time.

2. **Time is Life.**

   When we waste time we literally waste "life!" Since the Devil is subtle in the ways he tempts us to waste our time, many leaders are ineffective in the use of their time. When we stand before the Lord to give account for our lives, we will give account for what we did with our "time!"

3. **Time Lost Can Never Be Retrieved or Replaced.**

   You are always spending time, and once it is spent, you can never get it back. It is gone forever. This should drive us to spend time planning what to do with the rest of our time, and should make us desire to use every moment of time for the purpose that God created it.

4. **Time is Your Most Precious Commodity.**

   Your time is more valuable than anything else you have. God will hold you accountable for every minute that He has given to you, and Satan will tempt you to squander as many of those moments as he possibly can. Anything that God has given for us to do will require that time be assigned or budgeted to it.

Steps to Developing an Annual Theme and Plan

Choosing an Annual Theme

1. **Get alone with God.**

   Sometime during the mid-summer or early fall season, the pastor should schedule some time alone, away with God. It is often difficult to hear God's voice in the midst of the "daily ministry noise." Choosing an annual theme for your church is not something that should be done flippantly or quickly. The selection of this theme will create a spiritual emphasis that you will preach, teach, sing, and focus on all year long. This theme will probably become a memorable "sign-post" in the spiritual journey of every Christian in your church family. It is vital that the pastor spend quantity, quality time with God in prayer and Scripture reading.

2. **Consider the spiritual emphasis need of your church.**

   Every church is at a different point of spiritual development; therefore, what is right for one church may not be right for another. Your church is unique! The needs of your people are specific, and the desire of God for your church is specific. In addition to this, you may have a particular ministry focus that needs to be emphasized all year long such as soulwinning, building/construction, missions giving, family development, or spiritual maturity. You may be leading a group of new Christians who need a 12-month emphasis of basic truths—faith, trust, obedience, love, etc. Simply ask the Lord in prayer to lead you to the right emphasis in His Word. He will!

3. **Read God's Word with a sensitive heart.**

   Open the Word of God and look for- that Scripture that God would pin-point in your heart as "the theme verse!" You cannot go wrong having a theme that comes directly from the Scripture. Every theme for the Lancaster Baptist

Church has been chosen directly from a passage of Scripture—which also becomes the theme verse.

4. **Choose a scriptural theme.**

   You will know when God places the right theme on your heart. He will make it clear because He will first captivate you with the truth! He must! God will desire to use you in teaching, preaching, promoting, and challenging His people with this theme all year long, so you can expect that He will do a great work in your life through it first.

5. **Schedule major spiritual emphasis with your theme in mind.**

   After you have chosen your theme, you must begin seeking God's leading in how to apply that theme to various aspects of the Christian life and the growth of your church. For instance, you may choose to emphasize the family in a preaching series. How could you apply the new theme to "family life"? You will probably choose a season in your church year to emphasize giving and stewardship. How can you develop your theme in relation to giving? You may have a particular season when you re-emphasize soulwinning and outreach. How does the new theme tie to this? You will be shocked at how God will quickly tie your seasonal focus to the theme that He has placed upon your heart. Develop your whole year—spiritually—with this new theme in mind.

Involve Your Team in the Annual Plan

In August of every year, the staffs of Lancaster Baptist and its related ministries go away for a three-day training retreat. A big part of this retreat (other than ongoing training, policy revision, etc.) is the revealing of the annual theme to the staff team. At this retreat, the pastor shares what God has placed in his heart and begins to challenge the staff to understand, meditate upon, and personally invest their hearts into this new theme. This is vital, as the staff enters into a planning phase from September through December in preparation for the new year. It is critical that the new theme is embedded into the heart of every leader and into the core of every plan for the new year.

REQUIRE THE STAFF TO CREATE ANNUAL PLANNERS

This is a lengthy and potentially tedious process to describe, but it has become a critical part of the planning process at Lancaster Baptist Church. Every key leader of a ministry or department is required to create a six-month or a twelve-month detailed plan for every ministry that they oversee. This plan is to flow into the clearly defined biblical purposes of the ministry and into the new year theme as well (see CD 20.1 for a sample planner page).

Each plan is broken down by ministry and includes the vision, strategy, and goals for that particular ministry for 12 months. Each plan also includes a list of events, projects, and miscellaneous items that will serve to reach the goals. From this list, a detailed "action list" for every event or project is created. This "action list" breaks a project down to steps from a–z and includes dates that these actions will be "started" and "completed." Finally, these dates are entered into the daily calendar system for that particular staff member.

In effect, this calendar system becomes a twelve-month calendarized "to-do" list. If the staff member will commit to living by this calendar and to following through on these well-planned details, day by day, the plan will take shape and the goals will be reached for God's glory. This is the absolute best way for a staff member to accomplish more for God with less stress and pressure. This plan creates a trustworthy, well-thought-out approach to ministry, and it takes the burden of "remembering everything" off of a person's shoulders, so long as he follows the plan on the calendar.

You might be thinking, "Who has time to do this kind of planning." This is sort of like the person who is so busy "driving some place," they just do not have time to "get gas!" Every hour you spend in creating this type of plan—before the new year—will save you dozens of hours in the coming 12 months, while simultaneously making you more effective in both your ministry and your family life!

In actuality, the time it takes to create this plan depends upon the number of responsibilities you carry or oversee. If an assistant pastor in your ministry oversees three or four ministries, it will take him the better part of three or four days to create such a plan. It could be spaced out over several months or it could all be done in a short, dedicated period of time. It should be completed by early December.

The system used for this "calendar process" could vary widely. The key is that you have a page or physical "representation" for every day of the coming year, and that you will be committed to looking at that system every day! If you choose to use a computer program, consider the fact that seasonal events that recur every year can be entered as "repeating events" which in effect gives you a head start on your planners for years to come.

There are two keys to making this planner work. The first is, that as you live it out day to day, every "undone" task must be forwarded to another day! Leave nothing behind; otherwise you will have a trail of "undone" things lingering on past days that will only serve to "haunt you."

The second is that you must give yourself plenty of "lead time" on every project or task. Think three to six months ahead of every event and place things on the calendar with plenty of time in front of them. This will allow you to approach every task or project with a relaxed spirit of Christ-likeness, rather than an urgent spirit of frenzy and frustration. The further out in front, the safer you are!

For instance, as a pastor, place your "Christmas message planning" on the calendar for August rather than late November. Imagine the time you will have to research the Scriptures, look for other illustration resources, and simply meditate on what God might lead you to preach! Perhaps as a youth leader, you could place the enlistment of teen camp counselors on the calendar for

March or April—well in advance of summer planning for most adults in your church. You will have a much easier time enlisting people with that much "lead time."

Upon completion, this planner will be dozens of pages in length and will reflect a careful prayer plan for every ministry and every event within that ministry. This process will force you to have a "reason" behind everything you do, and will force you to tie that reason to your annual theme. Rather than having activity simply for activity's sake, you will now have a clear vision from God and a clear step-by-step strategy for seeing that vision become a reality! This is truly "setting things in order!"

HOST A PLANNER PRESENTATION LUNCHEON

The staff planner must have a deadline. If you are a pastor, set the deadline and stick with it. If you are a staff member, do not view this process as an unwanted college project or a begrudged high school science project. You are dealing with God's eternal purposes, the church that He died for, and the lives of people that He has redeemed! Do not approach this in a flippant or immature way. Approach it prayerfully and spiritually. Approach it meticulously. Recognize this as a vital process to being the steward that God has called you to be.

Also, as a staff member, recognize this as a huge spiritual blessing to your pastor! When a staff member lifts the burden of ministry off of the pastor's shoulders, he is truly doing what he is called to do. Nothing will lift a ministry burden off the pastor's shoulders and enable him to do more for God than a staff member who will personally own, plan, and follow through on his area of ministry.

Complete your planner on time, package it nicely in a notebook with dividers and page numbers, and schedule an early December luncheon when every key leader will take 15 or 20 minutes to present the plans for his ministry. After a great lunch and time of fellowship, present the plans. This process will allow everyone in the room to literally "marvel" at the job of "the other guy" and will have a huge impact as each player on the team recognizes the value and contribution of every other player! By the meeting's end, if the planners are well-prepared, the pastor will feel "lighter" and more energized than at any other time of the calendar year, and the whole team will be ready to charge into God's work for the new year! Everyone at this meeting will have a greater understanding and appreciation for the rest of the team.

DISCUSS THE CALENDAR WITH YOUR WIFE

The final step for the pastor in "involving the team" is to review the annual calendar and plan with his most valuable player! Not only will your wife need to be supportive of the vision and schedule, she will also be your most valuable advisor as the Lord will lead her to point out concerns, questions, and ideas. Listen carefully to the counsel and thoughts of your wife and give her a voice in the final decisions. God will use her in your life as a trusted counselor and completer.

Assign Events to the Church Calendar

As you emerge from the planner process, you will have a list of events that tie into your theme that will be added to your church calendar for every ministry. These events will need to flow through one key person who will be responsible for placing them on the church calendar (see CD 20.2 for sample Church calendar page). The pastor may want to choose the key dates for major events, and then perhaps a secretary could assign class activities, etc. to dates that are available. Flowing these dates through one person prevents conflicting events and allows for one person to coordinate the flow of the church calendar.

From year to year, you may find that similar events repeat themselves. You may be able to use a previous year's calendar as a "template" for the new year, but do not default into doing everything, every year, exactly the same as last year. The purpose behind the planning process is to get God's heart and mind for the new year. God is interested in spiritual change and spiritual growth, and most often this does not come from doing the same things the same way in a "status quo" approach. When God leads you to repeat an event, a focus, or a season project—do it. Just make sure of His leading rather than taking the "easy way out."

During the fall season, you should have a basic "New Year Calendar" that you can begin praying over and reviewing. This calendar should have all the events, dates, and theme focus for the new year built into it.

DEVELOP YOUR PERSONAL CALENDAR BY ROLE

One of the most important tools for any pastor is his personal calendar. This is different from the church-wide calendar as it reflects not only church events, but personal and family events as well. Your calendar ought to be one of your primary management, planning, and administrative tools for overseeing your entire life and ministry. Your personal calendar should include all major church events, major family events (vacations, time together, athletic events for the kids, etc.), and major personal events (study time, planning time, speaking engagements, etc.).

This "role-based" calendar starts by defining your personal, God-given roles in life. You could quickly list that you are a Christian, a husband, a father, and a pastor. In addition to this you might want to break down your pastoral roles or list others that God has given to you as well. Any God-given role should have time dedicated to it! It's that simple. What is not given time is just not important, no matter what we say we believe.

You may find, in defining your roles, that you have assumed a role that God has not given to you. Get rid of it as soon as you possibly can. Then, you may find that certain roles are faltering because of a lack of time commitment to that role. For instance, if your marriage is struggling, it is probably related primarily to the fact that the quantity and quality time you should be dedicating to it is being given to something else. Identifying your roles is the first step to resolving this problem.

In the light of all of your roles, take your twelve-month calendar and look at each month asking this question, "With this month will I fulfill the role of _____?" In other words, with the entire month in view, you can begin to get a feel for how "balanced" you are. You will probably need to schedule date nights with your wife, family days with your kids, study time, days off, and other non-urgent types of activities. Looking at the month with this type of approach will help preserve you from an urgent, crisis-driven life and will help you purposefully address those things which are God-given priorities in your life.

With today's computer technology, you may even choose to color code events on your calendar by role. Then, at a glance you could see where each role is being addressed each month.

Finally, in maintaining your personal calendar, it is suggested that you spend 30 minutes or so at the early part of each week reviewing your roles once again in light of the past week and the coming week. If, every seven days, you are deliberately and prayerfully reviewing your life in the light of God-given roles, you will never remain more than seven days "out-of-balance" without becoming aware of it. This short review time gives you opportunity to "flex" with the reality of how recent days have unfolded and give you a chance to make vital midcourse adjustments.

ADD MAJOR STEPS FOR MAJOR EVENTS TO YOUR CALENDAR

As a pastor, you will probably not be involved in planning and executing every major event. Yet, as a good overseer, you will want to stay in touch with key points along the journey to make sure that God's work is happening the way He has led. You will need to keep the staff accountable to their own planners by placing key dates and events on your calendar.

As the planners of other staff members are reviewed, you could identify key tasks or dates that you are acutely interested in. Flag those events and have a secretary add them to your personal calendar. Then, through the year you can periodically be reminded of important details. These details will form the basis for staff meeting discussions and further planning.

Which events should you add to your calendar? Here is a list of suggested events:

1. Key deadlines when a project is due

2. Key starting points for major projects

3. Key checkpoints along a project path

4. Key staff meetings

Prayerfully Review Your Church Calendar

Before you publish the church-wide calendar, it is vital that you prayerfully review the twelve-month plan, asking some critical questions in this review. It is also vital that other trusted leaders review it as well. During this review you are looking for balance. You need to determine if you have truly understood the mind of God, and you need to be able to present the calendar to your church family with confidence that God is pleased with it.

IDENTIFY CONFLICTS

During this review you will probably find potential conflicts or problems. When reviewing, look for unusually busy weeks. Perhaps you scheduled a Friday activity at the end of a missions conference week which means that your people will be away from home four out of five nights that week. It is probably best to avoid this as much as possible. Perhaps you overbooked the facility on one particular Saturday or maybe you scheduled a youth function and a couples' function on the same night. This would provide a conflict as couples try to line up babysitters. Perhaps you have a school which must schedule sporting events that need to be coordinated with the youth department.

As a side note, do not allow this review process to become a "turf war!" Every ministry leader should have a spirit of selflessness and submission toward this process. No event or activity is as important as a team spirit on the staff.

When identifying conflicts, get input from others and suggested solutions. Ask people with different ministry and family roles from you to review the calendar. In other words, a wife and mother might have a different perspective than a working father. A full-time staff member might have a different perspective than a godly layman. All of this counsel will help to anticipate problems, conflicts, and frustrations with the church schedule before they actually happen. This will be a blessing to the church family.

Inevitably, you will find conflicts on the calendar as you go through your year. It is impossible to avoid them all. Yet, if you keep good records of these conflicts with each passing year, your calendaring process becomes stronger and stronger. Over the years you will grow in your ability to avoid these conflicts. If you do not keep records, you will probably make the same mistake year after year.

IDENTIFY VULNERABILITY

Having an eye for vulnerability is a key responsibility for a pastor. You must review your calendar with an eye for seasons of vulnerability. For instance, what plan do you have in place to encourage people to stay faithful through the summer? What plan is in place to encourage lonely people during holiday seasons? Are there places on the calendar when nothing is scheduled and something *should be*? Anticipating these vulnerable times will help you deal with problems before they occur.

Allocate Resources According to Your Calendar

"What gets budgeted gets done!" The final step to creating your annual plan is to create your church budget. Depending on the size of your church this could be the effort of the pastor and the bookkeeper, or it could be a team effort with every leader working on his areas of responsibility. Ultimately this budget should be voted in by the deacons and by the church family. The budget preparation process should take place during the fall season and should address every major ministry, event, and operational aspect of the church.

Sometime in October, each ministry leader should be given a worksheet for each ministry that he oversees (see CD 20.3 for a sample budget planning sheet). This worksheet should reflect every expense category and event expense for each ministry and should show what month that expense will take place. For instance, if you must pay a $500 deposit in January for a June teen camp, this expense should show up on the ledger sheet in January.

Each ministry leader should go through the exercise of creating a budget for each event and each part of ministry showing both expense and income. This budget can then be entered into a master budget for the overall church ministry. It is a good idea for the deacons to approve this detailed budget. It would be suggested to reduce this lengthy budget to a simple one-page summary of major ministry categories for the church family to vote on sometime in early January.

Once the budget is in place, it should become a guide for the ministry. No budget is perfect, and every budget should be somewhat flexible to the leading of the Holy Spirit. The pastor must never relinquish faith in God to the domination of the "budget." Yet, this budgeting process over the years, will become more and more accurate and will effectually help you do more in ministry, not less. Disciplining yourself and your team to a budget process will force you to plan expenses and to be better stewards of God's blessings. In the light of this good stewardship, God will probably entrust you with more resources in the future, and your church family will be more confident in giving to God's work through your church.

Present the Plan to Your Church Family on Vision Night

A large portion of this annual plan is never really seen by the church family simply because of the details and the size of the plan. It would take too much time and thought to communicate every minute detail in a church service. There is really no need for that, and your church family will thank you!

It is critical, however, that you schedule an energetic "Vision Night" service sometime in early January to unveil the new year theme and to communicate the new year plan (see CD 20.4 for a sample Vision Night cue card). Perhaps this service could be the first Sunday night of the new year.

Vision Night at Lancaster Baptist Church has become a much anticipated and prayed over event each year. It is one of the most exciting nights in the calendar year. For months, ministry leaders and office staff are making preparations. Here is a list of ideas in communicating your vision and unveiling your theme.

1. **Create a theme graphic or banner for the unveiling.**
   Spend a few hundred dollars to create a banner or graphic that represents your theme for the year. This banner should be hung in a prominent place all year long and should be unveiled in a strategic moment during Vision Night. Share the Scripture that God laid on your heart, talk of what the theme means, and share what you pray God will do through it.

2. **Create theme-related materials to hand out.**
   A pen, a refrigerator magnet, a note pad, a bumper sticker—the list could go on at length. Hand out some gifts on Vision Night that depict the theme graphic and the Scripture verse.

3. **Hand out spiritually-motivating items.**
   One goal of Vision Night is to encourage God's people to get on track spiritually. It is a good idea to hand out a Bible reading schedule, a devotional notebook, a prayer

journal, or any other item that could challenge someone to grow spiritually in the new year.

4. **Print and hand out the church calendar.**
    Create a nicely designed calendar with the new year theme on it and a detailed schedule of ministry activities for the entire year. The pastor should go through the calendar with the church family and energetically share God's vision for the new year, pointing out key dates along the way.

5. **Reduce your collective planners to an abbreviated ministry goal sheet.**
    Print up a well-prepared goal sheet to hand out on Vision Night. This goal sheet should list the goals by ministry and should be explained by the pastor. It could literally become a prayer list for the church family as they consider each ministry of the church. It will most certainly excite and energize the church family behind a common set of goals. Finally, this goal sheet becomes a form of published accountability to those who are investing their lives and their resources into God's work in your church.

6. **Creatively develop the annual theme.**
    There are countless ways that the church theme can be promoted and developed. You could publish a list of new sermon series that revolve around the theme. You could teach the congregation a chorus related to your theme that will be sung periodically throughout the year. You could have special theme services where you recognize servant-hearted people who have exemplified the theme among your church family. Be creative in thinking of ways to develop the theme in the heart and life of your church.

Planning takes time, prayer, study, and deliberation. It is not easy, and it does not "feel" productive. Yet, planning has far-reaching implications in the long-term health, fruit, and life of your church.

Planning requires you to pull aside from the frenzy and the noise so that you can hear the voice of God. Once you have heard His voice, you can expect His blessing as you obey Him.

Perhaps you have never created such an annual plan. Perhaps the mere thought of it is somewhat overwhelming. Don't let that stop you. Start somewhere, even if it is small. Choose a strong theme, plan some great preaching, and schedule some key events to develop the spiritual strength of your church. You will be delighted and surprised at how God will bless your efforts. And, over the years, you will be shocked at how the plan develops as the ministry grows. God will truly do greater things than you could possibly imagine.

CHAPTER TWENTY-ONE

Missions Conference

*"Therefore said he unto them, The harvest truly is great, but
the labourers are few: pray ye therefore the Lord of the harvest,
that he would send forth labourers into his harvest."*
Luke 10:2

Missions have always been at the heart of the ministry of Lancaster
Baptist Church. In 1986, when we began serving the Lord in
Lancaster, the church was unable to pay us a salary; however, the
four or five families who were still gathering together upon our
arrival had committed to support two missionaries. One of the
church families suggested that we suspend missionary support
until the church could support its own pastor. I was determined
that we should maintain the support of the missionaries and truly
believe that God has blessed the faith of this decision.

I am thankful that God has allowed me to develop my missions
philosophy in the independent Baptist circles. Our approach to
missions is one of the greatest aspects of the independent Baptist
church movement. I say this for two reasons.

1. We believe the churches should send missionaries to the foreign field, much as the church in Antioch commissioned Paul and Barnabas on their first missionary journey. While we have various missions agencies and clearing houses serving our missionaries, it is our conviction that the missionaries are accountable to the local church and not to a denomination or missions board.

2. The second blessing of the independent Baptist missions movement is that the missionaries receive 100 percent of their support directly from the supporting churches. This insures that no percentage of the funds sent to the missions effort will ever go toward an institution that does not hold true to the fundamental doctrines of the Word of God.

The Lancaster Baptist Church family now supports 132 missionary families around the world. Hundreds of thousands of dollars each year are flowing to the foreign fields to support worldwide evangelization.

Much of the reason for our missions program growth has been due to our annual Missions Conference. This is a special time of year when we, as a local church, can develop relationships with the individual missionaries to learn how to pray for them and to understand their special challenges. Additionally, at this time we make financial commitments to their ministries that enable them to continue fervently serving the Lord overseas.

We who live in America are truly blessed with a high level of education, an abundance of Bibles and Christian books, and economic prosperity. At times, it is easy to forget that there are those in this world who do not live as we. There are millions of adults who have never been introduced to modern conveniences such as electricity and running water, children who will never learn to read, souls who have never heard of Jesus Christ or the Bible. The work is so vast, and we are so few; is it really possible to "*stand in the gap*" in this day and age (Ezekiel 22:30)?

During a missions conference, the church has the chance to see the Great Commission come alive before its eyes. Missionaries from all over the world—China, Brazil, India, Australia—gather together for a time of refreshment and fellowship with one another. They give testimonies and show slide presentations of their mission field, enabling church members in a mere two or three days to develop a stronger burden for the lost of this world.

Seeing the need of these mission fields will also increase the Christian's desire to give toward missions. Many churches find it very effective to have a time on the last night of the conference when the congregation can give specifically toward missions and decide on a missions offering commitment for the next year. By collecting commitment cards for these decisions, the church finance department will have a rough estimate of the total missions income for the year, and the pastor can prayerfully determine which missionaries to support.

Each missionary's testimony should be reviewed thoroughly prior to his admission to your missions conference. You should call his sending church to inquire about his background, his practices, and anything that could be of concern to your ministry.

The Missions Conference is also a great opportunity to get the children in the church excited about missions. Have each class bring in loose change to help with the missions offering. Allow time before and after services for children and adults to survey the missionary display tables, to talk with the missionaries, and for the children to get their Bibles or missions conference programs signed by the missionaries. If your church has a school or college, schedule special chapels or class times for the missionaries to speak with the students and answer any questions students may have. Many a young person have been called to the mission field or to full-time Christian service through a missions conference.

By scheduling the conference around the same time every year, both children and adults can look forward to its coming for months in advance. Most conferences begin on Sunday and revolve around special meetings Monday through Wednesday evenings, but some vary in duration from two days to a full week. The key is to help your members come into contact with the missionaries as much as possible in the time you have. Allow missionary wives to speak to the ladies of your church; have the missionary children sit in on classes or give testimonies in age-appropriate Sunday schools. If possible, gather all the missionaries together each afternoon for a special time of soulwinning with the church laymen. (Be sure to provide childcare for each event.) The impact these missionaries will have on your church members will far surpass any sacrifices made to attend these special meetings.

One great benefit of conducting a missions conference is that your church has the opportunity to be a blessing to those missionaries who attend. We suggest mailing a questionnaire (see CD 21.1) several months in advance to find out when they will arrive, how many will be attending, and whether or not they have a slide presentation. After you receive this information, try to coordinate as many arrangements as possible for the missionaries. Make sure they have food, lodging, transportation, directions to the church, and a map of the area including shops, restaurants, grocery stores, etc. Send a fruit basket or other such gift to the hotel or home where each will be staying. This will demonstrate to your church that missionaries are worthy of our respect and honor.

Once all the missionaries have arrived, the pastor should meet with the men to give an overview of the week's events and to let each missionary know what is expected of him. At this time, it is very helpful to have a packet ready for each missionary that tells him exactly where he needs to be at any given time. This packet may also include a welcome letter, a list of missionary policies and procedures, a missionary update notice (see CD 21.2), a map of the church building, and so on. The remainder of this chapter contains information that would be included in a missionary information packet, as well as a timeline for the Missions Conference.

Missions Conference

Preparation Timeline

*Dates are examples.

Letters to all missionaries about conference .... May 13, July 1
Confirm conference missionaries .... August 2
Put in a P.O. for S.S. children's gifts .... August 5
Choose a conference theme .... August 9
Order children's gifts .... August 12
Missions brochure to the pastor .... August 20
Send confirmation letter .... August 26
Brochure ready to print .... August 26
Autograph book ready to print .... August 30
Contact hosts of missionary families .... August 31
Put in a P.O. for all special gifts .... September 2
Organize housing for missionaries .... September 5
Put in a P.O. for buffet tablecloths .... September 6
Meeting with hosts of missionary families .... September 8
Complete conference schedule .... September 13
Order table decorations and tablecloths .... September 13
Begin sign-ups for international buffet .... September 15
Order tablecloths for mission displays .... September 16
International costume team .... September 16
Letter to hosts of missionary families .... September 16
Contact Filipinos regarding buffet .... September 16
Send Faith Promise cards to printer .... September 16
Complete individual schedules .... September 20
Complete missionary folders and gift packets .... September 27
Have flyer in bulletin .... October 6

Letter to the Missionaries

Dear Missionaries,

I want to welcome you to our Missions Conference. Our theme for this year's conference is Winning Our World. Our church has an overwhelming passion to make a difference in the lives of those around the world through our missions program. I hope that you will find the enclosed information helpful to you as we endeavor to heighten the awareness of world-wide missions to our church family this week.

I have included a schedule of all you will be involved in during our conference. I have arranged our speaking schedule according to the tenure of the missionaries and the time that each was scheduled to come to the conference. We consider every speaking opportunity to be very important. If you have any questions regarding your schedule or your involvement in our conference, please do not hesitate to see me.

Also, I would like to highlight some specific things that will help you understand what we would like you to do while you are with us. If you are involved in a children's class, it would be a great idea to bring visuals along with you to that class. Following the Sunday evening service, all missionaries are invited to go to the Student Life Center for the "Touring the World" buffet, cooked and prepared by the Spanish members of our church. Following the Monday evening service, the Filipino members of our church will be hosting a time of fellowship and a special dinner for you in the multi-purpose room as well. Following our evening services Tuesday and Wednesday, there will be a refreshment time for you and your family in the Student Life Center with our church family. There will be soulwinning opportunities Monday, Tuesday and Wednesday at 1:30 P.M., and Tuesday at 9:30 A.M. Childcare will be provided for you. On Tuesday morning at 8:00, we are asking all of the missionary wives to meet with the pastor's wife in the Student Life Center for a breakfast reception. She would like each missionary wife to be prepared to give a short greeting to all of the ladies.

Finally, let me reiterate to you that we count it a joy to have you with us for our Missions Conference, and we are thankful that we can serve the Lord together. It is my prayer that God will use you in a mighty way to increase our burden for world-wide missions. May the Lord bless you.

Sincerely,

Assistant Pastor

Missionary Policies and Procedures

1. It is our policy to support only Baptist missionaries.

2. Because a missionary is a church planter and will pastor churches on the field, it is the policy of this church that a missionary must meet the requirements of I Timothy 3 in his personal and public life.

3. A missionary will write no less than six times per year except those ministering in a Communist country or who have special circumstances outside of their control.

4. Each missionary must be a member of an Independent Baptist Church, and in agreement with the Lancaster Baptist Church doctrinal statement.

5. Requests for finances regarding projects and monthly support should be made directly to the senior pastor or missions director of our church. Questions about said support or church policies should be directed to the senior pastor or missions director.

6. No missionary may knowingly befriend or support in any way a former member of this church who has been removed from membership by the church due to discipline.

7. No missionary should make personal pleas for financial support to any member of the church unbeknownst to the senior pastor or missions director. It is understood that should a missionary change fields, his support by the church will be subject to review. It is understood that should a missionary change his doctrinal position, his

support will be dropped immediately, even while he is on the field.

8. It is understood that should a missionary change mission boards or home churches, his status for support will be reviewed at that time.

9. According to Acts 14–16, missionaries are to be accountable to the local church.

10. Any missionary who would argue with the doctrine or philosophy of a supporting church, in our opinion, should not be supported by the church.

_____   _____

Signature   Date

Guidelines for Missionaries

1. Communicate early and often with host church about itinerary.

2. Pray to be sensitive to the needs and burdens of the pastor and church.

3. Seek to endear the church to Christ, His commission and the pastor.

4. Do not fellowship in members' homes without checking with the host missions director first.

5. Do not correspond or solicit directly to members after the meeting.

6. Always use God's Word when you are preaching or teaching in the classes. Give biblical principles for missions and giving.

7. Do not discuss Fundamentalism or current issues with staff or lay members.

8. Do not make strong appeals in an effort to call people to your mission field. Let the Holy Spirit call and the local church separate members for missions.

9. Have a heart for soulwinning during the week.

10. Have a heart to serve during the week.

11. Give airfare expense amounts to the missions director early in the conference.

12. Share special offering needs with the pastor prior to your speaking time and seek his guidance on how to present the needs. (Typically, the church gets behind a project the pastor can push.)

13. Plan ample time to set up all equipment used for presentations.

14. Encourage people to love the church and pastor.

15. Do not place an undue emphasis on your particular mission board, but place the main emphasis on your mission field.

16. Realize the priority for speaking is given to returning missionaries who have been supported by this church.

17. If a church member talks to you about a desire to go to a mission field to visit or to be a missionary, direct them to a pastoral staff member.

18. Be flexible with your time and responsibilities.

19. Be sensitive to the pastor's schedule throughout the conference.

20. Be cognizant of the fact that the pastor has a heart to meet the needs of the church family, especially during service times.

Missions Conference Schedule

Saturday, October 13

5:00 P.M.	Men's prayer in Main Auditorium
6:00 P.M.	Meeting for all missionaries in room 210
7:00 P.M.	Set up displays in Main Auditorium

*Dinner with host family

Sunday, October 14

*International Breakfast Buffet served at 8:00 A.M.

7:30 A.M.	Morning prayer in room 206
8:30 A.M.	Early Service
10:00 A.M.	Homebuilders Class in North Auditorium
11:00 A.M.	Second Service
5:25 P.M.	Visit with the pastor
6:00 P.M.	Evening Service

*Touring the World Buffet (Spanish) following the evening service in the Student Life Center

Monday, October 15

10:00–12:00	College Chapel in North Auditorium
1:30 P.M.	Soulwinning in North Auditorium
7:00 P.M.	Evening Service

*Filipino Buffet in multi-purpose room following evening service

Tuesday, October 16

9:30 A.M.	Soulwinning in Main Auditorium
10:00–12:00	College Chapel in North Auditorium
1:30 P.M.	Soulwinning in North Auditorium
7:00 P.M.	Evening Service

Wednesday, October 17

10:00–12:00	College Chapel in North Auditorium
1:30 P.M.	Soulwinning in North Auditorium
7:00 P.M.	Evening Service

General Information

Unless otherwise indicated on your schedule, all Sunday through Wednesday meals will be served in the Student Life Center at the following times:

Breakfast:	7:00–8:00 A.M.
Lunch:	12:00–1:00 P.M.
Dinner:	5:00–6:00 P.M.

*Each missionary receives a personalized schedule displaying the areas of his involvement.

CHAPTER TWENTY-TWO

Stewardship Campaign

"But this I say, He which soweth sparingly
shall reap also sparingly;and he which soweth
bountifully shall reap also bountifully."
II Corinthians 9:6

Like many pastors, I had no way of knowing the importance of funding the ministry of the Lord Jesus Christ or the best biblical methods for accomplishing this task. Obviously, as any church grows, the need for space becomes more apparent.

The Lord has graciously allowed Lancaster Baptist Church to purchase 67 acres of property and build millions of dollars of buildings on our campus here in northern Los Angeles County. We have never used any high-pressure tactics nor ever mailed a desperation letter to our members pleading for funds. I believe the two critical components to seeing provision made for the ministry are first, solid Bible preaching and teaching on the subject of giving and second, leading the church family to seek the filling of the Holy Spirit and challenging them to allow God to lay on their hearts what He would have them do.

Giving is as much a part of the Christian life as any other thing. Jesus spoke often of money and its relation to our hearts and our spiritual lives. True spiritual giving is a grace that is produced by the inner working of the Holy Spirit through the power of God's Word. Though it is often hard for a pastor to teach or preach about giving, a godly pastor will earnestly help God's people grow in every grace and will teach and preach the whole counsel of God. In truth, when God's people trust the Lord with their financial resources, they will experience His provision and faithfulness in their lives in a way that nothing else provides. The heart and motivation for teaching or preaching about grace giving is to help God's people grow in their personal relationship with God. The fact that this is God's chosen way of providing for His work on earth is simply a by-product of spiritual growth in a healthy church. The focus should never be "fundraising" for the work of God. The focus should be helping God's people to trust Him, as He provides through them. God's providence is seen in Exodus 35 and 36, when Moses called on the people to help build the tabernacle:

> *The children of Israel brought a willing offering unto the Lord, every man and woman, whose heart made them willing to bring for all manner of work, which the Lord had commanded to be made by the hand of Moses... And they received of Moses all the offering, which the children of Israel had brought for the work of the service of the sanctuary, to make it withal. And they brought yet unto him free offerings every morning...And they spake unto Moses, saying, The people bring much more than enough for the service of the work, which the Lord commanded to make. And Moses gave commandment, and they caused it to be proclaimed throughout the camp, saying, Let neither man nor woman make any more work for the offering of the sanctuary. So the people were restrained from bringing. For the stuff they had*

was sufficient for all the work to make it, and too much.
Exodus 35:29, 36:5–6

What a wonder it must have been to watch God touch the hearts of His people to bring offerings with joyful and willing hearts until Moses had to ask them to stop! Imagine the shock of our communities if today's churches had to stop people from bringing in their offerings because of such a surplus.

An annual Stewardship Banquet will help keep an attitude of giving throughout the year at your church through commitments and pledges. There are two other methods of giving at a Stewardship Banquet; you may ask for a one-time offering on that night, or for tangible donations, such as jewelry, bonds, or other valuable items the people wish to give to the Lord. This money may be used for debt reduction, a new building program, or just to manage the church's everyday operational expenses, depending on the needs of your church. Prayerfully consider the avenue the Lord would have you to take regarding this special offering.

In Acts 2, the newly formed church, upon receiving the Holy Spirit, served the Lord together with a singleness of heart rarely found in our churches today. *"And all that believed were together, and had all things common; And sold their possessions and goods, and parted them to all men, as every man had need. And they, continuing daily with one accord...did eat their meat with gladness and singleness of heart"* (Acts 2:44–46). A special unity develops within the group of Christians that is striving together for a common objective. The petty quarrels and cliques that bring division to churches slowly fade away. You will find that having a yearly Stewardship Banquet will help your church to establish a purpose through giving that has an eternal focus—the saving of souls and edifying of the body of Christ.

To aid your members in establishing this goal, it is helpful to have a theme for each year's banquet that states your church's mission. Focus church services around the theme of the banquet, such as "Seeking the Lord" or "Giving by Faith," as the event draws near. Allow members of your church to share testimonies of God's faithfulness to them in the weeks preceding your banquet. Preaching, singing, testimonies, and drama can all be used by God to stir His people's hearts to give.

Although the main purpose of a stewardship banquet is to increase financial giving, it will also challenge your church members to grow in their Christian walk as they step out in faith and watch God provide. Nothing will encourage a new Christian more than to pray for a specific sum to give at the banquet and to have that prayer answered by God Himself.

The Home Fellowship Night will draw your church closer together and unite the church in their efforts to serve the Lord. Congregations that pray collectively and in small-group settings (prayer meetings, Home Fellowship Night) find their faith strengthened and spirits encouraged during this special time of preparation before the banquet.

If at all possible, provide your members with a meal at several people's homes before the service begins. If adequate space is available for the whole church, it is usually best in the early years to have the meal together with all the adults in the church. A time of fellowship over an elegant dinner in a nicely decorated room shows the congregation that you appreciate them and are grateful for all they already do as church members. It also gives them a chance to unwind from their day before entering into an evening where spiritual battles will certainly take place. Following the banquet, have a special time of singing, preaching, and prayer planned for the service, allowing the Lord to work in the people's hearts one last time before the offering is taken.

Once the offering has been counted, give all the glory to the Lord, regardless of the outcome. You may have received far more than anticipated—to God be the glory. It is also possible that your offering was not as high as it could have been—to God be the glory, Who knows the end from the beginning. He is the One who convicts and stirs His people to give according to His perfect plan, and we must trust Him completely for the results.

"Every man according as he purposeth in his heart, so let him give..." (II Corinthians 9:7)

The team leadership procedures that follow explain the specific requirements for each aspect of the stewardship banquet. Much planning and detail must go into every facet of the banquet itself (e.g., decorations, food, publicity, etc.) and leaders should be chosen with discretion (see CD 22.1 for the Stewardship Campaign Leadership Structure). Booklets should be distributed at least two months prior to the night of the banquet.

Team Leadership Handbook

A Word from the Pastor…

Dear Friends,

Thank you for taking time to attend this important meeting and for allowing me to share the vision and plan for our commitments from the Let God Arise *program and preparing our ministry for this new millennium.*

As you know by now, our theme for 2000 is Seek the Lord. *It is my prayer that our community will see a group of people in a church that truly does seek the Lord.*

The Seek the Lord *program is about much more than buildings or offerings. In fact, we have five distinct goals in this campaign which I would like to share with our team leaders today.*

I.   *To Grow Spiritually Mature*

    A.   *Through Bible reading and devotions*
    B.   *Through special prayer emphasis*
    C.   *Through church attendance*
    D.   *Through giving to God*

II.   *To Develop Fellowship as a Church Family*

    A.   *Through our home visitation program*
    B.   *Through working together*
    C.   *Through the Home Fellowship Night on February 27*

III. *To Help our Membership Find a Place of Ministry*

    A.   *Ministering during the campaign*
    B.   *Ministering after the campaign*

IV. *Worship and Thanksgiving to God*

    A.   *Through music/preaching/multi-media*

B. *Through testimonies*

V. *To Begin Mortgage Principal Reduction for God's Glory*

It is my prayer that as we team together, we will see God touch our lives and our church as never before. Let us die to ourselves and seek the filling of God's Spirit in this hour. Let us seek His face, and let us determine to honor Him in all that is accomplished.

I would ask you to study the material in your hand. Additionally, feel free to share input with me or the campaign director as we work together for God's glory. Most of all, let us pray that when the history of our church is written, it will be said that a group of faith-filled people decided to trust God in the early days of the twenty-first century. Thank you again for your prayers, your vision, and your support.

Your friend,

Pastor

Spiritual Purpose

To help God's people establish a closer walk with God by developing a pure heart and a clear vision for His will in their lives through prayer, the study of God's Word, and financial sacrifice.

Scope of Phase II

The *Seek the Lord* Offering takes into consideration prior commitments and principal reduction. Consequently, we will ask our church family on March 12, 2000, to give a one-time offering and to make commitments that will enable us to do ministry more effectively in the new millennium.

Seek the Lord Offering Calendar

1. Select team leaders ....December 27
2. Pass out prayer tents...................................December 31
3. Send out letter to church family......................January 12
4. Outline job descriptions and booklet ....January 20
5. Letter of invitations to team leaders................January 21
6. Send out testimony letter ....January 24
7. Send letter to home host team leaders ....January 24
8. Mail out church newsletter ....January 27
9. Team leaders' meeting ....January 30
10. Testimony team meeting .... February 2
11. All church letter for Home Fellowships .... February 4
12. Conduct a Home Fellowship meeting........... February 6
13. Design commitment cards and
    giving envelopes .... February 9

14. Testimonies begin .... February 13
15. *Seek the Lord* book goes to print.................... February 15
16. Spanish testimonies begin........................... February 20
17. Follow-up team leader meeting.................... February 20
18. Youth "Thanks for Seeking the Lord"........... February 27
19. Home Fellowship Night.............................. February 27
20. Youth Night .... March 5
21. *Seek the Lord* Offering (Victory Night) .... March 12

Seek the Lord Offering Information Summary

Pertinent dates for all team leaders

1. First team leader meeting............................... January 30
2. Team leader and home host meeting.............. February 6
3. Follow-up team leader meeting.................... February 20
4. Home Fellowships... February 27
5. *Seek the Lord* Offering (Victory Night) .... March 12

Proposed Seek the Lord Campaign Team Leaders

Campaign Director.................................. Jerry & Bonnie Ferrso
Babysitting ....Mark & Julie Hanna
Campaign Secretaries .... Lisa Stoner & Melanie Anderson
Finance..Ben & Carla Hobbs
Food Distribution.............................. Mark & Suza Rasmussen
Home Host ....Steve & Celise Tabor
Prayer ....John & Samantha Alvarez
Primary & Junior Care .... Tim & Nicole Christoson

General Information for Team Leaders

The team leaders should endeavor to convey the pastor's vision to all members of their committees. The team leaders will help organize and encourage each person in their groups.

During the first month, each team leader is encouraged to invite key members of his team over to his home for a time of fellowship and prayer.

Also, in the event that there is little or no response from a church member, the name of the member should be passed along to the campaign director.

On the following pages are job descriptions for each team leader. All of the team leaders should not only seek to do the minimum requirements that are outlined in this booklet, but they should also look for ways to expand their area of assignment.

Suggestions or questions regarding your area of service may be directed to the campaign director or to the senior pastor, who will be prompt in their reply to help follow-up in any way possible.

Campaign Director

The campaign director will work daily in giving oversight to the *Seek the Lord* Offering. This will include praying for and contacting the various team leaders regarding the progress of their specific areas.

The campaign director will work closely with assisting the home host team leader with home visits, responses to the home gatherings, and fellowship that will be conducted on February 27.

The campaign director will work with interfacing various aspects of the program and will be communicating to Pastor the total progress of the *Seek the Lord* Offering.

Nursery Team Leaders

The nursery team leaders' responsibilities include enlisting and training at least 30 qualified and responsible nursery workers and planning the babysitting program for newborns through three year olds on the night of the Home Fellowships and Victory Night. Most of these workers will be trained teenagers from our church. However, we must have four to six qualified adults as well. There should be ample videos for the children to watch, adequate food, diapers, and other supplies for younger children.

The nurseries should be cleaned and prepared. There should be a note for all parents thanking them for participating in our Home Fellowships. The greeters should wear matching outfits.

The team leaders should be available for checking in children from 5:00 until 6:10 P.M. The team leaders should leave their Home Fellowship a little early to greet the parents as they pick up their children.

The team leaders need to make note of the following dates:

1. All team members should be contacted and committed by February 6.

2. Twenty teenage workers to be committed by February 9.

3. Twenty college workers to be committed by February 9.

4. Training for these workers must be done by February 20.

5. Purchase orders should be submitted for nursery supplies by February 10.

6. The schedule and room assignments need to be finalized by February 9.

Campaign Secretaries

The team leaders' secretaries will be responsible for all mail-outs from any of the campaign team leaders during the *Seek the Lord* Offering program. The team leaders' secretaries will also help any other team leaders in mailing out articles or letters for meetings and instructions regarding the program.

The team leaders' secretaries need to make note of the following:

1. Letter to church family—January 12.

2. Letter to home host couples—January 24.

3. Take meeting minutes during *Seek the Lord* Administrative Team meetings.

4. Letter to team leaders for February 20 meeting.

Finance Team Leaders

The finance team leaders will be responsible for counting the money and commitment cards received at the *Seek the Lord* Offering. The finance team leaders are responsible for making sure there is a room for counting purposes at the church facility and then for checking to make sure there is a proper number of electrical outlets for calculators. The finance team leaders will work with the campaign director to make sure that the proper counting equipment is available for that day. The finance team leader should delegate the responsibility of counting the cards to some people, while others count cash and checks. Then there should be a detailed deposit count and a deposit made following the initial quick count.

The finance team leaders will work in close conjunction with the security team leaders to make sure there will be a safe and efficient deposit of funds.

The team leaders need to make note of the following dates:

1. Team members need to be contacted and committed by Sunday, February 6.

2. Secure any equipment that will be needed by February 27.

Food Distribution Team Leaders

As food distribution team leaders, you will work closely with the campaign director in choosing a food tray for our Home Fellowship Night. This would include ordering and preparing the food for both the Home Fellowships and also for our Spanish families who will be eating at the church on February 27. You will need to organize a plan that will distribute the food to each of the home-hosting families. Also, this will include the set-up, serving, and clean-up for the Spanish Ministry in the Student Life Center. The team members will consist of college students and will work with the nursery team leaders and the primary and junior care team leaders.

The team leaders need to make note of the following dates:

1. Have the menu finalized by February 9.

2. Contact and commit team members by February 9.

3. Schedule a planning meeting by February 16 with your team members to cast the vision for the *Seek the Lord* Offering and Home Fellowships and also to share your organizational plan for the meal preparation and delivery.

4. Turn in your purchase orders for the meal by February 16.

5. Distribute food to home host on February 27.

6. Serve Spanish families in SLC on February 27.

Home Host Team Leaders

The home host team leaders will be responsible for enlisting and training couples for the purpose of visiting or committing every member of our church to be part of the Home Fellowships. The goal of the visitation program has five major focuses:

1. Establish and build meaningful relationships.

2. Communicate our love and care for each member.

3. Inform them of our Home Fellowships for the *Seek the Lord* Offering.

4. Share updated building news.

5. Impart the need for each member to actively participate in the *Seek the Lord* Offering, to bring in all the commitments, and begin debt reduction.

The visitation team members must be enthusiastic in their presentation of the program; however, they must also be Spirit-filled and discerning with each call. The campaign director will mail a letter to the home hosts on Monday, January 24. The home host team leader should be prepared to explain the home host philosophy and teach the team members how to properly make the home visits at the meeting on Sunday, January 30, following the evening service.

At the home host meeting, Pastor will cast the vision for the upcoming *Seek the Lord* Offering, then the home host team leaders will proceed to train their couples. The home visits are scheduled to begin on Tuesday, February 1, and the goal is to have all the visits completed by February 20. Due to the allotted time, home host leaders may commit their families through phone calls. However, the goal is to have our entire church participate in our Home Fellowships on February 27.

The home host team leaders will work closely with each of the four team captains to make sure that every family has received a home visit and is committed to be in someone's home for the Home Fellowships on February 27.

The team leaders need to make note of the following dates:

1. Personally receive Home Visit Notebook by January 30.

2. Begin preparing for the home host meeting on January 30 with ideas and thoughts on:

    a. How to build meaningful relationships.

b. How to lead a home host gathering.

c. How to make a home visit properly.

d. Pass out co-host's assignments.

e. Pass out lists of families that have been assigned to visit.

3. On January 31, begin contacting and committing team members and informing them of the home host meeting on February 6.

4. Contact those who missed the February 6 meeting and reschedule a follow-up meeting for February 13.

5. By February 3, notify the campaign director of any team members who have not been committed to the Home Visitation Program.

6. During the weeks of January 31–February 13, contact the team captains regarding the progress of the home visit appointments.

7. Team leaders and host meeting on February 20 following the evening service.

Prayer Team Leaders

The responsibility of the prayer team leaders is to help develop a spirit of prayer and dependency upon God within the church as we enter the *Seek the Lord* Offering. The prayer chain will work through each adult Bible class care group leader. This year, we would like to continue the prayer chain throughout the year as an effort to maintain a spirit of prayer during the new millennium.

The first prayer chain night should be held on Thursday, February 24, to pray for the Home Fellowships on February 27. The next prayer chain night should be held on Thursday, March 9, to pray for the *Seek the Lord* Offering.

The team leaders need to make note of the following dates:

1. Contact your team members to be part of the prayer team by February 6.

2. Prayer chain needs to run on the following dates: Thursday, February 24, and Thursday, March 9.

Primary and Junior Care Team Leaders

The primary and junior care team leaders' responsibilities include preparing and planning a program for the night of the Home Fellowships. The team leaders should make sure there are adequate helpers, snacks, and other supplies.

Team leaders will also be responsible for working with the campaign director in assigning rooms for each of the different age groups.

The team leaders should be available for checking children in from 5:00 until 6:10 P.M. They should also be available to help dismiss the children at the close of the night.

The team leaders need to make note of the following dates:

1. Contact and commit your team members by February 6.

2. Enlist workers for the classes by February 9.

3. Organize and prepare the children's program by February 16. This should include the following areas:
   a. Materials for the teachers
   b. Selection of the teachers
   c. Games
   d. Videos
   e. Security
   f. Classroom assignments

4. Schedule and conduct one training session for your teachers and workers by February 23.

Publicity Team Leaders

The responsibility of the publicity team leader is to find creative ways to publicize the *Seek the Lord* Offering to our church family.

Publicity may include special advertisements (in the rest rooms, and hallways), electronic signs, skits, and the design of the *Seek the Lord* booklet that we will use for the Home Fellowship Night on February 27.

This year, in conjunction with the *Seek the Lord* Campaign, there will be a poster contest for children ages 4 years through 6th grade. The publicity team leader needs to contact the team leaders' secretary about graphs and charts showing attendance growth, salvations, baptisms, and other areas of growth of the church for display leading up to the *Seek the Lord* Offering.

The team leader needs to make note of the following dates:

1. Approximately 20 posters need to be hung around the building by Sunday, February 6.

2. Coordinate the children's poster contest with the primary and junior care tem leader beginning January 30.

3. Begin design of the *Seek the Lord* booklet on February 4.

4. Copy of the booklet to Pastor for approval on February 9.

5. Booklet goes to print on February 15.

6. Post the children's posters on February 26.

Testimony Team Leaders

The testimony team leaders will need to contact all people assigned to give testimonies and confirm that they will be there for their meeting on Wednesday, February 2, 2000. There is a brief introduction by the campaign director at this meeting. The testimony team leaders will proceed to explain the importance of these testimonies as well as explain how the testimonies should be given. Each testimony should include the words "Seeking the Lord." The testimony team leaders will offer any help in developing the testimonies as well as training the people in any necessary speech techniques. The testimony team leaders will remind the speaker a day or two before his appointed service. The testimony team leaders will notify the campaign director of any changes with the schedule.

The following people will be contacted by a letter from the campaign director and will need to be reminded by the testimony team leaders accordingly of the following calendar:

Sun., Feb. 13	A.M.	John Downey
	P.M.	Jack Smith
Wed., Feb. 16		Jennifer Jones
Sun., Feb. 20	A.M.	Del Hultman
	P.M.	Sam Jensen
Wed., Feb. 23		Bob Humphrey
Sun., Feb. 27	A.M.	Eric Pfeifer
	P.M.	Randy Wells
Wed., March 1		Don Schellenberg
Sun., March 5	A.M.	Paul Tierney
	P.M.	J.D. Thorogood
Wed., March 8		Juna Auldridge
Sun., March 12	A.M.	Bill Weible
	P.M.	Eldon Lofgren

Spanish Decorations Team Leaders

The decoration team leaders endeavor to set the mood and atmosphere of the Spanish Home Fellowship in the Student Life Center on February 27. The decoration team leaders should use creativity and should incorporate streamers, balloons, signs, and other forms of hanging decorations to create an exciting atmosphere.

The team leaders will need to stay in contact with the campaign director by way of purchase orders for decorations as well as scheduling times for decorators to be at the church on the night of the fellowship.

The team leaders need to make note of the following dates:

1. By Sunday, February 9, submit decorating ideas to the campaign director.

2. All purchase orders should be submitted by Thursday, February 10.

3. Each team member should be contacted and committed by February 13.

4. Confirm and remind team members regarding the decoration schedule by February 20.

Spanish Testimony Team Leaders

The testimony team leaders will need to contact all people assigned to give testimonies and confirm that they will be there for their meeting on Wednesday, February 2, 2000. There is a brief introduction by the campaign director at this meeting. The testimony team leaders will proceed to explain the importance of these testimonies as well as explain how the testimonies should be given. Each testimony should include the words "Seeking the Lord." The testimony team leaders will offer any help in developing the testimonies as well as training the people in any necessary speech techniques. The testimony team leaders will remind the speaker a day or two before his appointed service. The testimony team leaders will notify the campaign director of any changes with the schedule.

The following people will be contacted by a letter from the campaign director and will need to be reminded by the testimony team leaders accordingly of the following calendar:

Sun., Feb. 13	A.M.	Rufino Barrios
	P.M.	Edgar Solorzano
Sun., Feb. 20	A.M.	Carlos Broda
	P.M.	Manny Gonsales
Sun., Feb. 27	A.M.	Manny Rivera
	P.M.	Javier Ruiz
Sun., March 5	A.M.	Daniel Galdamez
	P.M.	Miguel Sandoval
Sun., March 12	A.M.	Morris Henriquez
	P.M.	Manny Morino

Visual Effects Team Leaders

The responsibility of the visual effects team leaders is to produce a video that can be shared with the church family during the weeks leading up to the *Seek the Lord* Offering. This video should last approximately five minutes.

Also, be prepared to use slides for the projection screens throughout the *Seek the Lord* Offering program.

Youth Night Team Leaders

The responsibility of the youth night team leaders is to produce a youth program to thank our church for Seeking the Lord. This will include the children's choir and a fifteen minute drama on Seeking the Lord.

This mini drama will be conducted on Sunday, March 5, during the evening service.

The team leaders need to make note of the following dates:

1. Submit drama and drama team to campaign director by February 4.

2. Begin practices with children's choirs and drama team on February 13.

Full Church-Wide Stewardship Campaign

This collection provides a complete outline of the annual stewardship campaign at Lancaster Baptist. God has blessed this campaign by allowing the church to give millions of dollars over the years. The collection includes the following:

- Campaign Leadership Notebook
- Leadership Team Meeting Video
- Stewardship messages and outlines
- Campaign print materials
- Campaign video
- Numerous starter ideas

For more information or to order this collection of materials call *Striving Together Publications* at 800-201-7748 or visit the website at www.strivingtogether.com.

CHAPTER TWENTY-THREE

Weddings

*"Therefore shall a man leave his father and his mother,
and shall cleave unto his wife: and they shall be one flesh."*
Genesis 2:24

The union of two Christian people in holy matrimony is a momentous and joyous occasion for all involved. The church has a critical role in the preparation, planning, and conducting of the wedding, as well as in the mentoring and establishing of a new family. Chances are, no matter what size your church, you will be called on frequently to provide premarital counseling, wedding arrangements, wedding ceremonies, and marriage counseling.

For your church family, these wedding ceremonies, over the years, will become joyful times of remembering young lives and seeing them come together in God's perfect will. As the years pass, these ceremonies will be a celebration of the fruit of your faithful ministry in one place for God's glory. There is great joy in staying in one place long enough to see young lives grow up in a church family and then come together to begin families of their own. This kind of long-term fruit is hard to put a price on. It is truly a glimpse at a ministry product that is years in creating by God's grace.

To your community—your church facility, your ministerial services, and your premarital counseling can be wonderful outreach opportunities. Over time, your community should be aware that you offer your church and your spiritual guidance for young couples preparing for marriage. Later in this chapter, you will find the guidelines that we have chosen to use in determining the extent of these services to the community. Many couples have been led to Christ and have begun their marriage as new Christians because of our willingness to counsel and marry couples who are not yet members of our church.

Over the years, many have opted not to take advantage of our services simply because our policies and guidelines were too confined in dealing with questions of music, alcohol, counseling, modesty, etc. We have chosen to keep the standard high when dealing with marriage from outside of our church family.

This chapter provides a look at the process that an engaged couple must complete to be married at Lancaster Baptist Church. Later in the chapter, there are some suggested ceremony details and an actual wedding ceremony script.

The Wedding Ceremony

After your salvation, your wedding day is the most important day of your life. Therefore, this little booklet has been written to help make this day a very memorable occasion.

This is certainly not exhaustive; however, what is written in these pages is designed for our church and the weddings conducted here.

It is expected that you carefully examine the following pages. Please make notes and write down any questions that come to mind.

Your wedding should be a happy and memorable occasion. The wedding service is not a show or for entertainment. Rather, it is a service to Almighty God. Therefore, we must meet together for prayer, preparation, and clarification of all that is necessary to assure you of a wonderful wedding service and for a godly home together. Thank you for giving us this opportunity to be of service to you.

Sincerely in Christ,

The Pastoral Staff

People to Meet With

    A. Wedding Counselor

    B. Wedding Planner

        1. Approves music, along with the music director (music must be submitted one week prior to wedding)

        2. Approves caterer (on property)

        3. Approves wedding dress and all attendants' dresses

    C. Wedding Coordinator

        1. Rehearsal, order of service

        2. The actual wedding ceremony

        3. Reception

The Officiating Pastor

The pastor who will preside at a particular wedding will depend upon the date requested on the calendar and the type of wedding being performed. The senior pastor will perform weddings as his calendar allows, primarily for faithful young people who have been raised in and are members of the church who have been faithfully attending all services for the previous six months. He will also perform the wedding of the bride or groom who is marrying someone from another church of like faith where he/she has been and is actively serving the Lord.

    An assistant pastor will be available to conduct the wedding of a couple that is from another church of like faith. He will also conduct a ceremony for marriage vows renewal for a faithful couple from the church or from another church of like faith.

Pre-Marital Counseling

    A. What to bring

        1. Notebook

    2. Pen/pencil

    3. Bible (King James Version)

B. Where and when

    1. In office of pastoral staff member

    2. During weekday office hours

C. How long

    1. Six sessions must be attended over a 12-week period. No one can be married at the church until all six counseling sessions are conducted. After mailing in the Preliminary Wedding Questionnaire (see CD 23.1), call the office to set up your first appointment. No wedding date is guaranteed until after the first pre-marital counseling session.

    2. The first appointment is strictly an introduction time concerning what to expect in pre-marital counseling and what the pastor expects of you.

    3. Be prepared to discuss your financial status. This church does not recommend couples marrying with an extreme debt situation.

Wedding Preparation

Announcements

1. DO NOT order announcements until the date has been cleared and approved by the pastor's secretary.

2. Announcements should be ordered at least four to six months in advance. This avoids any danger of having to send out misprinted invitations.

3. Announcements should be sent four to six weeks before the wedding date.

4. Announcements should be hand addressed in cursive writing. Address all announcements as such: Mr. and Mrs. George Brown (NOT George and Sally Brown).

5. Use the terms Dr., Mr., Mrs., or Miss (the appropriate title for the individual).

6. Do not write anything else on the announcement such as: Hi, Hello, Hope to see you, etc.

7. All this should be handled by the bride. However, both the groom and the bride can select the proper and appropriate invitation.

WHEN PARENTS ARE DIVORCED

When a daughter lives with her mother who is divorced from her father, the invitations are sent out in the mother's name. Her present husband's name may be included. Divorced parents never send invitations out together. In such circumstances, it is better that the wedding be given by the mother. To do otherwise might imply that the mother had been unfit to have the custody of her daughter.

The bride's mother should be seated in the regular pew reserved for the bride's mother, with members of her family and her current husband, if she is remarried. It is proper for the father to walk up the aisle of the church with his daughter and give her away, even though the invitations are sent out by his former wife. He then takes his place in one of the pews further back on the bride's side. If remarried, he may be accompanied by his current wife. If relations are strained, some other male relative may give the bride away, or her mother might if her father is not to attend the wedding.

If the groom's parents are divorced, again, the mother and family should be given the regular pew on the groom's side of the church, and the father seated several rows behind on the same side.

Every effort should be made to make the meetings of the divorced parents friendly and not conspicuously tense. The bride or groom needs to feel that those who brought her or him into existence are, on this day, brought together peacefully because of their mutual concern for their offspring's happiness.

If the bride's remarried mother gives the reception, her husband acts as the host, and the bride's father attends only as a guest. If the father gives the reception and he has not remarried, he stands first in the line to receive guests. If he has remarried, his wife acts as hostess. If the bride's mother attends the reception under the latter circumstances, she is present as a guest and should not stand at the side of her former husband nor share duties as hostess.

Flowers

1. Call a reputable florist at least four to six months in advance. Make an appointment to visit the business establishment and carefully review its catalogs. Be sure to order flowers that correspond to the season of the year. The flowers need not be extravagant. However, remember that flowers add real beauty to the wedding.

2. Where are flowers needed? (Some are optional.)

   a. Groomsmen
   b. Bridesmaids
   c. Instrumentalist
   d. Soloist
   e. Fathers and Mothers
   f. Pastor
   g. Ushers
   h. Front of the auditorium
   i. Pews
   j. Reception Hall
   k. Guest Book Attendant
   l. Candle Lighters

FLORAL DECORATIONS

A wedding is a time of simplicity and good taste, with particular moderation advisable in the selection of floral displays. There is no need for extreme decoration in the sanctuary.

Of course, the wish for a wedding of aesthetic beauty is normal, natural, and desirable. However, gaudiness and extremes should be avoided. Decorations should neither distract from nor obscure the furniture, the symbolism of the sanctuary, or the wedding service. The sanctuary itself should reflect, in symbols and beauty, the love of God and the spirit of Christ.

The coordinator should inform local florists of the rules of his church with regard to wedding decorations. Implicit understanding is needed with florists regarding the moving of furniture, where flowers are to be placed, and the use of tape and tacks.

Pictures

1. Seek a reputable photographer. Make an appointment at his office to see his work. Ask him to attend the rehearsal.

2. The photographer is not permitted to take pictures during the wedding ceremony.

Use of the Building and Wedding Fees

A. Buildings
No alcoholic beverages or tobacco are permitted on the church grounds. Please notify all guests of this policy (caterers, wedding party, etc.).

B. Wedding Fees

1. There will be a $50 fee required for the use of the building. This can be waived if the bridal party takes full responsibility for the clean-up (vacuuming,

mopping of floors, cleaning of restrooms, dusting, cleaning windows, etc.).
2. Pre-marital counselor—honorarium or gift
3. Presiding pastor—honorarium or gift
4. Instrumentalist—honorarium or gift
5. Soloists—honorarium or gift
6. Wedding coordinator—honorarium or gift
7. Wedding party—gifts at the rehearsal dinner
8. The bridal party is fully responsible for rental of tables and chairs (this includes delivery and pickup).

Who Is Responsible?

Often there comes confusion as to who is responsible for various functions and items for the wedding.

Duties of the Bride and Her Family

The date, place, and time of the ceremony are selected by the bride and her mother. They also schedule the church and the pastor, obtain an instrumentalist and a singer, choose music (to be cleared by the wedding planner and the music director), and arrange for the rehearsal of the wedding party at the church. The bride and her mother select the invitations, make up the guest list (after conferring with the groom's mother), and send out invitations. The selection of the style and color of the bridesmaids' dresses is up to the bride; however, she does not pay for them. Decorations and flowers for the church, the ring for the future husband, and the wedding reception are responsibilities of the bride's family. The bride also has the social obligation of acknowledging receipt of each wedding gift with a personal note.

Duties of the Groom

The groom purchases the marriage license, the ring, bouquet, and wedding gift for his bride. For the men of the wedding party, he purchases the ties, boutonnieres, or other gifts, as regional customs demand. He also arranges the rehearsal dinner. One of his most important duties is to make advance arrangements for the honeymoon trip so that accommodations are assured.

Financial Obligations of the Bride

1. Engraving of invitations and announcements
2. Mailing of invitations, cards, and announcements
3. Transportation for attendants to and from church
4. Hotel bills for her attendants when bride's parents cannot accommodate them
5. Instrumentalist
6. Soloist
7. Wedding reception
8. Groom's ring
9. Bride's trousseau
10. Wedding photographs
11. Gifts to the bridesmaids and maid (or matron) of honor
12. Bridesmaids' flowers
13. Church decorations
14. Gift to groom

Financial Obligations of the Groom

1. Marriage license
2. Bride's ring
3. Bachelor dinner (optional)
4. Rehearsal dinner

5. Gift to bride

6. Bride's flowers

7. Transportation for male attendants to and from church

8. Pastor's fee

9. Corsages for the mothers of the bride and groom

10. Boutonnieres for best man, ushers, groomsmen, groom's father, and the pastor

11. Gifts to male attendants and ushers

12. Ties and gloves for attendants (optional)

13. Hotel bills for his attendants from out of town

14. Wedding trip

Duties of the Maid (or Matron) of Honor

The maid of honor is the bride's most important attendant, usually being her sister or closest friend. She should be notified of her selection several months in advance, before invitations are sent, so that the date can be entered into her schedule and necessary adjustments and clothing preparations can be made.

Unless the bride can afford the expense and wants to give her the wedding outfit, the maid of honor buys her own wedding clothes. The flowers she carries, however, are given to her by the bride.

The duties and responsibilities of the maid of honor are as follows:

1. Attend the rehearsal.

2. Arrange the bride's train as the procession forms in the rear of the church and again at the altar if necessary, and straighten it behind the bride as she turns for the recessional.

3. Hold the bride's bouquet during the ring exchange.

4. Carry the groom's ring during the ceremony (unless there is a ring bearer), and give it to the pastor at the appropriate time.

5. If the bride wears a veil, the maid of honor helps to lift it back on her head at the end of the ceremony.

6. Stand in the receiving line to the groom's left.

7. Assist the bride in changing clothes and packing for her trip.

8. See that no tricks in bad taste are played.

Duties of the Best Man

The best man is the groom's primary attendant, usually his closest friend or a brother. He is chosen in ample time so that he can make whatever adjustments are necessary to be present.

The duties of the best man are:

1. Aid the groom in every possible way in preparation for the wedding. He protects the groom from pranks and, under no circumstances, participates in practical jokes played on the bride and groom.

2. Attend the rehearsal and aid the pastor in gaining the cooperation of the male attendants and see that they are on time for the wedding.

3. Help the groom dress for the wedding and go with him to the church at least half an hour before wedding time.

4. Deliver the license and wedding book to the pastor for his recording, sign his own signature as one of the witnesses, and deliver the same to the maid of honor for her signature.

5. Accompany the groom to the altar, carrying the bride's ring until the time the pastor asks for it in the ceremony.

If the groom wears gloves, the best man holds them during the ceremony.

6. Stand in the reception line to the left of the maid of honor. If the reception is at a place other than the church, he gets the hats and coats of the bride and groom and meets them at the front door. He chauffeurs the couple and maid of honor to the place of the reception.

7. Help the groom pack and take charge of the couple's luggage, seeing that it is placed safely in the going-away car.

8. Keep in safety the keys to the groom's car. When the time comes for the couple's departure, he helps them get away safely.

Checklist for Bride and Groom

Four to Six Months Before Wedding

1. Have conference with the pastor to arrange day and time.

2. Make reservation for church use for both wedding and reception. If reception is not in a church, you may have to make earlier arrangements.

3. Learn the policy of the church regarding costs, decoration, etc.

4. Make arrangements with organist, other musicians, and primary attendants.

5. Read through the wedding planning book.

Three Months Before Wedding

1. Make out wedding invitation list.

2. Make out reception list.

3. Order invitations and announcements.

4. Have conference with caterer.

Tenth Week Before Wedding

1. Select and get commitments from members of wedding party.

2. Choose general color scheme and flowers.

Ninth and Eighth Week Before Wedding

1. Order or begin making wedding dress (to be approved by wedding planner).

2. Arrange date, time, and place of rehearsal dinner.

3. Select china, glassware, and silver patterns.

Seventh Week Before Wedding

1. Make arrangements with florist.

2. Make arrangements with photographer.

3. Order printed napkins, etc., for reception.

Sixth Week Before Wedding

1. Pick out gifts for attendants.

2. Arrange for housing of guests from out of town.

3. Read literature recommended by the pastor.

4. Buy wedding rings.

Fifth Week Before Wedding

1. Buy going-away clothes.

2. Make honeymoon trip reservations.

Fourth Week Before Wedding

1. Have conference with physician.
2. Have blood test.
3. Recheck with all attendants to confirm that they will be present.
4. Send out invitations to wedding and to rehearsal dinner.
5. Submit a release to newspaper of announced wedding.
6. Give a bridesmaid's luncheon or tea.

Second Week Before Wedding

1. Get license.
2. Pose for a bride's picture for newspaper.

Last Week Before Wedding

1. Remind all participants regarding rehearsal attendance.
2. Have newspaper release ready.
3. Arrange for announcements to be mailed the day of the ceremony.

The Wedding Rehearsal

A. Who should attend

Please notify everyone in the wedding party of the exact time of the wedding rehearsal. Everyone is expected to be on time. (This means 5–15 minutes before the rehearsal time.)

B. How long

The rehearsal will be 45 minutes to one hour in duration.

C. Suggestions

No suggestions are permitted from the wedding party:

> First—The wedding coordinator will explain the format.

> Second—There will be a walk-through of the ceremony.

> Third—There will be a brief break. At this time the pastor will meet with the bride, groom, and parents. Please notify the wedding coordinator at this time of any changes.

> Fourth—A final walk through.

D. Attire

The wedding itself is a formal occasion. Thus, the wedding rehearsal is somewhat of a semi-formal occasion. Everyone must look and act very dignified. All participants in the wedding party must be dressed appropriately for rehearsal.

Men—Dress slacks or nice casual clothing are acceptable. (Please have an acceptable hair cut.)

Ladies—All ladies must wear modest, knee-length dresses. (Shoulders and back should be covered.)

(Anyone in the wedding party should dress modestly for both the rehearsal and the wedding day. Ladies, no pantsuits, please.)

E. Rehearsal dinner

This should be held immediately after the rehearsal. An invitation must be extended to everyone that you wish to have attend. Make it very clear that everyone in the wedding party and their mates are expected to attend.

EXAMPLE: The instrumentalist and his/her mate should be invited. This should be done weeks in advance. The tables should be pre-set with nametags at each setting. The bride and groom must act as the host and hostess. Make sure everyone knows one another, etc. The groom should begin the meal with a brief opening remark and prayer. After the meal, the groom should introduce the bride-to-be, at which time she acknowledges each bridesmaid in the wedding party with a word of introduction and a testimony regarding what that person means to her and then gives them a special gift. They should also recognize their parents at this time and give a testimony in their regard. Then the groom should recognize each groomsman with a word of introduction and testimony regarding that person and give them a gift. The pastor should be asked to close in prayer.

The Wedding

A. Bride

It is customary that the bride not see the groom that day until the wedding ceremony. It is suggested that she dress at the church in the bride's room rather than at home or at a motel. She should arrive at the church at least 1–1½ hours before the wedding. The bride's mother, the wedding coordinator, and the maid of honor are the only ones that should be together at this time.

B. Groom

He may dress in the designated groom's room before the service (arrive 45 minutes early).

C. Parents

The parents should stay out of public view until the wedding officially calls for their appearance. (A room will be designated for both sets of parents.)

D. Wedding party

Each one in the wedding party should arrive one hour before the service.

E. Dim lighting must be approved by the wedding planner.

F. Location

1. North Auditorium or Worship Center (depending on size of guest list)
2. Multi-Purpose Room (120 guests)

NOTE: The church does not provide childcare for weddings.

Music

All wedding and reception music must be pre-approved by the wedding planner and music director. The church policy is to have at least one hymn sung along with any other songs that are selected.

The Reception

We encourage you to hold your wedding reception at the church. Please make note of the following:

A. With advance permission obtained through our church wedding coordinator, you may use a designated room for your wedding reception. Tables and chairs may need to be rented.

B. It will be your responsibility to have the room set up for your reception and cleaned afterwards.

C. The church does not provide paper products, decorations, tablecloths, etc.

D. You may use the kitchen facility provided you clean and put away everything you use.

E. Childcare is not provided by the church for receptions.

F. No alcoholic beverages, smoking, or dancing are allowed on the church premises.

G. The reception should begin by introducing the wedding party and any special family members and guests followed by prayer for the meal. Any man serving must have a conservative hair cut (no ponytails) and no earrings. Women must not wear slacks.

H. All food preparation must be approved through the wedding coordinator.

The Honeymoon

The groom is responsible for the arrangements and is financially responsible for this memorable occasion.

Please make reservations ahead of time. The honeymoon must consist of a schedule that has been prepared by the groom:

1. Know the location of the motel.
2. Have it prepaid.
3. Have flowers in the room.
4. Set a schedule for every day (make plans to see places).
5. Save enough money to enjoy every meal at a restaurant.

The honeymoon should last four to ten days (approximately). Be sure to establish your home on your knees with an open Bible from day one.

Some Final Thoughts

You are both due for a real awakening! At times, you will be convinced you married a different person than the one that you dated.

Listed below are several suggestions:

1. Do not expect things from your mate. Expect things of yourself.

2. Have a personal prayer time and Bible study time daily.

3. Have family devotions.

4. Attend and BE ACTIVE in an independent, fundamental, Baptist church.

5. Tithe every week.

6. Support your church and pastor.

7. Show gratitude to those who have encouraged you.

May God Bless Your Home,

The Pastoral Staff

I have read this book in its entirety and agree to abide by its contents.

_____

Prospective Groom

_____

Prospective Bride

_____

Date

The Wedding Ceremony

- Lighting of Candles
- Seating of Grandparents

Song

(Parents will walk in together, light candles, and then are seated.)

Processional: Canon in D

- Aisle Runner
- Enter: Pastor, Groom, and Best Man
- Enter: Bridesmaids, Groomsmen, and Maid of Honor
- Enter: Flower girl and Ring Bearer

Bridal Chorus

- Enter: Bride and Father

Pastor: "You may be seated."

Pastor : Welcome/Prayer

Pastor: Introduction

"We are gathered here in the sight of God and in the presence of these witnesses to join together this man and this woman in the holy estate of matrimony, which is an honorable state, instituted by God, and signifying that union between Christ and the Church."

"Who gives this woman to be married to this man?"

Father of the bride: "Her mother and I do"

Father passes Bride's hand to Groom and then is seated.

Song
Charge to Couple

(Groom's name) and (Bride's name) have both given testimony...they have trusted Christ...

Song
Prelude to Vows

No other union is more tender. No other vows are more sacred than these you are about to assume.

(Groom's Name), will you have this woman to be your lawfully wedded wife, to live in the state of matrimony? Will you love her, comfort her, in sickness and in health, forsaking all others, keeping yourself for her so long as you both shall live?

Groom: I Will.

(Bride's Name), will you have this man to be your lawfully wedded husband, to live together after God's ordinance in the holy state of matrimony? Will you love, honor, obey and keep him in sickness and in health, forsaking all others keeping yourself only for him so long as you both shall live?

Bride: I Will.

Exchange Rings

What pledge do you give to show the sincerity of your vows?

Groom: A ring

Bride: A ring

With this ring, I thee wed, and all my worldly goods, I to thee endow.

Exchange Vows

(Groom's name) and (Bride's name), having come together in Christ, and now, this day in marriage, will you join right hands and repeat after me:

I,(Groom's name)/(Bride's name) take you, (Bride's name)/(Groom's name)

> to have and to hold…
> from this day forward…
> for better, for worse…
> for richer, for poorer…
> in sickness and in health…
> to love and to cherish…
> 'til death do us part.

Song

Lighting of Unity Candle

During song Groom and Bride will light Unity Candle then will kneel and pray together during the remainder of the song.

Prayer

By the power vested in me by God and this local church, I pronounce you man and wife. What God hath joined together, let no man put asunder. You may kiss your bride.

Ladies and Gentlemen, may I present to you ***Mr. and Mrs. (Groom's name)***

Recessional

CHAPTER TWENTY-FOUR

Funerals

"So when this corruptible shall have put on incorruption, and this mortal shall have put on immortality, then shall be brought to pass the saying that is written, Death is swallowed up in victory. O death, where is thy sting? O grave, where is thy victory?"
I Corinthians 15:54–55

The church is a body—when one member hurts, the body should sense and respond to that pain to the best of its ability. The church and its leadership can be a tremendous comfort and conduit of God's love and care during a time of loss, and there should be a heart to reach out, to assist with arrangements, and to provide comfort and care to those who are dealing with the loss. As the numbing impact of a loved one's death settles in, friends, care groups, pastors, and deacons can come to the side of a church family member to assist with funeral arrangements, paper work, notification of friends, and a myriad of other details. More importantly, the presence of the church body during this time brings an eternal perspective to something that is temporarily very painful.

The pastor and church family should have a plan of action—a process—that goes into effect the moment that notification of a death is received. This process is listed in more detail in this chapter but should include the notification of key care givers, assistance with funeral arrangements, planning a home-going service, providing meals and floral arrangements, and generally "being there" to give comfort and to bear the burden.

The care givers in this Christian's life (deacons, care group, pastoral staff) should be trained, ready, and willing to provide the following:

1. **Presence and companionship**—Nothing says more than just being there to pray, comfort, encourage, and even weep with those who are grieving.

2. **Encouraging Scriptures**—Know where to go in God's Word and make it a habit to give God's comfort in these situations.

3. **Meals**—Care groups can quickly arrange for meals to be prepared and delivered to the home for several days.

4. **Prayer support**—Few things say you really care like praying personally with someone. When you just don't know what to say—pray.

5. **Funeral arrangements**—Often, the family involved has little or no experience in planning a memorial service. A sample memorial service plan and cue card is offered later in this chapter. Be willing to suggest songs, Scripture passages, and special service details; be willing to listen to the desires and requests of the family as well.

6. **Use of church facilities**—More often than not, your church family will desire to use your auditorium for the memorial service. This will mean arranging for the cleaning and preparation of the room, sound system support, ushers, clean-up, etc. Also offer the use of

another room for a family reception if desired. (At LBC, there is no charge for these services, and local mortuaries are aware that they can call on our church for this support or for pastoral support, for non-members, at any time. On many occasions the Lord has opened doors of ministry with unsaved families through this avenue.)

7. **Follow-up care after the memorial service**—The hardest days for a grieving relative are usually after family and friends have gone. The church must still respond with loving care during this season of transition.

The following is a list of procedures that are followed when we receive notification of a death. At the end of this chapter is a sample cue card and message for a memorial service.

Funeral Procedures

A. Pastor (is notified by member, etc.)
The pastor will let the church staff know what he wants done for the family.

B. Assistant Pastor
He will find out what the family wants to do and will inform funeral assistant of details.

C. Funeral Assistant
This person will inform the deacon/care group leader what Pastor and the family want done as well the approximate number of people to prepare for.

D. Deacon or Care Group Leader

1. There may be a situation where the family needs to have meals in their home.
2. If a room at the church is to be set up for the family before the funeral, make available coffee, ice water, and cookies, depending on the time of day.
3. If the family wants the reception at the church, the deacon and his wife or the care group leader and his wife (who are assigned to the family) will line up three ladies to help with set-up, two ladies to help serve, and three ladies to help clean-up.
4. The food coordinator will purchase supplies, cold cuts, and rolls. She will also call upon ladies to help with the salads, chips, dips, and extras.
5. If the food coordinator is not available to do the purchasing, the church clerk will give the deacon or the care group leader a check to do the shopping.
6. After the reception, it is very important that the kitchen is tidied and all food either given to the family or put in the refrigerator.

7. If the family wants the reception at home, the deacon or care group leader will line up food to be taken to the home.

Sample Funeral Cue Card

Welcome: Pastor
Congregational: *It Is Well with My Soul*
Prayer: Pastor
Eulogy: Pastor
Scripture: Pastor
Special Song: *No More Night*
Message: Pastor
Closing Prayer: Pastor

Reception in the Multi-Purpose Room following graveside

Sample Funeral Message

Text: I Peter 12:1-9
Title: Homegoing Service for _____

Introduction:

The Apostle Peter wrote to Christians in the first century who were confused and dealing with incredible trials. As these Christians faced the tumultuous *rivers* of life, Peter's epistle pointed them to those giant *boulders* in the river. Boulders which would help them to cross safely.

We come here today as a people with heavy hearts, but we are not without a solid Rock—a sure footing of hope. Even as Peter pointed these Christians to "rocks of hope," let us notice what God provides for us...

    I. The Promise of God (I Peter 12:3)

        A. Begotten—Born = Saved

B. Hope—expectation of good

C. Because of Christ's resurrection

> *"And if Christ be not risen, then is our preaching vain, and your faith is also vain."* I Corinthians 15:14

> *"If in this life only we have hope in Christ, we are of all men most miserable. But now is Christ risen from the dead, and become the **first-fruits** of them that slept."* I Corinthians 15:19–20

> NOTE: The promise is found in the words *"first-fruits."*

> *"...It is sown in corruption; it is raised in incorruption: It is sown in dishonour; it is raised in glory: it is sown in weakness; it is raised in power: It is sown a natural body; it is raised a spiritual body..."* I Corinthians 15:42–44

> *"...to be absent from the body, and to be present with the Lord."* II Corinthians 5:8

II. The Place of God (I Peter 12:4)

A. Incorruptible

B. Undefiled

> *"...God himself shall be with them...And God shall wipe away all tears from their eyes; and there shall be no more death, neither sorrow, nor crying, neither shall there be any more pain: for the former things are passed away."* Revelation 21:3–4

C. Reserved—Now how do we **reserve** a place in heaven? Is it that concise? YES—our names are written down.

Turn to John 14:1–6

> NOTE: The place of God is **Heaven**—you can reserve a place today!

Promise of God—eternal life
Place of God—Heaven

III. The Power of God (I Peter 12:5)

    A. Power to keep us

        "...[I] am persuaded that he is able to keep that which I have committed..." II Timothy 1:12

    B. Power to comfort us

        "The LORD is nigh unto them that are of a broken heart..." Psalm 34:18

        "God is our refuge and strength, a very present help in trouble." Psalm 46:1

    C. Power to redeem us

        "The LORD redeemeth the soul of his servants: and none of them that trust in him shall be desolate." Psalm 34:22

        *"But I would not have you to be ignorant, brethren, concerning them which are asleep, that ye sorrow not, even as others which have no hope. For **if we believe** that Jesus died and rose again, even so them also which sleep in Jesus will God bring with Him."* I Thessalonians 4:13–14

Conclusion:

The Promise of God—Eternal Life
The Place of God—Heaven
The Power of God—To comfort and redeem

CHAPTER TWENTY-FIVE

Going to Two Services

"And the lord said unto the servant, Go out into the
highways and hedges, and compel them to come in,
that my house may be filled."
Luke 14:23

Looking back over the history of Lancaster Baptist Church, there
are several men who counseled and guided me in the development
of this ministry. In particular, I remember a special meeting we
had with Dr. Lee Roberson from Chattanooga, Tennessee. At that
time, we were meeting in our downtown building in Lancaster,
awaiting the construction of our new building on the east side. I
was seriously contemplating going to two services, as the building
was packed and, for the evening services, people literally were
sitting outside the church listening through the windows. This
was especially true during special meetings with men such as Dr.
Tom Malone, Dr. Lee Roberson and Dr. Curtis Hutson.

My habit was, and continues to be today, to get as much
counsel as possible from godly pastors who will take time with

me. I remember specifically asking Dr. Roberson if we should go to two services at that time. His counsel to me was to keep the auditorium packed and overflowing while we were in the midst of a building program. This was fantastic counsel! I followed his counsel until God allowed us to move into our new building about a year later.

Our first auditorium on the east side of Lancaster had a seating capacity of around eight hundred. To our surprise and excitement, on the Dedication Sunday of the new building our attendance grew from 1,600 the previous week to over 2,300. Nearly 1,200 of those people crammed into our brand new auditorium. It was exciting and a little deflating, all at the same time!

Shortly after moving to this property I spoke to Dr. Curtis Hutson. Dr. Hutson became a dear friend and counselor in the ministry and, while he was a solid, fundamental, Bible-believing preacher, he was a man who was not willing to allow a few critics to stop him from using various innovative methods to reach souls for the Saviour. Dr. Hutson strongly encouraged me to consider a two-service schedule.

At that time, I did not know a single pastor who was using a two-service schedule. I remember taking our pastoral staff to a conference room off the property of our church and spending a day and a half trying to consider all of the variables of a two-service schedule. There were so many facets of the situation that needed to be discussed. First, we wanted to make sure that our philosophy was correct. We were not simply making a new schedule for the convenience of people, but for the purpose of reaching souls.

Second, we wanted to make sure that no person was left behind. It was vital to me that we did not divide families when the new schedule was announced. For example, we did not want to create a situation in which a wife, who was in the choir, was not able to attend a Sunday school class with her husband.

Ten years have come and gone since the initial decision to go to two services. We are still conducting two preaching services every Sunday morning and believe that God has used this method to help us reach souls for our Saviour.

Currently, at Lancaster Baptist Church, we conduct Sunday school at 8:15, 9:30, and 11:00 A.M., and morning worship services at 9:30 and 11:00 A.M. For many years we conducted morning services at 8:30, Sunday school at 10:00, and another morning service at 11:00. The current program allowed us to develop many new Sunday school classes.

On the following pages we will share with you some of the training that was given to our church family as we approached the two-service schedule.

Philosophy

(Transcribed from a training meeting with Pastor Chappell)

A growing church is always in transition.

Learn that from the very beginning. I used to tell the Sunday school teachers, "Do not get all emotionally attached to your class location because we might have to move you to another one." We have had classes meeting in buses, on the grass out front; we have had classes meet in tents, public high schools, in garages, in houses, under stairwells—you name the little spot, we have had a class there. We have just tried to teach the Word everywhere we possibly can. Maintaining flexibility is key to making this transition.

Methods are many, principles are few. Methods may change; principles never do.

When it comes to doctrine, the principles of the church, soulwinning, the various distinctives of the church, those things are written down from the Word of God. The Bible says, "remove not the ancient landmarks." For example, we have a principle about the kind of music we use, the version of the Bible that we use, and the way we go out soulwinning. These principles will not change.

Different types of methods can be used from time to time without being unscriptural. Such is the case when it comes to the scheduling of services. For example, services can be held seven days a week. They can be held all day long on Sunday, as I understand the Word of God. Traditionally in America, morning services have been held primarily at 11:00. The main reason they were established at that time, as history records, was so that the farmers could milk the cows, get cleaned up, and get to church. That is why church has been at 11:00. That is a good explanation, but it does not mean you are unscriptural if you have church at another time.

Honestly, I struggle with a two-service schedule because I am a big "*T*"—Traditionalist. I like doing things in a traditional way. I love, and will always love, the 11:00 service. I love church on Sunday morning, Sunday night, and Wednesday night. That is the way I am. So, in one respect, going to two worship services is not changing anything, it is just adding to what is already there. You may say, "All right, I like 10:00 and 11:00." That is great and you don't have a thing to worry about, but we definitely need to make some more room somehow until the new building gets built. So we are going to try something (beginning Easter Sunday) that we have done for the last three Easters already, and that is to have a morning service at 8:30, Sunday school at 10:00, and then the morning service at 11:00. Then we are going to roll with it for a while and see if that helps us accommodate the needs.

Some of you are not aware that we have people, every Sunday morning, who drive into the parking lot, cannot park, and they leave. Others come in and see the auditorium, and they are not sticking around. This morning at least 100–150 chairs were set up. Now, someone who is a Bible-believing, fundamental Baptist would sit on that front step to hear the preaching of the Word of God without compromise. I do not believe that you or I should come to church because it is convenient, or because we are comfortable. We should come to church and want to be here because of the message that is being preached. But, there are people who are either not saved, not committed, or whatever, who need to have that little bit of comfort until they grow in conviction to say, "Bless God, I will sit on a hard, steel chair for four hours to hear a good message." It takes a while to develop that type of commitment.

Now, I know there are a lot of inconsistencies with people, because these same people who would feel uncomfortable sitting on a folding chair at church would go to a Dodgers' game and sit for four hours getting beer spilled on them, yelling, screaming, and acting like a bunch of nuts. That is telling us a little about their spiritual level also. I believe that in our hearts we need to develop a desire that says, "I want to be in the house of God and it is more exciting that any athletic event that I could go to." I think you have that kind of dedication tonight or you would not be here at 5:25. So, there are a lot of considerations, and I want to give you four things that will help you to know distinctly the philosophy that we have in adding an additional service.

Our Concern

What is the driving force behind doing this?

Souls

We are doing what we are doing to reach people with the Gospel of Jesus Christ. If we were almost done with the new building and the ushers were telling me, "Pastor, they are driving in and then driving out," I would probably say what I said at the old building, "Let's just pack this baby out; let's just hang on; let's risk losing some folks and as soon as we get into that new building, everything will take care of itself." And that is what we did! We got into this new building, and now it is filled up. So I believe we need to be a people who would say, "I am willing to adjust some things here and there." Most of you will not have to adjust much. The choir will have to adjust a little bit. But, I am willing to make some adjustments so that people can get saved. Our number-one concern, more than our comfort (and most of you will not feel any discomfort with this), is the souls of men.

The stewardship of the resources that we have

We want to use these buildings as often as we possibly can to proclaim the Gospel of Christ. We had prayer meetings and other meetings yesterday morning; at 11:00 we had 300 boys and girls come in for Saturday Bible school, and we had a prayer meeting Saturday night. Then at 8:00 and 9:00 this morning the Spanish folks were using these rooms around us. At 10:00 and at 11:00 we had services. We are going to add one more time, basically, to the overall schedule because we want to be good stewards of the resources we have. I believe, if we use what we have to its fullest, if we keep it clean and take care of it, then God will bless us with more facilities that we can use for His honor and glory.

The same vision

Our Vision Statement is on your bulletin. It says, "To aggressively impact the Antelope Valley and the regions beyond with the Gospel of Christ." Our program is simply to reach men and women, boys and girls, being sensitive to the culture around us (meaning single-parent families, Spanish-speaking families, etc.), wherever they are. We want to equip them with the Word of God so they can go out and tell other people about Jesus Christ. We want to "aggressively impact the Antelope Valley." This new service schedule will help us do that in a way that will be more effective, until we can get our building built.

Our Continuity

People will sometimes ask, "How will we keep the continuity?" That is a question that I like to ask. I like the continuity that we have as a church family. I am very concerned that we maintain that continuity.

First of all, you let the pastor be the judge of whether or not we are maintaining continuity. Let me tell you how we are going to maintain that family-like spirit. Some people say, "Well, if you have two services, you have a divided church—you have two separate groups." Do you know why they say that? Because churches that say that do not have a strong Sunday school or a strong Sunday night ministry. We are going to maintain continuity because of our strong adult Bible classes and our strong Sunday night service. This is the tragedy—most of the churches in the Antelope Valley and America that have two services have done it for convenience sake. They have not done it because they are out of room. They have done it for Sunday morning golfers and the lukewarm Christians, so a guy can go to the 8:30 service and still get an 11:00 tee time and not even think about the Sunday night service.

We are not here to please a lukewarm Christian. We are here to keep the standard high and to try to bring them to a standard where they will take up the cross and follow Jesus Christ. These churches that have the early service for the sake of convenience also have done something very cute on Sunday nights called "home Bible studies." The latest report by a Christian pollster named George Barna says, "churches that have opted out of the Sunday night service and have opted to have the 'home Bible study' approach had only 12 percent of their Sunday morning attendees in those home Bible study groups in 1994." In other words, "home Bible studies" are a failure. In 1992 they peaked at 22 percent of the morning crowd going to something at night.

The reason that this church will maintain continuity while we have this new service schedule is because 65 percent of our morning crowd is here every Sunday night. Why, when you are having a return of that percentage, would you go to something called "home Bible studies?" The answer is, you don't! Listen, America does not need God's people sitting around a coffee table eating donuts, drinking coffee, gossiping, and trying to say, "Mildred, what do you think that verse says? Joey, what do you think it says?" America needs old-fashioned, leather-lunged prophets of God to get down on their faces before God, to study, to pray, to seek the face of God, and to come in on a Sunday night and set the pulpit on fire. God's people will come to watch it burn!

What I am saying is, we need to figure out that the need today is the preaching of the Word of God and the thing that will give the continuity is when God's people say, "All right, we are going to get back to that Sunday night service." I know what you are going to say. "Well, we are going to pack it out on a Sunday night." Yes we are! But the Sunday night crowd will "pack" a little easier than the Sunday morning visiting crowd that we are trying to reach and win for the Lord Jesus Christ.

Let's review. How will we keep our continuity? First of all, every adult needs to be a part of an adult Bible class. We are going to be starting more adult Bible classes. We are going to be getting another modular. We will be starting one class on Easter Sunday. These classes we are starting are intended to help maintain the continuity. Of course, we will continue to emphasize our theme— "Three to Thrive: Sunday morning, Sunday night, Wednesday night." Our continuity will be kept through the evening services.

Let me tell you a third way to feel a part or to keep continuity in the ministry. Be a part of a ministry! Get up in the choir; be an usher; find a group in which you can serve; work in the nursery. We are going to need folks to help in the Parking Lot Ministry, because we are going to have to coordinate our parking a little better to accommodate multiple services. Maybe you would like to help with that—directing people in. We are going to have to save some spots for folks coming in at 11:00. As you serve with other brothers and sisters in Christ, you will feel more a part of what is going on so we will maintain continuity that way. There is a place of service for everyone at Lancaster Baptist Church. Our goal is to have "every member a minister."

Our concern is for souls; our continuity will be maintained through our adult Bible classes and our evening services. For those of you who have come from situations where you have felt like there were just two separate things going on, you can be guaranteed there is one thing going on around here, and that one thing is called winning souls and preaching the Word of God. We are going to keep that continuity.

Our Conviction

Our conviction is that the two-service philosophy is not for convenience. We are living in a day when people are trying to "market the church" ministries and make everything convenient. We are doing this for the simple fact that we have run out of room. Also, we are not doing it to be trendy—just because someone else has done it. If I were just someone trying to be trendy, we would have done this six years ago. In fact, I have bucked the trend. Now, I feel God's leading to go ahead and take this step. We are not doing it for convenience, to be trendy, to keep up with the Jones', or anything of that nature, but for the purpose of reaching the lost. Of course, our Bible classes and Sunday school will be a key to maintaining our continuity.

Our Commitment

Here are some things we are committed to. First of all, we are committed to having the same service both hours. At 8:30 there will be a full choir, specials, and the preaching of God's Word. We will have the same thing at 11:00. That is important for you to know. Also, the purpose of the church remains the same and that is to develop "hearts for God."

Please understand this in the right way. Someone might say, "Well, if we have two services, it will be like we have two churches on Sunday morning." First of all, I like this one pretty well, and I would not mind having another one just like it. Do you follow what I am saying? Do you understand that one of the reasons we are establishing West Coast Baptist College is so that young men can get training here and go and do likewise. So, we are going to do it here at home twice on a Sunday morning.

Some people have a hard time with a growing church ministry, but you should't, because it is a blessing from the Lord. Statisticians tell us that in a church of 60, you are going to get to know about

60 people. In a church of about 120, you are going to get to know about 60 people. In a church of about 180, you are going to get to know about 60 people. Most of you do not know 60 people, and if you have been around here a long time, you might know about 60 people. Get into a church of about 240 and you will still get to know about 60 people. The idea of not getting to know everybody because you are not going to the early or late service is really misleading because you don't know everybody anyway. If that is a real burden of your heart, you can go to both services. I suggest that approach for some of you anyway because you are not getting it, folks. You need both services! In any event, we need to prayerfully give over to the Lord some of the things that pop into our minds.

Conclusion

Why would we do this? What is our concern? It is the same concern that we have always had—to win the lost to Jesus Christ. That is why we are here in the Antelope Valley. Last year, 2,000 people trusted Christ, and nearly half of those were baptized. That is why we are here.

Sometimes folks come from another church (although very seldom), but when they come, we are very glad to have them. But our primary purpose is to win the lost to Jesus Christ. That is what we are doing!

Why have two services? Why have a Bus Ministry? Why have a Sunday School Ministry? Why support missionaries? The reason we do what we do must be reflective of our Vision Statement, and that is to "win the lost to Jesus Christ!"

So our **concern** is for souls and to be good and wise stewards of the resources that we have.

Our **continuity** will be kept through our adult Bible classes and through our evening services. Again, if you will check, the churches who feel they have no continuity have a very weak Sunday night service. We plan to keep the pulpit hot on Sunday nights. I expect every worker of the church to be here, and I believe every mature Christian ought to be here on Sunday night. Third, our **conviction**—it is not being done for convenience or to be trendy. We are going to maintain the same philosophy. Our **commitment** is to maintain the same services both hours, the same preaching, the same music, and the same program.

Our goal is to do this more efficiently than any church has ever done it. Also, we will maintain better continuity with more vim, vigor, and fire in this ministry than in any ministry that has ever made this transition. And, I will go ahead and tell you this, if I feel that we were losing anything by this, I will cancel the whole thing. I do not think we will, though. In fact, I think we will fill this auditorium both times within a matter of just a few months. If we fill it twice a week and more people are coming to the Lord, AMEN. That is what we are here to do!

Schedule

8:30 A.M.—Early Worship Service
10:00 A.M.—Sunday School
11:00 A.M.—Worship Service

Transition

- Have print materials, brochures (see CD 25.1), and posters to advertise the new schedule.

- Teach church members the philosophy of going to two services.

- Visualize the necessity of going to two services by producing a video or a PowerPoint presentation.

Sample Service Schedules

Below are two service schedules we have used here at Lancaster Baptist Church. The first one was used to add an additional worship service allowing space for more people to attend the morning services. The second schedule is used not only to allow for more people to attend the worship services, but also to add more space for adult Bible classes and teen classes. This was accomplished by having three separate hours of Sunday school as well as two morning services.

Schedule 1

8:30–9:45 A.M.	10:00–10:50 A.M.	11:00 A.M.–12:15 P.M.
Worship Service		**Worship Service**
Nursery	Adult Classes	Children's Classes
	Teen Classes	Nursery
	Children's Classes	
	Nursery	

Schedule 2

8:15–9:15 A.M.	9:30–10:45 A.M.	11:00 A.M.–12:15 P.M.
	Worship Service	**Worship Service**
Adult Classes	Adult Classes	Adult Classes
Teen Classes	Teen Classes	Teen Classes
Children's Classes	Children's Classes	Children's Classes
Nursery	Nursery	Nursery

CHAPTER TWENTY-SIX

Other Special Days

"For God so loved the world, that he gave his only
begotten Son, that whosoever believeth in him should
not perish, but have everlasting life. "
John 3:16

One glance through a calendar and you will see many holidays or special days set aside to celebrate something or honor someone. These special days can be used effectively to reach the lost in our neighborhoods. Some, such as Mother's Day, are obvious, but others can be used creatively to reach out to the community. Many special Sundays can be invented, such as "Bring Them In Sunday" or "Law Enforcement—Firefighter Appreciation Day."

By promoting these special days both to the public and to your members, your church can see many different segments of society reached with the Gospel.

This chapter outlines a sample calendar year of special Sundays. All special days include ideas for activities/promotions.

"Great-Start Sunday"

- First Sunday of New Year
- Complete membership mailout
- Promote through announcements as a day to "start your year off right!"
- Announcements/inserts in main bulletin and adult Bible class bulletins

"Family Month"

- Preaching series on the family
- Special music—family singing groups each week

"Family Picture Day"

- Each family that brings a visiting family to the morning service gets to have a family portrait made. The visiting family also gets to make a family portrait.
- Have a professional from within the church membership take these portraits or have this hired out.

"Commuter Sunday"

- All commuters (people who drive a long distance to a job or to church) receive a gift packet including goodies that they will enjoy on their commute during the next week. These packets can include a CD greeting from the pastor with special music recorded during the last few weeks, edible goodies, and gifts such as a flashlight for the car that has the church name imprinted on it, etc.
- Promote through pulpit announcements and bulletin inserts
- The pastor may choose to preach on "The Last Commute" (the rapture).

"I Love My Church Sunday"

- Sunday closest to Valentine's Day
- Complete membership mailout
- Promoted for 100 percent membership attendance
- Phone calls/cards to all members of every Sunday school class

"Revival Sunday"

- Sunday before start of Winter Revival
- Two complete membership mailouts
- Promote through announcements and bulletins
- Starts the annual Winter Revival (Sunday–Wednesday)

"Celebration Sunday"

- Sunday following "Victory Night" (see Chapter 22)
- Four complete membership mailouts about banquet/dinners and "Celebration Sunday"
- The purpose of this day can vary. The annual "Victory Offering" can be taken on this day or the total can be announced on this day (if offering was taken on Friday night). Either way, this is truly a celebration day!

"Resurrection Sunday"

- Complete membership mailout
- Choir/orchestra presents Easter musical
- Promote through pulpit announcements and bulletin inserts

"Pop Ahead Sunday"

- Time change Sunday in April

- Complete church mailout reminding of time change
- Pulpit/bulletin announcements
- Adult Bible class leaders announce the day and many care group leaders will make little gifts for their groups. These gifts have to do with "pop"—things like "Pop" Tarts, "pop" rocks, "pop" (soft drinks), etc.
- All class teachers, bus workers, and care group leaders call their enrollment lists on Saturday night to remind class members.

"Bring Them In Sunday"

- "Big Day" for the Bus Ministry.
- Promotions, giveaways, refreshments, clowns, games, etc. on the bus routes
- Rallies should be held at rented public schools for each area. The bus routes attend the rally in their respective area.
- Every home in every bus route area receives flyers, brochures, tracts during the week before.

"Law Enforcement/Firefighter Appreciation Day"

- Mailout and personal visit from pastor/associate pastor to every fire station and police station in area
- Have a meeting with members who are law enforcement officers or firefighters. Equip them with flyers, business cards, and brochures about the day. They may be in-roads to inviting entire precincts and firehouses.
- Honor them during worship service and give each a small gift for his service to the community.

"Mother's Day"

- Promote through pulpit announcements and bulletin inserts

- Gift to all moms
- Honor with a token gift or flowers—"specials" such as mom with most children present in church, newest mom, oldest mom, mom who has been saved the longest, etc.

"God and Country Sunday"

- Sunday before Memorial Day
- Patriotic decorations and music
- Pledge of Allegiance in worship service
- Honor/thank those who have given their lives in service for the United States

"Promotion Sunday"

- First Sunday in June
- Mailout to all parents/children/teens about room changes
- Pulpit/bulletin announcements
- Call parents on Saturday to inform as to where to pick children up after Sunday school.

"Father's Day"

- Gift given to all fathers in the worship service

"I Love America Sunday"

- Sunday closest to July 4
- Patriotic music and decorations
- Pledge of Allegiance in worship service
- Choir/Orchestra—patriotic musical—performed at area military base
- Promote through pulpit announcements and bulletin inserts
- Patriotic video

"Anniversary Sunday"

- Complete membership mailout
- Honor Pastor/long-time members
- Share history of the church and the pastor's vision for the future
- Sunday night fellowship with new members

"Aloha Sunday"

- Encourage members to modestly dress Hawaiian, such as Hawaiian shirts with pants for the men and Hawaiian print dresses for the ladies.
- Give out leis as people enter church
- Gospel music with a Hawaiian sound
- Hawaiian-style refreshments outside before or after the service
- Promote through pulpit and bulletin announcements

"Super Summer Sunday"

- Any Sunday during the summer
- Slices of cool watermelon after the morning service
- Promote through pulpit and bulletin announcements

"Back-to-School Sunday"

- First Sunday in September
- Purpose—To get people back in church after the summer slump
- Complete membership mailout
- Promote through pulpit announcements and bulletin inserts
- "School" related gift to all children 3 years–6th grade

478

"Grandparents' Day"

- Gift for all grandparents present in morning service
- Complete membership mailout
- Promote through pulpit and bulletin announcements
- Can honor grandparent with most grandchildren present in church

"Armed Forces Appreciation Day"

- Patriotic decorations and music
- Honor all who have served or are serving in the various branches of the military.
- Encourage them to dress in uniform if possible.
- Mailout to all area military bases, advertise in their newspapers if possible.
- Invite military V.I.P.'s and honor them by name in the service.
- Have meeting weeks prior with church members currently working at area bases. Encourage them to invite co-workers and hang posters on work bulletin boards if permitted. Equip these members with brochures, flyers, and tracts made especially for this day. (Can have pizza at this meeting to help promote positive atmosphere and to thank them ahead of time.)
- Can have a meal after the service for all military families in attendance
- Can give small present to all military during the service
- Promote through pulpit announcements and bulletin inserts

"Educators' Appreciation Day"

- Special gift for anyone working in education

- Have meeting weeks prior with church members currently working at area public schools. Encourage them to invite co-workers and hang posters on work bulletin boards if permitted. Equip these members with brochures, flyers, and tracts made especially for this day. (Can have pizza at this meeting to help promote positive atmosphere and to thank them ahead of time.)
- Call all public schools in the area and let administration know that you are honoring educators.
- Equip all children/teens in their Sunday school classes the week before this day with brochures/flyers. Encourage all children/teens to invite their teachers to be honored.
- Promote through pulpit and bulletin announcements

"Country Harvest Days"

- All of these Sundays are explained in Chapters 19 and 21.
  1st Sunday—"Open House Sunday"
  2nd Sunday—"Missions Sunday"
  3rd Sunday—"Dinner on the Grounds Sunday"
  4th Sunday—"Harvest Sunday"
  Last Sunday—"Round-Up Sunday"
- If the month has only four Sundays, eliminate Harvest Sunday.
- Mail brochure advertising all Sundays to complete membership.

"Veterans' Sunday"

- Sunday nearest Veteran's Day
- Special gift for all veterans present in the morning worship service
- Honor all veterans by having them stand.
- Encourage members to dress in uniform if possible for this day.

• Promote through pulpit and bulletin announcements

"Christian Music Sunday"

• Special music groups
• Special/more than usual congregational singing
• Can have sermon on the effects of listening to the right kinds of music
• Visitors receive Christian music CD.
• Can have tables set up to sell discounted Christian music

"Thanksgiving Sunday"

• Sunday before Thanksgiving
• Special music
• Thanksgiving offering—offering for special projects such as building fund, new bus, missions project, etc.
• Promote weeks in advance through pulpit announcements and bulletin inserts
• Weeks following show pictures/slides of what was done with the offering.

"Christmas Musical"

• Purpose—To invite friends, family, neighbors, and co-workers who might attend church only during the Christmas season to give a simple, clear presentation of the Gospel
• Choir/Orchestra/Drama Team present the Christmas musical.
• Promote through pulpit announcements and bulletin inserts
• Have free tickets professionally printed for church members to give to people who say they would like to attend.
• If Sunday performance becomes too crowded, a Saturday night performance can be offered.

• Complete membership mailout

"Christmas Gifts to Jesus"

• Can be done on a Sunday night close to Christmas or the Christmas Eve service
• Several weeks ahead of time have the different ministries turn in a "wish list" of items that could be used in their ministry such as "Children's Ministries—crayons, Bibles, craft items" or "Christian School—office supplies, playground items, books, etc."
• Promote the special service and "wish lists" on a bulletin insert for two Sundays prior. Encourage families to purchase an item or items on the list and gift wrap them.
• During the "Christmas Gifts to Jesus" service, have a special time for families to bring their gifts up to the altar. It is a special time to see the wrapped presents being given and it teaches the children the joy of giving to the Lord and His church.
• People not wishing to purchase a gift may give a cash offering designated to the ministry of their choice.

"Christmas Eve Candlelight Service"

• Can be held on Christmas Eve or the Wednesday night closest to Christmas
• Lights dimmed
• Choir presents special music and holds candles
• Special reading of the Christmas story (Luke 2)

Conclusion

It is my prayer that some of the ideas in this book have been a help and encouragement to you and your ministry. In fact, we pray that this book will be a resource for years to come, as you consider beginning new ministries or facilitating ongoing training in your church.

We believe it is entirely possible, by the grace of God, to build an aggressive, soulwinning church for the glory of God in these days. It is vital that each of us, as church leaders, determines to make Jesus Christ his goal in the ministry. Success is a moving target, but leadership has a fixed goal and the goal is Jesus Christ.

Of all of the methods and programs that can be discussed and developed, I want to give a final urging to the reader not to neglect the area of personally taking time each week to get out into the community and share the Gospel of Christ with others. The Apostle Paul was persistent in this method of going from place to place with the Gospel. The Bible tells us that he was "bold in his God to preach the Gospel." He did not test the winds to see if there was an easier or more popular method. He was not a faddist looking for a new technique and he certainly never surveyed a community, asking an unregenerate man what kind of message he would like to hear. He simply stayed faithful, preaching the unchanging truth of the Lord Jesus Christ.

It is vital, as we develop the ministries of the local church and preach the Gospel of Jesus Christ, that we likewise follow the Apostle Paul in maintaining a heart that is pure before God. In I Thessalonians 2:3–6, Paul expressed to the Thessalonian believers the following truths:

> For our exhortation was not of deceit, nor of uncleanness, nor in guile: But as we were allowed of God to be put in trust with the gospel, even so we speak; not as pleasing men, but God, which trieth our hearts. For neither at any time used we flattering words, as ye know, nor a cloke of covetousness; God is witness: Nor of men sought we glory, neither of you, nor yet of others, when we might have been burdensome, as the apostles of Christ.

His motives were neither deceitful nor self-centered nor covetous. His one desire was to please the Lord Jesus Christ. We see Paul as a man who was persistent in his method of soulwinning and pure in the motive of his heart. I also see that he was a man who was personal in his ministry. I Thessalonians 2:7–8 says:

> But we were gentle among you, even as a nurse cherisheth her children: So being affectionately desirous of you, we were willing to have imparted unto you, not the gospel of God only, but also our own souls, because ye were dear unto us.

What an amazing thought that this rough preacher was as gentle as a nursing mother! It has been said that people do not care how much you know until they know how much you care. The reasons we have taken time to develop so many ministries, such as discipleship, care groups, adult classes, etc., is to love and to care for the people of God and to help them as they grow from being babes in Christ to fully committed followers of Christ.

Each of us is required to be a steward of those people God entrusts to the membership of his church. May He be pleased in using the methods in this book for the purpose of helping you properly steward and oversee His purchased possession.

Other books written by Dr. Paul Chappell

The Right Path

This new book challenges the reader to return to the right path for serving, building, growing, and laboring in church ministry. Through its pages you will examine your motives and be challenged to serve God's way.

Guided by Grace

Do you want to grow in an understanding of Christ-like leadership? Written from a transparent heart, *Guided by Grace* will challenge, encourage, and motivate you to lead God's people more effectively.

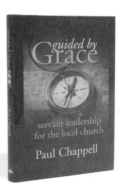

A Heart for God

There is no greater priority than to develop a heart for God. All service rendered to God must first flow from a heart for God, and these pages will help you begin the journey.

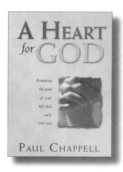

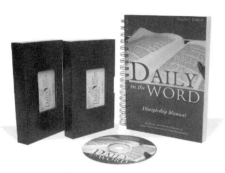

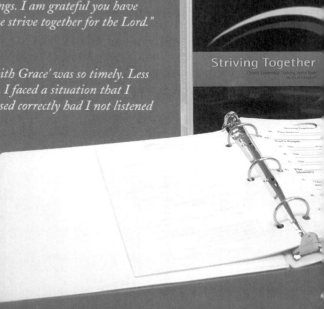

Individual Lessons $15 each

- Leading in a Hostile Culture
- Structuring Your Ministry to Develop Leaders
- Project Management and Completion
- Development of an Annual Plan
- The Work of the Ministry
- Building a Happy Family and a Growing Ministry
- The Servant Leader in the Local Church
- Attributes of a Godly Leader
- A Biblical Strategy for Reaching Your Community
- Establishing Leadership Requirements
- How to Build an Adult Bible Class
- Leading Through a Crisis
- Developing a Life Changing Message
- Characteristics of a Winning Team
- First Things Resolution
- Confronting Needs with God's Grace
- The Leader and His Friendships
- How to Approach an Unfaithful Church Worker
- Building a Soulwinning Church
- Laboring with Understanding
- Qualities of an Effective Leader
- Conducting an Effective Staff Meeting
- Leading through a Building Program
- Leading Together with God
- Biblical Qualifications of Pastoral Leadership
- Developing the Church in the Early Years
- Ten Signs of a Healthy Church
- Making a Difference
- Casting Biblical Vision
- Seven Principles for Building a Soulwinning Church
- Seven Qualities of an Effective Youth Worker
- Characteristics of an Effective Christian Worker
- Strategy for Leadership Development in the Local Church